Strategic Enterprise Resource Planning Models for E–Government:

Applications and Methodologies

Susheel Chhabra
Lal Bahadur Shastri Institute of Management, India

Muneesh Kumar
University of Delhi South Campus, India

Senior Editorial Director:	Kristin Klinger
Director of Book Publications:	Julia Mosemann
Editorial Director:	Lindsay Johnston
Acquisitions Editor:	Erika Carter
Development Editor:	Mike Killian
Production Editor:	Sean Woznicki
Typesetters:	Chris Shearer, Lisandro Gonzalez
Print Coordinator:	Jamie Snavely
Cover Design:	Nick Newcomer

Published in the United States of America by
Information Science Reference (an imprint of IGI Global)
701 E. Chocolate Avenue
Hershey PA 17033
Tel: 717-533-8845
Fax: 717-533-8661
E-mail: cust@igi-global.com
Web site: http://www.igi-global.com

Library of Congress Cataloging-in-Publication Data

Strategic enterprise resource planning models for e-government: applications and methodologies / Susheel Chhabra and Muneesh Kumar, editors.
  p. cm.
 Includes bibliographical references and index.
 Summary: "This book reviews enterprise resource planning frameworks for government enterprises along with their applications and methodologies to improve effectiveness of processes and enhancement of citizen-centric services"--Provided by publisher.
 ISBN 978-1-60960-863-7 (hardcover) -- ISBN 978-1-60960-864-4 (ebook) -- ISBN 978-1-60960-865-1 (print & perpetual access) 1. Internet in public administration. 2. Information technology--Management. 3. Management information systems. 4. Administrative agencies--Customer services. I. Chhabra, Susheel. II. Kumar, Muneesh.
 JF1525.A8S885 2011
 352.3'802854678--dc22
                              2011012087

British Cataloguing in Publication Data
A Cataloguing in Publication record for this book is available from the British Library.

All work contributed to this book is new, previously-unpublished material. The views expressed in this book are those of the authors, but not necessarily of the publisher.

Editorial Advisory Board

Table of Contents

Section 2
ERP Processes and Applications for E-Government

Detailed Table of Contents

Section 1
Strategic ERP Framework and Methodologies for E-Government

Chapter 1

Asmare Emerie Kassahun, RMIT University, Australia
Alemayehu Molla, RMIT University, Australia
Pradipta Sarkar, RMIT University, Australia

Government Process Reengineering (GPR) is the most important component for designing ERP frameworks. The chapter presents introduction, synthesis and analysis of literature from 1997 to 2009. It has also reviewed normative studies that examine the nature and characteristics of government process reengineering, challenges and problems of undertaking government process reengineering, and relationships between government process reengineering and IT-especially enterprise resource planning (ERP)-based E-Government. The chapter also encompasses the methods, techniques and tools for undertaking GPR; analytical and conceptual GPR models and frameworks; and empirical studies that evaluate GPR implementation outcomes and identify the critical success or failure factors. The authors conclude the chapter by summarizing selected articles in terms of research types, methods, theories, and contexts.

Chapter 2

Girish H. Subramanian, Penn State University at Harrisburg, USA
Alan R. Peslak, Penn State University, USA

A sound and effective implementation approach is the basis for success of ERP in E-Government. The authors have developed phased ERP implementation model having four phases – preparation and training, transition, performance and usefulness, and maintenance. The empirical support for this model is provided through research findings and content analysis of interviews which helped them to come up with the recommendations and applications. Using data from two manufacturing divisions that implemented ERP, the chapter aims to identify major phases in ERP implementation process.

Chapter 3

John Douglas Thomson, RMIT University, Australia

E-government agencies in developed and developing countries are anticipating efficiency and effectiveness gains from the evolution of new e-business models. The adoption of Enterprise Resource Planning (ERP) is one of these e-business models. The chapter explores the adoption of ERP by the Australian Department of Defence through longitudinal action research. This development may be of interest to other public sectors wishing to avoid unnecessary expense and to achieve an efficient and effective outcome in minimum time.

Chapter 4

Catherine Equey Balzli, University of Applied Sciences, Switzerland
Emmanuel Fragnière, University of Applied Sciences, Switzerland

The strategic nature of ERP facilitate the organizations to standardized and provide common frontend interfaces. The chapter is an attempt to understand why the accounting function of a Swiss public administration has significantly changed following the implementation of an ERP system. To study this social phenomenon, an ethnography research strategy was followed. The analysis has been structured around organizational structure changes, standardization and centralization processes, and centralization's effect on accounting tasks. Research findings and analyses indicate that the power of each public administration department under review is very strong to the point that it has negatively impacted the necessary standardization imposed by an ERP system implementation. Consequently, authors advocate that an ERP implementation project cannot be managed in the same manner as those realized in the private sector.

Chapter 5

Sangeeta Sharma, University of Rajasthan, India

The impediments and fallouts in the formulation, implementation and evaluation of ERP solutions for E-government are directly related to the societal approach. The author has proposed ERP III with moral epicenter assuming that societal approach can be attained if individuals are trained in the moralistic values which eventually redefine the entrepreneurial goals such that it adopts befitting approach in pursuing specific targets. This chapter highlights concept, strategic paradoxes, and rebuilding through didactic approach by e-initiative and prognostic strategy for ERP III.

Chapter 6

Susheel Chhabra, Lal Bahadur Shastri Institute of Management, India
D. N. Gupta, Government of Orissa, India

The basic objective of E-Government framework is to enhance quality of services provided to citizens. The chapter evaluates service quality, and suggests E-Government Citizen Centric Framework for Citizen Service Centers (CSC) of Haryana State in India. Citizen Centric framework is suggested using responses collected from 300 users of five (5) E-Government citizen service centers. This framework can be used in other similar E-Government citizen service centers to evaluate service quality.

Section 2
ERP Processes and Applications for E-Government

Chapter 7

Lars Frank, Copenhagen Business School, Denmark

A distributed modular ERP system is a set of systems that operate in different locations where each module can use the resources of the other ERP modules in its own or in other ERP locations. These systems use a common database and therefore use modules supported by the ERP suppliers. Keeping in view the fact that ERP uses heterogeneous database modules and hence it becomes difficult to use the traditional ACID (Atomicity, Consistency, Isolation and Durability) database properties and inconsistency and anomaly arise. The users cannot trust the data they are reading and they can undermine the validity of the databases if they update the databases by using such inconsistent information. The author has recommended the possibility of using relaxed ACID properties to avoid this problematic situation.

Chapter 8

Christopher G. Reddick, The University of Texas, USA

New Public Management (NPM) and CRM e-government models have commonly been cited in the public administration literature as drivers of organizational reform and change. The author has examined common characteristics of these two models with data from a survey of local government chief administrators. The results indicate that local governments that used more advanced CRM technology are more likely to report organizational change from these models. The implications of these findings suggest researchers to understand both the NPM and e-government principles important for understanding organizational change. In addition, CRM and in its ability to integrate information systems create a more enterprise approach to governance.

Chapter 9

Hakikur Rahman, SchoolNet Foundation, Bangladesh

Ever-growing and evolutionary technologies of the Internet have lured nations in utilizing information and communication technologies to upgrade the livelihood of their citizens. Governments of most countries have initiated multi-faceted programs and initiatives to provide enhanced services through means and methods that are being facilitated by the Internet. However, forms and norms of services have taken shapes and domains depending on the ground context, expansion and maturity of ICTs in their countries and communities. The chapter explores situations of electronic forms of the government, which it argues is a pre-requisite for good governance and thus enable governments to reach the people at large. Particularly, the chapter reviews the emancipation of ICTs in eight countries of the South Asian Association for Regional Cooperation (SAARC). It investigates some basic parameters of ICTs retrieving archived data from various institutions and organizations. Later on, the chapter tries to generalize the situation in terms of recommendations.

Chapter 10

Muneesh Kumar, University of Delhi South Campus, India
Mamta Sareen, University of Delhi, India

The increasing use of Enterprise Resource Planning (ERP) Systems in E-Government is shifting the focus of such initiative to internal integration of processes. However, any e-government initiative with focus on optimization of internal processes will serve only a limited purpose. Rather, use of ERP systems should enable governments to provide a more effective platform for delivery of information and service to citizen more conveniently and in a transparent manner. The channel used for providing access to information and services is generally a web site/portal. In this chapter, an attempt has been made to evaluate municipal websites of twenty major cities in India. It also examines relationship between the income levels of the city and the quality of municipal website. While the significant differences were observed among municipal web sites of different cities, no significant relationship could be established between the quality of municipal websites and income levels in the city.

Chapter 11

Geetanjali Sahi, Lal Bahadur Shastri Institute of Management, India
Sushila Madan, University of Delhi, India

The government has become more dependent on modern technologies that have the potential to create seamless, responsive and citizen-centric government for the benefits of all. It has become increasingly vulnerable to a range of risks, from interruption of operations that are based on computers to loss of confidential data. Information security requires a combination of business, management, and technical measures in an on-going basis. The chapter helps to understand threats and risks, clarification and investigation techniques in mitigating these challenges and issues involved in improving E-governance ERP security.

Preface

Enterprise Resource Planning is playing a strategic role in designing, and managing E-Government resources. Governments all over the world are facing challenges in designing robust Enterprise Resource Planning applications & methodologies to align themselves with the expectations of citizens and stakeholders. The existing standard Enterprise Resource Planning solutions are proprietary, inflexible and expensive to implement in Government Enterprises. There is a growing demand for action-oriented research to provide insights into challenges, issues, and solutions related to the design, development, implementation and management of government resources through Enterprise Resource Planning Systems.

The objective of this book is to suggest Enterprise Resource Planning frameworks for government enterprises along with their applications & methodologies to improve effectiveness of processes & enhancing citizen-centric services. The research initiatives presented in this book is expected to ease the process of implementing customized Enterprise Resource Planning solutions in E-Government.

The book is useful for professionals and researchers working in the field of E-Government including policy makers, academicians ICT vendors, consultants, and implementing agencies.

The call for chapters was sent to 1000 research institutions, consultants, academicians, and industry experts all the over world, that attracted enormous interest in addressing various e-government issues. After a stringent blind refereeing process and coupled with well-focused persuasive, qualitative IGI Global's book editing style, 11 contributions were selected for publication in this book.

The book is logically sequenced into chapter having two sections to examine major themes: Section 1 proposes Strategic ERP Framework & Methodologies for E-Government and Section 2 suggests ERP Processes & Applications for E-Government.

Government Process Reengineering (GPR) is the most important component for designing ERP frameworks. Chapter 1 in Section 1 present introduction, synthesis and analysis of literature of GPR from 1997 to 2009. It reviews normative studies that examine the nature and characteristics of government process reengineering, challenges and problems of undertaking government process reengineering, and relationships between government process reengineering and IT-especially enterprise resource planning (ERP)-based E-Government. The analysis also encompasses the methods, techniques and tools for undertaking GPR; analytical and conceptual GPR models and frameworks; and empirical studies that evaluate GPR implementation outcomes and identify the critical success or failure factors.

A sound and effective implementation approach is the basis for success of ERP in E-Government. The authors in Chapter 2 have suggested phased ERP implementation model consisting of four phases – preparation and training, transition, performance and usefulness, and maintenance using data from two manufacturing divisions that implemented ERP,. The empirical support for this model is provided through research findings to identify major phases in ERP implementation process.

E-government agencies in developed and developing countries are anticipating efficiency and effectiveness gains from the evolution of new e-business models. The adoption of Enterprise Resource Planning (ERP) is one of these e-business models. The Chapter 3 explores the adoption of ERP by the Australian Department of Defense through longitudinal action research. This development is of interest to other public sectors wishing to avoid unnecessary expense and to achieve an efficient and effective outcome in minimum time.

ERP facilitates the organizations to standardize and to provide common user interface. The Chapter 4 is an attempt to understand why the accounting function of a Swiss public administration has significantly changed following the implementation of an ERP system. To study this social phenomenon, an ethnography research strategy has been followed. The analysis is structured around organizational structure changes, standardization and centralization processes, and centralization's effect on accounting tasks. Research findings and analyses indicate that the power of each public administration department under review is very strong to the point that it has negatively impacted the necessary standardization imposed by an ERP system implementation. Consequently, authors advocate that an ERP implementation project cannot be managed in the same manner as those realized in the private sector.

The impediments and fallouts in the formulation, implementation and evaluation of ERP solutions for E-government are directly related to the societal approach. The author in the Chapter 5 of this section has proposed ERP III with moral epicenter assuming that societal approach can be attained if individuals are trained in the moralistic values which eventually redefine the entrepreneurial goals such that it adopts befitting approach in pursuing specific targets. This chapter highlights concept, strategic paradoxes, and rebuilding through didactic approach by e-initiative and prognostic strategy for ERP III.

The basic objective of E-Government framework is to enhance quality of services provided to citizens. The Chapter 6 evaluates service quality, and suggests E-Government Citizen Centric Framework for Citizen Service Centers (CSC) of Haryana State in India. Citizen Centric framework is suggested using responses collected from 300 users of five (5) E-Government citizen service centers. This framework can be used in other similar E-Government citizen service centers to evaluate service quality.

Section 2 contains four chapters covering various aspects of ERP Processes & Applications for E-Government. The Chapter 7 portrays architecture for ERP system integration with heterogeneous E-Government modules. A distributed modular ERP system is a set of systems that operate in different locations where each module can use the resources of the other ERP modules in its own or in other ERP locations. These systems use a common database and therefore use modules supported by the ERP suppliers. Keeping in view the fact that ERP uses heterogeneous database modules and hence it becomes difficult to use the traditional ACID (Atomicity, Consistency, Isolation and Durability) database properties and inconsistency and anomaly arise. The users cannot trust the data they are reading and they can undermine the validity of the databases if they update the databases by using such inconsistent information. The author has recommended the possibility of using relaxed ACID properties to avoid this problematic situation.

New Public Management (NPM) and CRM e-government models have commonly been cited in the public administration literature as drivers of organizational reform and change. The author in Chapter 8 has examined common characteristics of these two models with data from a survey of local government chief administrators. The results indicate that local governments that used more advanced CRM technology are more likely to report organizational change from these models. The implications of these findings suggest researchers to understand both the NPM and e-government principles important for understanding organizational change. In addition, CRM and in its ability to integrate information systems create a more enterprise approach to governance.

Ever-growing and evolutionary technologies of the Internet have lured nations in utilizing information and communication technologies to upgrade the livelihood of their citizens. Governments of most countries have initiated multi-faceted programs and initiatives to provide enhanced services through means and methods that are being facilitated by the Internet. However, forms and norms of services have taken shapes and domains depending on the ground context, expansion and maturity of ICTs in their countries and communities. The Chapter 9 explores situations of electronic forms of the government, which it argues is a pre-requisite for good governance and thus enable governments to reach the people at large. Particularly, the chapter reviews the emancipation of ICTs in eight countries of the South Asian Association for Regional Cooperation (SAARC). It investigates some basic parameters of ICTs retrieving archived data from various institutions and organizations. Later on, the chapter tries to generalize the situation in terms of recommendations.

The increasing use of Enterprise Resource Planning (ERP) Systems in E-Government is shifting the focus of such initiative to internal integration of processes. However, any e-government initiative with focus on optimization of internal processes will serve only a limited purpose. Rather, use of ERP systems should enable governments to provide a more effective platform for delivery of information and service to citizen more conveniently and in a transparent manner. The channel used for providing access to information and services is generally a web site/portal. In Chapter 10, the authors have made an attempt to evaluate municipal websites of twenty major cities in India. It also examines relationship between the income levels of the city and the quality of municipal website. While the significant differences were observed among municipal web sites of different cities, no significant relationship could be established between the quality of municipal websites and income levels in the city.

The government has become more dependent on modern technologies that have the potential to create seamless, responsive and citizen-centric government for the benefits of all. It has become increasingly vulnerable to a range of risks, from interruption of operations that are based on computers to loss of confidential data. Information security requires a combination of business, management, and technical measures in an on-going basis. The last, Chapter 11, helps to understand threats and risks, clarification and investigation techniques in mitigating these challenges and issues involved in improving E-governance ERP security.

Susheel Chhabra
Lal Bahadur Shastri Institute of Management, India

Muneesh Kumar
University of Delhi South Campus, India

Acknowledgment

This book reflects contributions of several individuals. First of all, we would like to express our gratitude to all the authors of chapters in this book. Second, we are grateful to the several research institutions, companies, and generous individuals who supported the research that formed the basis of chapters' contributions.

Due to large number of submissions received, reviewing all the chapters was not a trivial task. We would like to thank everyone who helped with the review process. Without their timely efforts and constructive criticism, this book would not have been possible. Unfortunately, we are unable to thank each of them individually here due to the large number of people involved, but their support is greatly appreciated.

We are grateful to Kristin M. Klinger and Heather A. Probst for giving us the opportunity to bring this publication into reality. Mike Killian and his staff deserve special appreciation for providing guidance during the development of this book.

We would remiss if we failed to thank all the encouragement and support provided by Dr. Gautam Sinha, Director Lal Bahadur Shastri Institute of Management, Delhi and Professor Dinesh Singh, Vice Chancellor, University of Delhi, India.

We would also like to place on record a word of appreciation for our family members, Mrs Shilpa Chhabra, Bhavya & Ram Vaibhav, and Mrs. Raj Kumari, and Richa, who sacrificed their time to bring this project a reality.

Susheel Chhabra
Lal Bahadur Shastri Institute of Management, India

Muneesh Kumar
University of Delhi South Campus, India

Section 1
Strategic ERP Framework and Methodologies for E-Government

Chapter 1
Government Process Reengineering:
What we Know and What we Need to Know

Asmare Emerie Kassahun
RMIT University, Australia

Alemayehu Molla
RMIT University, Australia

Pradipta Sarkar
RMIT University, Australia

ABSTRACT

Despite differences between public and private sectors, business process reengineering (BPR) principles have been widely used in reengineering government processes. This has led to a growing body of literature on government process reengineering (GPR). This chapter presents synthesis and analysis of the literature on government process reengineering from 1997 to 2009. It reviews normative studies that examine the nature and characteristics of government process reengineering, challenges and problems of undertaking government process reengineering, and relationships between government process reengineering and IT-especially enterprise resource planning (ERP)-based E-Government. The review also encompasses the methods, techniques and tools for undertaking GPR; analytical and conceptual GPR models and frameworks; and empirical studies that evaluate GPR implementation outcomes and identify the critical success or failure factors. The chapter summarizes the selected articles in terms of research types, methods, theories, and contexts. Based on the review, areas for future research are defined.

DOI: 10.4018/978-1-60960-863-7.ch001

INTRODUCTION

Governments of both developed and developing economies are reforming the public sector to promote good governance (Linden, 1994). Process reengineering together with appropriate information and communications technology (ICT) implementation are recognized as key reform tools. Consequently, there are now several cases of government process reengineering (GPR) implementations that exploit the enabling and transforming power of ICT including strategic enterprise resource planning (ERP) systems for realizing E-Government. As government process reengineering is characteristically different from private sector process reengineering, several researchers have been contributing to the cumulative body of knowledge on the subject. Therefore, there is a need for synthesizing and analyzing the literature on GPR.

The purpose of this chapter is, therefore, to examine the literature on GPR from 1997 to 2009. The aim is to

a.   appraise what is known about GPR,
b.   identify gaps in the literature, and
c.   highlight and suggest areas future research shall be heading to.

To achieve these aims, we first analyze the GPR literature by research methods (case study or survey), informing theories, study contexts (developed economy or developing), and journals outlet.

Second, we synthesize the research articles in terms of

a.   normative studies focusing on distinguishing characteristics of GPR, unique challenges and problems of GPR, relationship of GPR and ICT such as ERP system enabled E-Government,
b.   approaches and methodologies for undertaking GPR,

c.   theoretical/conceptual models of GPR, and
d.   GPR adoption and implementation and evaluation.

Third, we define a research agenda for future GPR research.

The rest of the chapter is organized into five sections. The second section offers a brief background discussion of public organisations and business process reengineering. Section three discusses the methodology used for selecting and classifying the relevant articles used in this review. Section four presents results of the literature review and its discussion. The fifth section discusses the areas identified for future research. Finally section six presents the summary and conclusion.

BACKGROUND

Public organizations across developed and developing economies are experiencing challenges to meet the ever increasing demands for efficient public service delivery, more transparent and accountable governance system, and better performance by citizens, businesses, and Governments (Thong, Yap, and Seah, 2000; Linden, 1994). The adoption and implementation of ICT such as ERP-enabled E-Government systems could help to improve operational efficiencies of public sectors. However, addressing effectively all the above demands calls for undertaking a more radical transformation of the organizational model and accompanying business processes. Business process reengineering (BPR) is one of the principal practices for radical transformation of organizations. Public sector organizations have embraced the practice of BPR under the banner of GPR as an instrumental reform tool to transform the public sector from its traditional hierarchical bureaucratic model to customer-oriented horizontal/process model (Sia and Neo, 2008; Anderson, 1999; 2006).

Although the academic interest for BPR in the private sector appears to have saturated, BPR in the public sector (i.e. GPR) is an active area of research (MacIntosh, 2003). The principles of BPR such as fundamental rethinking, radical process redesign, and technology enablement remain appealing and powerful transformative ideas for the public sector (Sia and Neo, 2008). Previous reviews of the literature on process reengineering are predominantly in the context of private sector (see O'Neill and Sohal, 1999; Motwani, Kumar, and Jiang, 1998; Al-Mashari, Irani, et al., 2001). However, the public administration literature acknowledges that the public sector has its own specifics and unique characteristics that distinguish it from private sector. These can include absence of market exposure; existence of multiple stakeholders with conflicting goals and higher political influences (including impacts of interest groups) (Thong, Yap, and Seah, 2000; Halachmi and Bovaird, 1997; Indihar Stemberger and Jaklic, 2007). In addition, the public sector usually face more level of financial, legal, and rule/red tape constraints and mandatory reporting requirements due to the unique sanctions and coercive power of governments (Dzhumalieva and Helfert, 2008: Thong, Yap, and Seah, 2000). Further, more frequent turnover of top-management due to elections and political appointments, and limited autonomy of public officials to devise incentives for individual performance differentiate public organisations from private sector businesses (Rainey and Steinbauer, 1999; Thong, Yap, and Seah, 2000; Martin and Montagna, 2006).

The above differences have implications on the methods, models, principles, and lessons to be applied in public sector. As a result, there is now a growing body of literature on GPR. Nevertheless there has never been any review of the GPR literature on its own. This limits our knowledge about GPR and its future research direction. The central aim of this chapter is to address an essential research gap (i.e. to uncover areas that are sufficiently researched and areas where further research is needed and contribute to the advancement of knowledge on the area).

APPROACH AND METHODOLOGY

This review is conducted based on a three-stage (input-processing-output) literature review approach and method (Levy and Elliss, 2006). A literature review method is appropriate when the purpose of the review is to lay a firm foundation for advancing knowledge and theory development (Webster and Watson, 2002). A systematic literature review entails carrying out those three stages of input-processing-output activities sequentially. The input stage involves carrying out literature gathering and screening. The processing stage comprises knowing/comprehending the literature, analyzing, synthesizing and evaluating the screened literature. The output stage represents the activity of writing the literature review report/paper.

Accordingly, in the first step (i.e. input stage), relevant journal articles covering the period from 1997 to 2009 were identified from Scholar Google, Science Direct, Emerald, SCOPUS, EBSCO and ProQuest databases. The articles were identified using the following keywords: "public sector business process reengineering," "government process reengineering," "public sector business process change," "business process reengineering and eGovernment," and "public sector business process reengineering and Enterprise Resource Planning systems." The initial search identified 86 articles. In order to further screen the articles, the abstracts of all of the articles and in some cases the whole paper were reviewed. The screening process considered mainly academic journal articles that discuss GPR as their main theme instead of those that make a passing reference to it. This process reduced the number of articles from 86 to 40 only.

In the second step, which represents the processing stage of the literature review process, we adopted Motwani, Kumar, and Jiang (1998) framework to classify the articles into one of the four research themes. The four research themes are:

1. normative GPR studies,
2. GPR methodology studies,
3. GPR theoretical framework /conceptual model studies, and
4. GPR adoption, implementation and evaluation studies.

Table 1 provides a description of each research theme as well as the selection criteria.

Normative GPR studies help us to assess conceptual clarity of process reengineering as applied to the public sector (definition, scope, principles, benefits and problems) and how the concept has evolved since it was first coined as business process reengineering (BPR) or simply

as reengineering in the early 1990s. GPR methodology studies help us to assess adequacy and extent of these methodologies and analyze to what extent these are different from those used in the private sector. Conceptual model studies, besides helping to take stock of the existing GPR conceptual models, allow understanding and assessment of their scope (comprehensiveness, from GPR initiation to post-GPR evaluation/assessment) and scale (organizational, inter-organizational business process) of applicability. As such the articles under this theme can be conceptually or empirically derived. However, they are supposed to be theory based. GPR adoption and implementation and evaluation studies help to determine GPR implementation outcomes, the factors contributing to it, and research gaps that may exist.

Finally, in the third step (i.e. output stage), this literature review chapter is written up and compiled.

Table 1. Classification framework description

Theme	Description	Inclusion Criteria: *If the main theme of the article refers to*
Normative GPR Studies	This refers to GPR studies whose main goal is to describe and show the unique and distinguishing characteristics of public sector process reengineering. Articles under this category can be both conceptual and empirical but often lack foundational theory.	• Definition and concept of GPR • Distinguishing characteristics of GPR and its implication • Principles and approaches for GPR • Relationship of GPR and ICT such as ERP-based E-Government, • Benefit/importance or applicability of process reengineering to the public sector
GPR Methodology Studies	Refers to GPR studies whose main goal is to develop methodologies, tools, and techniques that are appropriate to public sector process reengineering.	• development of GPR methodologies • Development of business process modeling tools and techniques for the public sector
Conceptual Model Studies	Refers to articles whose main thrust was developing a conceptual model /theoretical framework of GPR or validating an already existing GPR conceptual model. The articles can be conceptual or empirical but they are supposed to be theory based.	• Development of GPR theoretical /conceptual framework • Validation and testing of GPR conceptual/theoretical framework • Development of measurement instrument for one or more than one elements of a proposed GPR framework
GPR adoption, implementation and evaluation Studies	Refers to articles whose main intent is to assess or evaluate GPR implementation outcomes and report the lessons learnt from GPR implementation experiences in the form of critical success/failure factors. As such the articles are all empirical studies.	• reporting GPR implementation outcomes • reporting GPR critical success /failure factor studies based on empirical case studies • discussion of lessons learnt from GPR implementation experiences

REVIEW RESULTS AND DISCUSSION

This section presents profile of the reviewed articles and a discussion of the review results from research rigor and quality perspective and along the four research themes already stated above. The section also pinpoints and determines research issues and gaps under each of the four themes.

Profile of the Reviewed Articles

The articles selected for review have appeared in over 30 Journals (see Appendix 1). The top four most frequently used journals for GPR research are Business Process Management Journal which published 10% of the 40 articles; Electronic Journal of e-Government, Government Information Quarterly, and Total Quality Management each publishing 5% of the articles. The remaining 75% of the articles were published across 25 journals.

Regarding the distribution of articles by year of publication, most of the articles (about 60%) have been published from 2004 on wards (the largest part being in 2007 (17.5%) and the second largest in 2008 & 2006 (12.5% each)) (See Table 2). This suggests that GPR research is receiving more attention by the academia now than it used to have before.

Rigor and Quality of GPR Research

The use of existing theories and existence of a clearly elaborated research methodology can tell about the rigor and quality of the research. In this regard, out of the 40 articles reviewed 25 did not use any theory (are atheoretical). Six of the articles used business process theory, two used institutional theory, and seven articles used other theories (see Table 3).

Table 2. Distribution of journal articles by year of publication

Year	No of articles	Reference
1997	4 (10%)	Halachmi and Bovaird (1997); Buchanan (1997); Davidson (1997) ; Harrington, McLoughlin, Riddell (1997)
1998	3 (7.5%)	McAdam and Mitchell (1998); Coulson-Thomas (1998); Narsimhan and Jayaram (1998)
1999	2 (5%)	Aldowaisan and Gaafar (1999); Anderson (1999)
2000	1 (2.5%)	Thong, Yap, Seah (2000)
2001	2 (5%)	Adenso-Diaz and Canteli (2001); McAdam and Corrigan (2001)
2002	3 (7.5%)	Aversano, Canfora, De Lucia, and Gallucci (2002); Gulledge and Sommer (2002); Kwak and Lee (2002)
2003	1 (2.5%)	MacIntosh (2003)
2004	4 (10%)	Bliemel and Hassanein (2004); Martinez-Moyano and Gil-Garcia (2004); McNulty and Ferlie (2004); Ongaro (2004)
2005	2 (5%)	Alpar and Olbrich (2005); Scholl (2005)
2006	5 (12.5%)	Martin and Montagna (2006); Mengesha and Common (2006); Hughes, Scott, and Golden (2006); Anderson (2006) ; Greasley (2006)
2007	7(17.5%)	Frye and Gulledge(2007); Gauld (2007);Ilesson (2007);Ilesson, Al-Ameed, and Samaka (2007); Indihar Stemberger and Jaklic (2007); Meneklis and Douligeris (2007); Dwivedi, Weerakkody, and Williams (2007)
2008	5 (12.5%)	Dzhumalieva and Helfert (2008); Knox (2008); Tarokh, Sharifi, and Nazemi (2008); Sia and Neo (2008); Groznik, Kovacic, Trkman (2008)
2009	1 (2.5%)	Limam Mansa, Reijers, and Ounnar (2009)
Total	40	

Table 3. Type of theories used

Theories used	No. of articles using the theory	Author/s and year of publication
Business process theory (implied or not explicitly stated)	6 (15%)	McAdam and Mitchell (1998); Narasimhan and Jayaram (1998); Ongaro (2004); Thong, Yap, Seah (2000); McAdam and Corrigan (2001); Anderson (2006),
Conceptual lens of Panopticon	1(2.5%)	Sia and Neo (2008)
Decision Theory	1 (2.5%)	Limam Mansa, Reijers, and Ounnar (2009)
Event driven process chain theory	1 (2.5%)	Alpar and Olbrich (2005)
Institutional theory and Principal agent theory	2 (5%)	Martinez-Moyano and Gil-Garcia (2004); Knox (2008)
Organizational change theory	1 (2.5%)	McNulty and Ferlie (2004)
Resources based view theory (knowledge based view)	1 (2.5%)	Dzhumalieva and Helfert (2008)
Sociotechnical and dynamic system theory	1 (2.5%)	Dwivedi, Weerakkody, and Williams (2007)
Structuration Theory	1 (2.5%)	Meneklis and Douligeris (2007)
No theory	25 (62.5%)	Kwak and Lee (2002); Indihar Stemberger and Mojca (2007); Aldowaisan and Gaafar (1999); Martin and Montagan (2006); Greasley (2006); Harrington, McLoughlin, Riddell (1997); Scholl (2005); Frye and Gulledge(2007); Hesson, Al-Ameed, and Samaka (2007); Hesson (2007); Adenso-Diaz and Canteli (2001); Aversano, Canfora, De Lucia, and Gallucci (2002); Bliemel and Hassanein (2004); Anderson (1999); MacIntosh (2003); Mengesha and Common (2006); Tarokh, Sharifi, and Nazemi (2008); Coulson-Thomas (1998); Hughes, Scott, and Golden (2006); Buchanan (1997); Halachmi and Bovaird (1997); Davidson (1997); Groznik, Kovacic, Trkman (2008); Guald (2007); Gulllege and Sommer (2002)
Total	40	

Regarding the research methodology employed while 30% of the articles never clearly state about their research design and method, 55% used single case study method; 7.5% used multiple case study method; 5% used survey method; and one article followed mixed method (Table 4). The fact that many of the studies did neither use existing theories nor clearly state the research methodology used suggest that most of the GPR research lack rigor and quality.

GPR Studies in the Context of Developing Countries

Out of the interest to understand whether the GPR experiences and practices of developing countries are presented or not, the review identified those articles that explored and investigated cases of developing economies. Although relatively few, the review revealed that six articles out of the 40 are in the context of developing economies (Table 5). The remaining 34 articles are in the context of developed economies.

Review and Classification of the GPR Literature

As it was stated earlier in this chapter, this review adopted four research themes for the purposes of analysis and synthesis of GPR researches. Concerning the distribution of the articles along those four research themes, 35% of the articles are GPR adoption, implementation and evaluation studies; 25% are normative GPR studies;

Table 4. Research methodology used by the articles selected for review

Research Method	No of Articles using the Method	
Single Case Study	22(55%)	Kwak and Lee (2002); Indihar Stemberger and Mojca (2007); Aldowaisan and Gaafar (1999); Martin and Montagan (2006), Greasley (2006); Limam Mansa, Reijers, and Ounnar (2009); Knox (2008); Narsimhan and Jayaram (1998); Dzhumalieva and Helfert (2008); Dwivedi, Weerakkody, and Williams (2007); Hesson, Al-Ameed, and Samaka (2007); Hesson (2007); Adenso-Diaz and Canteli (2001); Thong, Yap, Seah (2000); Anderson (1999); McNulty and Ferlie (2004); McAdam and Corrigan (2001); Coulson-Thomas (1998); Gulledge and Sommer (2002); Hughes, Scott, and Golden (2006); Buchanan (1997); Groznik, Kovacic, Trkman (2008)
Multiple Case Study	3 (7.5%)	Scholl (2005); Ongaro (2004); MacIntosh (2003)
Survey	2 (5%)	Mengesha and Common (2006); Tarokh, Sharifi, and Nazemi (2008)
Mixed Method	1 (2.5%)	Sia and Neo (2008)
No research design / Method	12 (30%)	Alpar and Olbrich (2005); Frye and Gulledge(2007); Meneklis and Douligeris (2007); McAdam and Mitchell (1998); Martinez-Moyano and Gil-Garcia (2004); Aversano, Canfora, De Lucia, and Gallucci (2002); Bliemel and Hassanein (2004); Anderson (1999); Anderson (2006); Halachmi and Bovaird (1997); Davidson (1997); Harrington, McLoughlin, Riddell (1997)
Total	40	

Table 5. GPR studies in the context of developing countries

Reference	Country	Research Themes
Dzhumalieva & Helfert (2008)	Bulgaria	Conceptual model
Knox (2008)	Kazakhstan	Normative studies
Tarokh, Sharifi, and Nazemi (2008)	Iran	GPR adoption, implementation and evaluation
Mengesha and Common (2006)	Ethiopia	GPR adoption, implementation and evaluation
Martin and Montagna (2006)	Argentina	Conceptual Model
Hesson (2007)	UAE	GPR adoption, implementation and evaluation
Hesson, Al-Ameed, and Samaka (2007)	UAE	GPR adoption, implementation and evaluation

22.5% are GPR theoretical/conceptual model studies; and the remaining are GPR methodology studies (Table 6). Subsequent part of this section provides a discussion of the articles under each research theme.

Normative GPR Studies

The articles under this theme are consistent in their tone that government organizations have a unique culture and face unique challenges which have a bearing on the process and outcome of GPR. For example, Thong, Yap, Seah (2000) point out the institutional/environmental factors such as absence of market exposure, presence of more formal constraints, and existence of higher political influences and organizational factors like multiple goals which are often contradictory, leaders with more political role than organizational affairs, frequent turnover of leaders as a result of elections, and rigid reward and incentive schemes.

Appreciating the differences between the public sector BPR and private sector BPR and in recognition of political environment's coexistence

Table 6. Distribution of Articles by the research themes

Research themes	No. of articles	Author(s) and publication year
Normative GPR Studies	10 (25%)	Thong, Yap, Seah (2000); Anderson (2006), Scholl (2005); Knox (2008); Gulledge and Sommer (2002); Hughes, Scott, and Golden (2006); Buchanan (1997); Halachmi and Bovaird (1997); Davidson (1997)
GPR methodology Studies	7 (17.5%)	Kwak and Lee (2002); Indihar Stemberger and Jaklic (2007); Aldowaisan and Gaafar (1999); Limam Mansa, Reijers, and Ounnar (2009); Alpar and Olbrich (2005); Greasley (2006); Groznik., Kovacic, Trkman (2008)
GPR conceptual model Studies	9 (22.5%)	Frye and Gulledge(2007); Dwivedi, Weerakkody, and Williams (2007); Martinez-Moyano and Gil-Garcia (2004); Dzhumalieva and Helfert (2008); Meneklis and Douligeris (2007); McAdam and Mitchell (1998); Martin and Montagna (2006); Ongaro (2004); Narasimhan and Jayaram (1998)
GPR adoption, implementation and evaluation Studies	14 (35%)	Hesson, Al-Ameed, and Samaka (2007); Hesson (2007); Adenso-Diaz and Canteli (2001); Aversano, Canfora, De Lucia, and Gallucci (2002); Bliemel and Hassanein (2004); Anderson (1999); Harrington, McLoughlin, Riddell (1997); MacIntosh (2003); McNulty & Ferlie (2004); McAdam and Corrigan (2001); Sia and Neo (2008); Coulson-Thomas (1998); Mengesha and Common (2006); Tarokh, Sharifi, and Nazemi (2008)
Total No of Articles	40 (100%)	

with any managerial rationalism in the former, Anderson (199; 2006) proposes political value chain model as basis for public sector process rebuilding. The model acknowledges the existence of several stakeholders with conflicting interests, who will subjectively judge the value of the GPR as opposed to objective measures of the private sector. On the other hand, McAdam and Michell (1998); Harrington, McLoughlin, and Riddell (1998); and McNulty & Ferlie (2004) argue that because of the differences between public and private sectors, the private sector BPR models and methodologies can't directly be transferred to the public sector. They cite the following characteristics of public organizations to have a bearing upon GPR: rigid hierarchies, culture, multiple stakeholders for a single process, possibility of sudden and dramatic changes in policy and direction, overlap of initiatives, wide scope of activities, and staff with the attitude of lifelong employment (Hutton, 1996 as cited in McAdam and Mitchelll, 1998). Furthermore, some of the studies indicate the difficulty of applying the clean slate approach and undertaking a radical BPR in public organizations due to stated characteristics of public organizations (MacIntosh, 2003; Scholl,

2005; Gulledge and Sommer, 2002; Halachmi and Bovaird, 1997; Buchanan, 1997; Davidson, 1997; and Martin and Montagna, 2006).

The other dimension considered in characterizing public sector BPR (GPR) is the close relationship between GPR and ICT such as ERP-based E-Government. GPR presupposes ICT as its essential enabler and as its integral element (Hammer and Champy, 1993; Davenport, 1993). As such, GPR can be considered as the tool and methodology for the transformation of the public sector and for realizing E-Government (Martin and Montagna, 2006). While the first two stages of E-Government (that is the cataloguing and transaction stages), according to Layne and Lee (2001), appear relatively easy to attain, the higher two stages (i.e. vertical integration and horizontal integration are difficult to achieve without undertaking GPR). GPR is essential to reengineer the back office activities (government business processes, procedures, structures, and underlying culture) and interorganizational transactional processes (network processes) of each public organization (Hughes, Scott, and Golden, 2006; Gulledge and Sommer, 2002; Martin and Montagna, 2006). In relation to this,

Hughes, Scott, Golden (2006) and Gulledge and Sommer (2002) investigate the role of GPR in E-Government implementation and established that GPR is instrumental and is a prerequisite for effective E-Government implementation.

In summary, the articles under this theme outline

1. public sector BPR (GPR) is characteristically different from private sector BPR;
2. GPR has important role in E-Government implementation; and
3. application of the clean slate approach and attaining of radical transformation through GPR is practically difficult in government organizations.

The review findings suggest that private sector lessons, experiences, methods, tools, and techniques might not readily be transferred to the public sector.

GPR Methodology Studies

The journal articles under this theme present research findings on methodologies, tools, and techniques for GPR implementation. Indihar Stemberger and Mojca (2007) acknowledge the importance of GPR for effective implementation of the higher stages of E-Government and propose a six stage methodology with detail activities and tools. In the same vein, Groznik, Kovacic, Trkman (2008) develop a GPR methodology for modeling, renovating, and informatizing the business process of a public organization as part of E-Government implementation. Alpar and Olbrich (2005) also show the applicability of event-driven process chain modeling of government business processes and business rules in the context of E-Government implementation. The rest deal with methods of redesigning government business processes using BPR best practices (Limam Mansa, Reijers, and Ounnar, 2009) and process mapping and simula-

tion tools (Greasley, 2006; Kwak and Lee, 2002; and Aldowaisan and Gaafar, 1999).

All the methodology studies also maintain that public sector BPR has its own specifics that distinguish it from private sector BPR and attempt to adapt their methodology to the public sector context. These studies, although stop short of empirically testing and validating their methodologies, have identified several attributes for GPR methodologies. First, GPR methodologies need to be reasonably precise. This is because whenever a methodology is loose or lacks precision, it invites some politically motivated actors to maneuver or manipulate the reengineering process and its outcome in their favor. On the other hand, whenever a methodology is so prescriptive and detailed, it reduces or restricts creativity of the reengineering team in adapting or tailoring the methodology to the contextual realities (Coulson-Thomas, 1998; Buchanan, 1997). In this respect, the benefit of a well-validated GPR methodology, if exist, is so immense. Second, besides being reasonably precise, GPR methodologies need to be comprehensive, that is, they should address all the activities that are bound to take place while performing GPR, such as those stated by Indihar Stemberger and Mojca (2007). Third, they need to be explicit about inter-organizational networking and the use of IT (such as ERP-based E-Government) for attaining radical transformation and achieving dramatic gains in performance.

In general, although the studies propose various methodologies for use in GPR implementation, there is still lack of well validated, integrated (integrating and embedding IT with GPR) and comprehensive (from envisioning and scoping up to monitoring, measurement and evaluation) GPR methodology that is instrumental to the realization of IT enabled E-Government. While measurement and evaluation of the GPR outcome is essential, no single article under this theme has tried to incorporate this feature into its methodology.

Conceptual Model Studies

The review identified nine articles under this theme which can further be divided into two groups based on their focus:

1. those which focus on proper GPR implementation model, and
2. those which focus on developing framework or model for integrating GPR and E-Government to realize one-stop government (OSG).

Within the first group, we find Narasimhan and Jayaram (1998), McAdam and Mitchell (1998), and Ongaro (2004) who develop a model for GPR implementation based on BPR theory. Narasimhan and Jayaram (1998) propose a three-stage process model (assessment effectiveness stage, reengineering design effectiveness stage, and implementation planning effectiveness stage) based on longitudinal case study. The model also proposes critical success factors in the form of testable propositions that would ensure effective accomplishment of each stage. However, the model overlooks evaluation stage of the GPR which measures and assesses the outcomes achieved at process performance and organizational performance level. Further, while processual factors were considered in the model, contextual factors such as organization type, organization size, and GPR complimentary factors such as performance measurement, process management, reward system, employee empowerment and work monitoring are neglected.

The second model in this group is the process model proposed by McAdam and Mitchell (1998) based on BPR theory. The elements of the model include as-is assessment, proposed to-be design, public sector critical success factors (such as culture, strategy and policy, structure, processes, people, technology, and communication), actual to-be, and feedback loop to ensure continuous monitoring and improvement. As such, the model

appears simple but lacks testable propositions and empirical validation besides its omission of contextual factors.

The model proposed by Ongaro (2004) is the third model in the first group which uses BPR theory and is empirically tested. The elements in the model include macro-institutional and contextual factors such as legal and cultural settings together with macro enabling factors, public sector reform program with specific enabling conditions and pressures, micro-level/individual organizations and their relationships, executive leadership, and implementation of process management together with enabling ICT and organizational culture. As such, the model integrates macro level contextual institutional factors and micro organizational factors that are deemed to influence any GPR implementation. That being its strength, it requires further validation and consideration especially in evaluating the degree of process-orientation achieved.

Martin and Montagna (2006), Dzhumalieva and Helfert (2008), Martinez-Moyano and Gil-Garcia (2004), Meneklis and Douligeris (2007), Dwivedi, Weerakkody, and Williams (2007), and Frye and Gulledge(2007) constitute the second group of articles. These articles focus on developing frameworks that integrate GPR into the development of E-Government with a view to realize one-stop government. Except Martin and Montagna (2006) and Frye and Gulledge(2007) that are not based on existing theory, all others are theoretically grounded such as the resource based and knowledge based views, principal-agent, institutional, structuration, system dynamic and socio-technical theory. Regarding research method used, all followed the interpretive research paradigm based on single case study method excepting Martinez-Moyano and Gil-Garcia (2004), Meneklis and Douligeris (2007) and Frye and Gulledge(2007), who didn't state the method used. The articles by Martin and Montagna (2006) and Dzhumalieva and Helfert (2008) stand out to be special. The former fuses GPR principles, methodologies, tools and techniques within the E-Government development framework and the latter links organizational resources (organization knowledge and service delivery capabilities) with process level performance and organizational level performance in the context of public sector.

In summary, the research articles under this theme propose models for use while implementing GPR. While several of the models are empirically grounded in and theory supported, they need further testing and empirical validation. The articles under this theme are also mainly qualitative single case studies, which indicate lack of a complementary quantitative-based research. Further, several of the articles fail to model the contextual variables (macro and institutional) and complimentary competences necessary to further enhance and sustain the GPR outcome. Although evaluation and monitoring (measurement & assessment) of the GPR outcome is critical, all except Dzhumalieva and Helfert (2008) have not considered it in their model.

GPR Adoption, Implementation, and Evaluation Studies

There are 14 articles under this theme. Analysis of contents of these research articles revealed that the articles emphasize on three areas:

1. lessons learnt from implementation experiences (issues, factors contributing to success, factors contributing to failure, etc),
2. assessment /evaluation of implementation outcome, and
3. GPR impact on work environment (employees empowerment and work monitoring).

Notable works under the lessons learnt are research articles by Hesson (2007); Hesson, Al-Ameed, and Samaka (2007); McNulty and Ferlie (2004); Harrington, McLoughlin, and Riddell (1997); MacIntosh (2003); and McAdam and

Corrigan (2001). All these articles report problem of undertaking the radical type of BPR in public organization due, primarily, to top management's reluctance to lose its approval power to lower level employees who directly interface with service recipients. Although the GPR implementation entails employees empowerment and requires putting in place process-based organizational structure, middle and top level management are less committed to make that happen. Indeed, they try to maintain their power through preserving the existing status quo (Hesson, Al-Ameed, and Samaka, 2007; Harrington, McLoughlin, and Riddell, 1997; and McNulty and Ferlie, 2004). In addition, McNulty and Ferlie (2004) indicate difficulty of realizing process-based transformation in professionalized public organizations, such as in the health care and educational sector. Professionals in such kind of organizations are powerful enough to compromise or maneuver the anticipated change outcome in a way that suits them. Despite the aforementioned factors that limit radical transformation, there are important lessons learnt that are critical to GPR success. These include:

*   efficient database design, search facilities, electronic document archive (Hesson, 2007 and Hesson, Al-Ameed, and Samaka, 2007);
*   synchronizing the process based organizing that GPR requires with the demands of functional-based organization structure (McNulty and Ferlie, 2004);
*   use of reasonably precise GPR methodology which discourages politically motivated individuals from influencing the GPR process and outcome in their favor (MacIntosh, 2003); and
*   top management support, commitment and understanding of GPR; communication, empowerment, alleviation of downsizing fears, preparedness for organizational

change; choosing the reengineering team; and training (McAdam and Corrigan, 2001).

Getachew and Common (2006) and Tarokh, Sharifi, and Nazemi (2008) focus on assessment and evaluation of GPR implementation outcome. While the former assesses GPR outcome of two Ministry Offices (Ministry of Trade and Industry and Ministry of Education) in Ethiopia and reports the result as success, the latter carries out a similar survey of 13 public organizations in Iran and report the finding as failure due, primarily, to lack of preparation and readiness for a change that GPR entails. On the other hand, Sia and Neo's (2008) study of Inland Revenue Service in Singapore reveals that employees were more empowered and that work monitoring was more heightened for work activities (especially routine activities) post-BPR. Contrary to the common assumption (see Harrington, McLoughlin, and Riddell, 1997), the finding suggests that empowerment doesn't necessarily lead to control risk so long as the necessary internal control systems are in-built (embedded) within the system and the work activities assigned to employees are made visible, traceable, and transparent. Further implication of such a finding by Sia and Neo (2008) suggests the importance of bringing the literature on empowerment and monitoring into one in process reengineering.

When all the article under this theme are assessed in terms of use of existing theory, none except Sia and Neo (2008) use any existing theory that would guide their investigation and analysis. Concerning research method, Mengesha and Common (2006) and Tarokh, Sharifi, and Nazemi (2008) used descriptive survey method; Sia and Neo (2008) used mixed method; and the remaining used case study method (MacIntosh, 2003 and Anderson, 1999). In terms of context of the studies, while four of the studies are in the context of developing countries, the rest are cases of developed countries (Table 4).

In sum, the articles under the adoption, implementation and evaluation studies theme explore and investigate GPR implementation practices in order to understand the lessons that can be learnt, the outcome of GPR implementation, and the impact of GPR implementation on employees' empowerment and work monitoring. Analysis of findings of the reviewed articles revealed that there is a limit to radical GPR due to managements' reluctance to lose power and professionals' tendency to preserve the existing status quo. The review also disclosed important lessons that can be learnt, such as the importance of enabling IT, synchronizing the process based structure with the functional based structure, using precise GPR methodology, importance of top-management support, commitment, and understanding. Contrary to the common understanding that GPR increases empowerment at the expense of compromising the control system of the organization, the reviewed articles show that work monitoring is rather heightened post-BPR. Different from the previous themes, the research articles under this category include experiences and practices in the context of developing economies.

FUTURE GPR RESEARCH DIRECTIONS AND RECOMMENDATIONS

As it becomes evident from the discussion of reviewed articles, there are GPR related issues and gaps that need to be addressed in the future. This section presents the areas identified for further research based on research gaps, which the literature review revealed. The research issues are grouped into the following five categories which are same as the research streams used for purpose of literature review discussion:

1. GPR research rigor and quality,
2. GPR theoretical frameworks/conceptual models,

3. GPR Methodologies (including techniques and tools),
4. GPR adoption, implementation, and evaluation, and
5. Normative GPR studies.

GPR Research Rigor and Quality

The review revealed that several of the research articles are atheoretical and did not present their research design and method. This practice has negative implication to GPR research quality and relevance. Thus, future GPR researches shall clearly state the research method and shall use existing theory that would dictate formulation of the research question/hypothesis, guide/inform data collection, and govern data analysis and interpretation.

Furthermore, most of the research articles were predominantly qualitative case studies along the interpretive paradigm. While such studies are useful to understand the context and provide detail explanation about the why and how types of questions, they will have limitation to make statistical generalization and validation. Thus, in order to complement findings of the studies made so far and validate some of the GPR frameworks/models proposed, future GPR researches need to focus more on quantitative studies.

GPR Theoretical Frameworks/Models

The literature review disclosed that, GPR literature lacks well validated and theoretically grounded frameworks and models. Considering the fact that GPR is undertaken as means to achieve better organizational performance, future research shall aim for developing and/or validating a model that will link the GPR effort to organizational performance based on established theory. We, therefore, like to suggest the following areas for future research.

- Development of theoretically grounded frameworks and models for measuring the effect of GPR on public organization performance and the factors that affect success. Such studies can draw from the resource based view theory to define and test the effect of GPR complimentary competencies and capabilities (such as continuous improvement and process management activities). Future research can also consider developing and validating measurement instruments for important constructs such as public sector organizational performance and GPR complimentary competences.
- Extension and validation of existing GPR models such as those proposed by Narasimhan and Jayaram (1998); Martin and Montagan (2006); and Ongaro (2004). While extending the models, it would be worthwhile to take into consideration contextual variables and measurement and evaluation of GPR outcomes.
- Considering that measurement of the effect of GPR on public organization performance is more complex than measurement of the effect of BPR on private sector performance, developing models for measuring organizational performance effect of GPR will also be a significant academic and practical contribution. Thus, future research should build upon the work of Dzhumalieva and Helfert (2008) that used process performance and organizational performance constructs.

GPR Methodologies

The review also revealed that there is no widely accepted GPR methodology that is comprehensive enough (guiding from GPR readiness assessment to post implementation and evaluation) and that integrates the enabling role of information technology. There is also lack of high level (less technical) process-aware enabling tools that GPR adopters can use while undertaking process design, process modeling and simulation. Thus, there is a need for further research towards a more comprehensive, integrated, well validated methodology embracing all the essential process mapping, modeling, and management tools and techniques. We, therefore, like to suggest the following areas for future research.

- Development and validation of GPR methodologies that are comprehensive and explicit about the enabling techniques and tools;
- Development of high level process-aware tools, which facilitate and increase effectiveness of the GPR such as process mapping, modeling and simulation. In this connection, further extension and validation of the work of Limam Mansa, Reijers, and Ounnar (2009) may be a worthwhile research endeavour.

GPR Adoption, Implementation, and Evaluation

The review disclosed existence of contradictory findings among GPR adopters about their practices, implementation outcomes, and post-GPR impact (some repot success while others report failure and some say empowerment weakens control while others report a case of strengthened control). There is, therefore, a need for further research on GPR implementation practices, outcomes, and post-GPR impact in order to gain more insight about the critical factors that contribute to GPR success/failure and issues/problems (people as well as organization related) that emerge post-BPR. Given that GPR is being embraced by developing economies as part of their reform program (Mengesha and Common, 2006), more empirical research about their GPR practices and outcomes is also commendable. Further, the GPR literature is silent about issues

and problems that take place post GPR. One of these problems relates to how the process-based form of organizing, which GPR introduces, coexist and gradually takes precedence over the existing functional-based structure.

We, therefore, like to recommend the following areas for future research in relation to GPR adoption, implementation, and evaluation.

- More GPR adoption and implementation studies; especially in a developing economy context. Besides reporting the implementation experiences, GPR adoption and implementation studies can be more relevant if they explore antecedent patterns of successful and/or failed GPR cases (as measured based on the degree of radical transformation and resultant organizational performance achieved). Among others, the antecedent factors can include GPR project coordination and management arrangement (leadership), resource deployment (financial, technological as well as expertise), depth and breadth of GPR undertaken, implementation problems experienced, complimentary process management competences and capabilities, the role IT played during the GPR implementation (automation, informational, innovation/strategic, and infrastructural/ communication/), and contextual factors such as organization type, nature, culture, and leadership. The research may be designed as longitudinal single/multiple case study or quantitative study surveying large number of organizations that undertake GPR using well validated framework and instrument. Given that prior studies were mainly qualitative single case studies, longitudinal multiple case studies and model-based quantitative studies can help to complement earlier studies and validate earlier findings obtained based on qualitative singe case studies.

- Further studies exploring GPR's impact on employees' empowerment and work monitoring along the direction of Thong, Yap, Seah (2000). Further study in this direction (empowerment and monitoring pre-GPR and Post-GPR) can help to validate previous findings and inform practitioners how to effectively deal with the control risk often associated with employees' empowerment.

- Study on impact of GPR on control (administrative control and principle of check and balance); on performance measurement and management; on human resource practices such as promotion and remuneration; on leadership and management; on organizational culture, on existing IT resources and services which were designed and developed with the functional-based organization in mind; on process management and governance; on organizational structure and government arrangement; and on government laws and regulations.

- Research on conditions or factors that should be put in place in order to attain high level of process orientation; how to balance the process-based organizing which the GPR necessitates and the continuing demand for functional mode of operation.

Normative GPR Studies

The review also determined research gaps that require further normative kinds of studies by practitioners and academicians. These relate to the following areas:

- *Sustaining the result of GPR:* What are the conditions and mechanisms that would safeguard the GPR result from backsliding? Future research can explore and investigate the role of complementary competences in IT, performance measurement and management system, process manage-

ment and governance system, and continuous process improvement strategy in enhancing and sustaining the effect of the GPR.

- *Linking the GPR and E-Goverment initiatives:* The two are complementary and undertaking one in absence of the other can be less effective. Cognizant of the fact that GPR involves IT such as ERP-based E-Government as its enabler and effective E-Government is hardly possible to achieve without undertaking associated GPR, future research shall explore how the two can seamlessly fused one another. In this connection, future research can consider to build up on the work of Martin and Motagna (2006).

- *Limitation of ERP systems to the public sector:* In spite of the fact that ERP systems have embedded customizable features and several best practices with in them, those features are the results of primarily private sector experiences. Considering that public sector is characteristically different from the private sector, further normative studies about opportunities and limitations of ERP system adoption and implementation for the public sector in general and of a developing country context in particular will have practical contribution because the way government of a developing economy functions (system, arrangement, services) is different from that of a developed economy in several aspects.

- *Coordination problem:* Public administration functions involve a number of independent public agencies at different levels of government, which undertake same functions such as procurement, finance (budgeting and accounting), human resource and payroll, general service and logistics, record/document management, IT services, government fixed asset management, internal control and auditing. Thus, further normative GPR studies that inform how GPR of support and management processes needs to be coordinated and managed (including accountability and responsibility for different kinds of government business processes) would be significant in preventing /avoiding emergence of unnecessary dissimilar processes and systems and in promoting and ensuring standardized support & management processes.

- *Readiness studies for GPR implementation (including breadth/scope and depth of GPR)*: GPR implementation is a high-return and high-risk venture/undertaking. In order to reduce the chance of failure and increase chance of success, it would be significant to develop GPR readiness assessment measures /indicators that would help to determine one's areas of strength and weakness and adjust oneself before formally launching and embarking on the project.

- *Conceptualization and classification of government business processes*: For purpose of gaining clarity and achieving consensus among GPR steering and implementation teams, there is a great need for normative studies that clarify concepts such as cross-functional, end-to-end, clean slate, and radical, business process using the language and context of the public sector. For example, does end-to-end refer to cross organizational; if so where is the end point and beginning point in a government organization context? Moreover, taxonomy and classification studies of government business processes would permit to better understand the government functions irrespective of the actual government arrangements (in terms of ministries, agencies, authorities, etc) which is subject to change from period to period. Hence, future normative GPR studies shall focus on developing government business process taxonomies and classifications.

Table 7 summarizes the research gaps identified and discussed above and the future research directions that are recommended in order to fill up those gaps.

CONCLUSION

This chapter has presented a review of the literature on government process reengineering (GPR). It reviewed 40 peer reviewed academic articles that appeared in about 30 journals, covering the period from 1997 to 2009. While extant GPR literature made significant contributions to both academic research and practice, the review also determined research gaps that need to be filled in the future. The research gaps identified include:

a. failure to use established theory that guides/ informs the research and lack of stating and elaborating the research method used; both of which negatively affect quality of the GPR research;

b. domination of qualitative case studies along the interpretive paradigm with little quantitative studies along the positivism paradigm due to which there is lack of validated frameworks/models and validated instruments for measuring some constructs already proposed based on findings using qualitative case studies;

c. absence of widely accepted comprehensive GPR methodology that guides the implementation activity from inception of the GPR through implementation to post-implementation and evaluation with explicitly stated tools, techniques, and procedures for each phases of the methodology;

d. lack of well-validated and theoretically grounded conceptual models for the implementation of GPR and evaluation of the process and its outcome;

e. insufficient number of empirical GPR studies (especially in the context of developing economies) assessing the effect of GPR on

Table 7. Summary of GPR research gaps and recommended future research areas

Themes	Research issues and gaps	Recommendations
Rigor and quality	• The extant literature suffers from lack of clearly stated research methodology and supporting theory	• Research that are theoretically and methodologically rigorous; that follow explicit research method; and that develop conceptual models and measurement instruments for relevant GPR constructs and that empirically test the contribution of GPR to public sector performance
GPR theoretical frameworks/ conceptual models	Lack of a well validated GPR model that is based on well established theory	• Research that develops and validates theoretical frameworks/ models useful for assessing the effect of BPR on organizational performance taking necessary antecedent factors including complimentary competences, technological resources, processual and contextual factors; that develops a validated measurement instruments for important constructs such as public sector organizational performance and GPR complementary competences.
GPR methodology	• Lack of a GPR methodology that is widely accepted to guide GPR implementation from readiness assessment up to post-implementation activities and evaluation with explicit consideration of critical success factors including information technology	• Research that develops and tests a comprehensive GPR methodology which explicitly integrates the technology, critical success factors, and process mapping and modelling tools and techniques
GPR adoption, implementation, and evaluation	• Lack of empirical GPR research assessing implementation outcome and post-implementation impact of GPR	• Research that evaluates outcomes of GPR implementation (can be quantitative, longitudinal multiple case study); that assesses post-implementation impact of GPR on employees empowerment, internal control (principle of check and balance), performance measurement & management, human resource practice, IT services, government structure, laws, regulations and policies; that examines antecedents factors to a successful/failed GPR implementation
GPR normative Studies	• Lack of normative studies dealing with issues on GPR project coordination and management, fitting/aligning existing ERP systems to the reengineered government processes and vice versa, GPR readiness assessment; and strategies of sustaining the results of GPR.	• Research that explores and investigates GPR project coordination and management (who should be responsible for what during GPR implementation involving different layers of government); limitations and opportunities of ERP systems as GPR enabler, GPR readiness assessment instrument; taxonomies and classification of government business processes; and strategies for sustaining the positive results of GPR

organizational performance and exploring post-GPR issues, problems, and impacts; and

f.   lack of normative GPR studies on enhancing and sustaining positive results of GPR; on opportunities and limitation of ERP systems as GPR enabling technology; and on GPR project coordination and management.

With the view to address the above research gaps, the review indicated the direction that future GPR research shall be heading to in the form of recommendation. While one can refer to section five for details of the recommended research directions/areas, we like to draw the attention of future

GPR researchers to use existing theories to guide and inform the research; state and elaborate the research method; undertake a research to develop GPR methodology that guides from readiness assessment through implementation and post implementation-evaluation; carry out research to develop tools that facilitate and increase GPR implementation success; undertake research to develop/validate GPR models and instruments to measure some constructs of existing models /proposed models; and conduct empirical and normative research on post-GPR issues, problems, and impacts.

In conclusion, analysis of the review findings revealed weak and strong aspects of extant GPR studies. As strength, GPR research is live and active in all areas (GPR methodology, GPR models/frameworks, GPR adoption & implementation, and GPR normative studies) and both in developed & developing economies. As weakness, extant GPR literature is largely atheoretical and as such can lack the rigor and quality required for academic research. Further, although the purpose of undertaking GPR is for achieving performance gains, only a few of the extant studies did try to assess GPR's effect through linking the GPR effort with organizational performance. In order to further increase its quality and relevance, future GPR research needs to focus more on developing and validating GPR theoretical frameworks (models) and assessing effect of GPR on performance using well-established theoretical framework taking into account all the essential factors antecedent to the GPR implementation and essential GPR complementary competences/capabilities that need to be put in place post-GPR.

Finally, the literature review (approach and methodology pursued) was not without limitation; however. The review is limited chiefly to peer-reviewed academic journal articles, ignoring conference papers, book chapters, and professional magazine articles. Further, classifying articles along the four themes is not a straight forward process. Articles are classified into one of the four categories based on the understanding of the first author, which is subjective and can be questioned.

REFERENCES

Adenso-Di'Az, B., & Canteli, A. (2001). Business Process Reengineering and University Organisation: a normative approach from the Spanish case. *Journal of Higher Education Policy and Management*, *23*(1), 63–73. doi:10.1080/13600800020047243

Al-Mashari, M., Irani, Z., & Zairi, M. (2001). Business process reengineering: a survey of international experience. *Business Process Management Journal*, *7*(5), 437–455. doi:10.1108/14637150110406812

Aldowaisan, T., & Gaafar, L. (1999). BPR: An approach for process mapping. *Omega*, *27*, 515–524. doi:10.1016/S0305-0483(99)00015-8

Alpar, P., & Olbrich, S. (2005). Legal Requirements and Modelling of Processes in e-Government. *The Electronic. Journal of E-Government*, *3*(3), 107–116.

Andersen, K. (1999). Reengineering public sector organisations using information technology. *Reinventing government in the information age*: 312-330.

Anderson, K. (2006). Reengineering Public Sector Organizations Using Information Technology. *Research in Public Policy Analysis and Management*, *15*, 615–634. doi:10.1016/S0732-1317(06)15027-7

Aversano, L., Canfora, G., De Lucia, A., & Gallucci, P. (2002). Business process reengineering and workflow automation: a technology transfer. *Journal of Systems and Software*, *63*(1), 29–44. doi:10.1016/S0164-1212(01)00128-5

Bliemel, M., & Hassanein, K. (2004). E-health:applying business process reengineering principles to healthcare in Canada. *International Journal of Electronic Business*, *2*(6), 625–643. doi:10.1504/IJEB.2004.006129

Buchanan, D. (1997). The limitations and opportunities of business process re-engineering in a politicized organizational climate. *Human Relations*, *50*(1), 51. doi:10.1177/001872679705000103

Coulson-Thomas, C. (1998). Managing innovation in public services: European and international experience. *Total quality management & Business Excellence, 9*(2), 213-222.

Davidson, G. (1997). Managing by process in private and public organizations: Scientific Management in the Information Revolution. *Journal of Post Keynesian Economics, 20*(1), 25–45.

Dwivedi, Y. K., Weerakkody, V., & Williams, M. D. (2007). Interorganzational Information Integration: A key enabler for digital government. *Government Information Quarterly, 24,* 691. doi:10.1016/j.giq.2007.08.004

Dzhumalieva, S., & Helfert, M. (2008). A Conceptual Framework for Handling Complex Administrative Processes in E-Government. *Information Systems and E-Business Technologies, 417-428.*

Frye, D., & Gulledge, T. (2007). End-to-end business process scenarios. *Industrial Management & Data Systems, 107*(6), 749–761. doi:10.1108/02635570710758707

Greasley, A. (2006). Using process mapping and business process simulation to support a process-based approach to change in a public sector organization. *Technovation, 26*(1), 95–103. doi:10.1016/j.technovation.2004.07.008

Groznik, A., Kovacic, A., & Trkman, P. (2008). The role of business renovation and information in eGovernment. *Journal of Computer Information Systems, 49*(1), 81–89.

Gulledge, T., & Sommer, R. (2002). Business process management: public sector implications. *Business Process Management Journal, 8*(4), 364–376. doi:10.1108/14637150210435017

Halachmi, A., & Bovaird, T. (1997). Process reengineering in the public sector: Learning some private sector lessons. *Technovation, 17*(5), 227–235. doi:10.1016/S0166-4972(96)00123-X

Harrington, B., McLoughlin, K., & Riddell, D. (1997). Business Process Re-engineering in the Public Sector: a Case Study of the Contributions Agency. *New Technology, Work and Employment, 13*(1), 43–50. doi:10.1111/1468-005X.00037

Hesson, M. (2007). Business process reengineering in UAE public sector A naturalization and residency case study. *Business Process Management Journal, 13*(5), 707–727. doi:10.1108/14637150710823174

Hesson, M., Al-Ameed, H., & Samaka, M. (2007). BPR in UAE Public Sector: a town planning study. *Business Process Management Journal, 13*(3), 348–378. doi:10.1108/14637150710752281

Hughes, M., Scott, M., & Golden, W. (2006). The role of business process redesign in creating e-Government in Ireland. *Business Process Management Journal, 12*(1), 76–87. doi:10.1108/14637150610643779

Indihar Stemberger, M., & Jaklic, J. (2007). Towards E-government by business process change-A methodology for public sector. *International Journal of Information Management, 27*(4), 221–232. doi:10.1016/j.ijinfomgt.2007.02.006

Knox, C. (2008). Kazakhstan: modernizing government in the context of political inertia. *International Review of Administrative Sciences, 74*(3), 477. doi:10.1177/0020852308095314

Kwak, N., & Lee, C. (2002). Business process reengineering for health-care system using muticriteria mathematical programming. *European Journal of Operational Research, 140*(2), 447–458. doi:10.1016/S0377-2217(02)00082-6

Layne, K., & Lee, J. (2001). Developing fully functional E-government: A four stage model. *Government Information Quarterly, 18*(2), 122–136. doi:10.1016/S0740-624X(01)00066-1

Levy, Y., & Ellis, T. (2006). A systems approach to conduct an effective literature review in support of information systems research. *Informing Science: International Journal of an Emerging Transdiscipline, 9,* 181–212.

Limam Mansar, S., Reijers, H. A., & Ounnar, F. (2009). Development of a decision-making stategy to improve the efficiency of BPR. *Expert Systems with Applications, 36*(2), 3248–3262. doi:10.1016/j.eswa.2008.01.008

Linden, R. (1994). *Seamless Government: A Practical Guide to Re-engineering in the Public Sector*. Jossey-Bass Publishers.

MacIntosh, R. (2003). BPR: alive and well in the public sector. *International Journal of Operations & Production Management, 23*(3/4), 327–345. doi:10.1108/01443570310462794

Martin, R., & Montagna, J. (2006). Business process reengineering role in electronic government. *The past and Future of Information Systems:1976-2006 and Beyond: 77-88*

Martinez-Moyano, I., & Gil-Garcia, J. (2004). Rules, Norms, and Individual preferences for action: An Institutional Framework to Understand the dynamics of eGovernment Evolution. *Electronic. Journal of E-Government*, 194–199. doi:10.1007/978-3-540-30078-6_32

McAdam, R., & Corrigan, M. (2001). Re-engineering in public sector health care:a telecommunication case study. *International Journal of Health Care Quality Assurance, 14*(5), 218–227. doi:10.1108/09526860110401340

McAdam, R., & Micheli, P. (1998). Development of Business process reengineering Model applicable to the public sector. *Total Quality Management, 9*(4), 160–163. doi:10.1080/0954412988802

McNulty, T., & Ferlie, E. (2004). Process transformation: Limitations to radical organizational change within public service organizations. *Organization Studies, 25*(8), 1389. doi:10.1177/0170840604046349

Meneklis, V., & Douligeris, C. (2007). Enhancing the design of e-government: identifying structures and modelling concepts in contemporary platforms. *Proceedings of the 1st international conference on Theory and practice of electronic governance:* ACM, 108-116.

Mengesha, G., & Common, R. (2007). Public sector capacity reform in Ethiopia: a tale of success in two ministries? *Public Administration and Development, 27*(5), 367–380. doi:10.1002/pad.456

Motwani, J., Kumar, A., Jiang, J., & Youssef, M. (1998). Business process reengineering: a theoretical framework and an integrated model. *International Journal of Operations & Production Management, 18*(9/10), 964–977. doi:10.1108/EUM0000000004536

Narsimhan, R., & Jayaram, J. (1998). Reengineering Service Operation: a longitudinal casse study. *Journal of Operations Management, 17*(1), 7–22. doi:10.1016/S0272-6963(98)00029-1

O'Neill, P., & Sohal, A. (1999). Business Process Reengineering A review of recent literature. *Technovation, 19*(9), 571–581. doi:10.1016/S0166-4972(99)00059-0

Ongaro, E. (2004). Process management in the public sector: the experience of one-stop shops in Italy. *International Journal of Public Sector Management, 17*(1), 81–107. doi:10.1108/09513550410515592

Rainey, H., & Steinbauer, P. (1999). Galloping elephants: Developing elements of a theory of effective government organizations. *Journal of Public Administration: Research and Theory, 9*(1), 1.

Scholl, H. (2005). "Organizational transformation through e-government: myth or reality?" *Electronic Government*: 1-11.

Scholl, H. (2005). E-government: A Special Case of ICT-enabled Business Process Change. *International Journal of E-Govemment Research, 1*(2), 27–49. doi:10.4018/jegr.2005040102

Sia, S., & Neo, B. (2008). Business process reengineering, empowerment and work monitoring: An empirical analysis through the panopticon. *Business Process Management Journal, 14*(5), 609–628. doi:10.1108/14637150810903020

Tarokh, M., Sharifi, E., & Nazemi, E. (2008). Survey of BPR experiences in Iran: reasons for success and failure. *Journal of Business and Industrial Marketing, 23*(5), 350–362. doi:10.1108/08858620810881629

Thong, J., Yap, C., & Seah, K. (2000). Business process reengineering in the public sector: The case of the housing development board in Singapore. *Journal of Management Information Systems, 17*(1), 245–270.

Webster, J., & Watson, R. (2002). Analysing the past to prepare for the future: Writing a literature review. *Management Information Systems Quarterly, 26*(2), 13–23.

ADDITIONAL READING

Abdolvand, N., Albandvi, A., & Ferdowsi, Z. (2008). Assessing Readiness for Reengineering. *Business Process Management Journal, 14*(4), 497–511. doi:10.1108/14637150810888046

Al-Hudhaif, S. (2009). Process redesign: reengineering core process at computer department–a case of SWCC. *Business Process Management Journal, 15*.

Al-Mashari, M., & Zairi, M. (2000) Revisiting BPR: a holistic review of practice and development", *Business process management, 6*(1), 10-42.

Altinkemer, K., Chaturvedi, A., & Kondareddy, S. (1998). Business Process Reengineering and Organizational Performance: An Exploration of Issues. *International Journal of Information Management, 18*(6), 381–392. doi:10.1016/S0268-4012(98)00030-9

Davenport, T. (1993). *Process innovation: reengineering work through information technology*. Cambridge, MA: Harvard Business School Press.

Davenport, T., & Short, J. (1990). The New Industrial Engineering: Information Technology and Business Process Redesign, in. *Sloan Management Review*, (Summer): 11–27.

Grover, V., & Malhotra, M. K. (1997). Business process reengineering: A tutorial on the concept, evolution, method, technology and application. *Journal of Operations Management, 15*, 193–213. doi:10.1016/S0272-6963(96)00104-0

Hammer, M. (2007). *The Process Audit*. Cambridge, MA: Harvard Business Review.

Hammer, M., & Champy, J. (1993). *Reengineering the Corporation: A Manifesto for Business Revolution*. New York

Hansen, J. (2007). Strategic Management when Profit isn't the End: Differences between Public Organizations.

Hassan, N. (2009). Using social network analysis to measure IT-enabled business process performance. *Information Systems Management, 26*(1), 61–76. doi:10.1080/10580530802557762

Hutton, G. (1996). *Business process re-engineering–a public sector view. Managing Business Processes±BPR and Beyond*. New York, NY: Wiley.

James, Y., Chee-Sing, Y., & Kin-Lee, S. (2000). Business Process Reengineering in the Public Sector: The Case of the Housing Development Board in Singapore. *Journal of Management Information Systems, 17*, 245–270.

Janssen, M., Kars, M., & Van Veenstra, A. (2007). Integrating information architecture and process management: experiences from the development of a digital safe by the Dutch Inland Revenue Service. *International Journal of Technology. Policy and Management*, *7*, 378–395.

Kaplan, R., & Murdoch, L. (1991). Core process redesign. *The McKinsey Quarterly*, *2*, 27–43.

Kim, H., Pan, G., & Pan, S. (2007). Managing IT-enabled transformation in the public sector: A case study on e-government in South Korea. *Government Information Quarterly*, *24*, 338–352. doi:10.1016/j.giq.2006.09.007

Klempa (1995). *Understanding Business Process Reengineering*. Business Process Change: Concepts, Methods, and Technologies.

Kliem, R. (2000). Risk Management for Business Process Reengineering. *Information Systems Management*, *17*(4), 1–3. doi:10.1201/1078/431 93.17.4.20000901/31256.12

Ma, L., Chung, J., & Thorson, S. (2005). E-government in China: Bringing economic development through administrative reform. *Government Information Quarterly*, *22*, 20–37. doi:10.1016/j.giq.2004.10.001

Ray, G., Barney, J., & Muhanna, W. (2004). Capabilities, business processes, and competitive advantage: choosing the dependent variable in empirical tests of the resource-based view. *Strategic Management Journal*, *25*(1), 23–37. doi:10.1002/smj.366

Sia, S., & Neo, B. (1996). The impact of business process reengineering on organizational controls. *International Journal of Project Management*, *14*(6), 346–348.

Stebbins, M., & Shani, A. (1998). Business Process Reengineering at Blue Shield of California: The integration of multiple change initiatives. *Journal of Organizational Change Management*, *11*(3), 216–231. doi:10.1108/09534819810216256

Teng, J., Grover, V., & Fiedler, K. (1994). Redesigning business processes using information technology. *Long Range Planning*, *27*, 95–106. doi:10.1016/0024-6301(94)90010-8

Vergidis, K., Turner, C., & Tiwari, A. (2008). Business process perspectives: Theoretical developments vs. real-world practice. *International Journal of Production Economics*, *114*, 91–104. doi:10.1016/j.ijpe.2007.12.009

KEY TERMS AND DEFINITIONS

Business Process Reengineering (BPR): It is used mostly in relation to private sectors and refers to fundamental rethinking and radical redesign of business processes using the power of information technology in order to achieve spectacular gains in process and organization performance.

Functional-Based Organization: This is the traditional model of hierarchical / bureaucratic organization that organizes its functions and employees along areas of specializations (or following the principle of division of labour).

Government Process Reengineering (GPR): Fundamental rethinking of government functions & administration processes and radical redesign of them leveraging information technology for achieving dramatic gains in organizational performance.

GPR Outcome: The performance impact (both at process and organizational performance level) that the implementation of GPR brings about to the organization.

One Stop Government Services (OSG): Providing businesses and customers all government services in one location (which can be a single portal or satellite service provision sites). Such is possible through integration of the processes and services of the various public agencies and harnessing the power of information technology.

Process-Based Organization: This is the type of organization GPR tries to introduce and it essentially organizes tasks and teams from the perspective of customers (service recipients) and results as opposed to areas of specialization.

Seamless Integration: This is similar to the concept of OSG and refers to bringing the various fragmented government services into one for the convenience and comfort of the service recipient (businesses and citizens). As such the service recipients don't know and see what is going on behind the front desk.

APPENDIX

Figure 1. Articles by Journals they appeared in

Journals	No. of Articles	Articles
Business Process Management Journal	4	Gulledge and Sommer (2002), Hesson (2007), Hesson, Al-Ameed, and Samaka (2007), Sia and Neo, 2008; Hughes, Scott, and Golden (2006).
Electronic Journal of e-Government	3	Martinez-Moyano and Gil-Garcia (2004); Alpar and Olbrich (2005), Meneklis and Douligeris (2007)
Government Information Quarterly	2	Dwivedi, Weerakkody, and Williams (2007), Gauld (2007)
Public Administration and Development	2	Berman and Tettey (2001), Mengesha and Common (2006)
Technovation	2	Halachmi and Bovaird (1997), Greasley (2006)
Total quality management	2	McAdam and Mitchell (1998); Coulson-Thomas (1998)
European Journal of Operation Research	1	Kwak and Lee (2002)
Expert Systems with Applications	1	Limam Mansa, Reijers, and Ounnar (2009)
Reinventing government in the information age	1	Anderson (1999)
Human Relations	1	Buchanan (1997)
Industrial Management & Data Systems	1	Frye and Gulledge(2007)
International Federation for Information Processing (IFIP)	1	Martin and Montagna (2006)
International Journal of Information Management	1	Indihar Stemberger and Jaklic (2007)
International Review of Administrative Sci.	1	Knox (2008)
International Journal of E-Government Res.	1	Scholl (2005)
International Journal of Health Care Quality Assurance	1	McAdam and Corrigan (2001)
International journal of operations & production management	1	MacIntosh (2003)
International Journal of public sector management	1	Ongaro (2004)
International Journal of Electronic Business	1	Bliemel and Hassanein (2004)
Journal of Business and Industrial Marketing	1	Tarokh, Sharifi, and Nazemi (2008)
Journal of Post keynesian Economics	1	Davidson (1997)
Journal of Higher Education Policy & Management	1	Adenso-Diaz and Canteli (2001)
Journal of Management Information System	1	Thong, Yap, Seah (2000)
Journal of Operations Management.	1	Narsimhan and Jayaram (1998)
New Technology, Work & Employment	1	Harrington, McLoughlin, Riddell (1997)
Omega	1	Aldowaisan and Gaafar (1999)
Organizational studies	1	McNulty and Ferlie (2004)
Research in Public Policy and Management	1	Anderson (2006)
The Journal of Computer Information Systems	1	Groznik, Kovacic, Trkman (2008)
Information Systems and e-Business Technologies	1	Dzhumalieva and Helfert (2008)
Total	40	

Chapter 2
ERP Implementation Model, Research Findings, and its Applications to Government

Girish H. Subramanian
Penn State University at Harrisburg, USA

Alan R. Peslak
Penn State University, USA

ABSTRACT

An ERP implementation model is developed with the help of a review of relevant literature. This implementation model has four phases: preparation and training, transition, performance and usefulness, and maintenance. Research findings from our study provide empirical support for the ERP implementation model. For the purpose of this chapter, we use content analysis of the structured interviews to come up with solutions and recommendations for ERP implementation in government. We finally present the conclusion and future directions.

INTRODUCTION

Enterprise Resource Planning (ERP) Systems have been developed to help organizations integrate and better manage information within and also with their business partners. ERP systems match the information flow with the physical flow of goods, from raw materials to finished goods.

ERP is also an efficient approach to fine tune a company's internal value chain. Most mid-size to large organizations have or will have ERP systems. The government sector (example: state of Pennsylvania in USA) also has adopted ERP systems. Many difficult and costly implementations of ERP systems have been tried in many organizations including FoxMeyer Drug, Dell Computer, Applied Materials and Dow Chemi-

DOI: 10.4018/978-1-60960-863-7.ch002

cal (Davenport, 1998). Some studies point to more than half of ERP implementations end in failure (Banker et al, 1988). Poorer results with 75% of ERP projects judged to be unsuccessful are mentioned in other research (Hong and Kim, 2002). Studies also state that it is believed that 90% of ERP projects are late (Scott and Vessey, 2002). As a result, it is extremely important to understand ERP implementation and specifically for government applications.

A phased implementation approach is highlighted from our research (Peslak et al, 2008). Our main thesis is that it is important to have a structured approach, similar to systems development, for the implementation and maintenance of ERP systems. We substantiate this statement based on our research study (Peslak et al., 2008) that shows that preparation and training, transition, performance and usefulness, and maintenance phases exist in ERP implementation of organizations and these phases positively influence the preferred use of ERP systems. The purpose of this chapter is to present this phased ERP implementation approach, our findings from (Peslak et al, 2008), and content analysis of interviews to help us come up with recommendations and applications of our ERP implementation model to government. Specifically, the main contribution of the chapter is to illustrate how the ERP implementation approach is helpful to government, supported by examples from a content analysis of interviews.

Using data from two manufacturing divisions that have implemented an ERP, our research (Peslak et al, 2008) aims to identify major phases in ERP implementation. We would like to see if these ERP implementation phases would be as helpful in ERP implementation as the Systems Development Lifecycle (SDLC) is to traditional systems implementation. The SDLC, per se, is not applicable to ERP implementation as ERP is often associated with "buying" software and implementing it within the organization.

BACKGROUND

Boudreau and Robey(2005) suggest that it is important to obtain acceptance of ERP systems. Currently they note that if not successfully implemented, users may work around the system and otherwise doom the project to costly duplication of effort, or worse, system failure. A phased implementation approach is highlighted in Robey et al, (2002).

Systems development theory uses the concept of a lifecycle and stages in the lifecycle to indicate development of information systems. The waterfall model, incremental model, RAD (rapid application development) model and spiral model are some of the systems development methods prevalent in the literature (Pressman, 2004). Newer approaches to systems development address component-based development using off-the-shelf packages, agile development and the unified process for object-oriented software development (Pressman, 2004). The newer approaches have fewer stages in the development of systems. For example, the unified process model which draws upon the best practices of conventional software process models (Pressman, 2004) has inception, elaboration, construction and transition phases.

Empirical research has addressed issues that organizations face during and after implementation of systems. Specifically, several studies have looked at ERP implementation ([Akkermans and van Helden, 2002], [Hong and Kim, 2002], [Robey et al., 2002]). The implementation and performance stage model ([Kwon and Zmud, 1987], [Cooper and Zmud, 1990]) is a useful tool for understanding the implementation of the ERP technology and provides six stages: initiation, adoption, adaptation, acceptance, routinization, and infusion. This six-stage model sets the framework to investigate the implementation and performance issues of utilizing an ERP system within an organization. The initiation stage analyzes the factors that influence the decision to utilize an ERP system such as incompatibility, need for connectivity, top management vision, and need to change. Implementation issues are addressed in the adoption and adaptation stages including: investment decisions, cost/benefit analysis, and choice of appropriate technology. Implementation and performance measures such as system modifications, training, integration of functional units, enhanced performance, user acceptance, flaws corrected, and organizational integration realized, are identified during the acceptance and routinization stages. Finally, the infusion stage addresses future innovations including IT integration at global levels and future opportunities.

Parr and Shanks (2000) review different models of ERP implementation and suggest a PPM/CSF hybrid model that incorporates a project phase model (PPM) with critical success factors (CSF). The phases included in their model are planning, project, and enhancement. Our work is both an extension and a testing of their project phase model for ERP implementation. Parr and Shanks (2000) are the first to suggest that there is justification for creating a project phase model (PPM) of ERP implementation which is centered on the individual, discrete phases of the implementation project itself rather than one which treats the project as just another phase in the whole implementation enterprise.

What happens after ERP implementation, and the benefits derived from ERP implementation, is specifically addressed by Gattiker and Goodhue (2005). The model by these researchers looks at the subunit level of the organization, similar to our study, and looks at determinants of ERP benefits. Task efficiency, coordination improvements and data quality explain a large amount of the ERP benefits of the sub-unit (Gattiker and Goodhue, 2005).

Based on an exploratory study, Rajagopal(2002) revealed that at Owens Corning, marketing and manufacturing each had its own sales forecasting numbers prior to implementing their ERP system. As a result, there were discrepancies in the information used for strategic

decision making in the same organization. This was a result of the incompatibility among the information systems used in various functions at Owens Corning (Rajagopal, 2002). System incompatibility can also impede performance, as observed at Eastman Kodak Company. At one point, Eastman Kodak was operating their business on 2600 different software applications, more than 4000 system interfaces, and about 100 different programming languages running on legacy-type mainframe systems (Stevens, 1997). It thus can be concluded that proper preparation and planning is needed for ERP implementation. Implementation planning influences ERP system performance (Yang et al., 2006).

We also summarize some key literature that supports the existence of a few stages in ERP implementation. An organization has to prepare itself for ERP implementation before the actual ERP decision is taken (Bagchi et al, 2003) and these researchers believe that such preparation is key to ERP success. It may take information technology diffusion and infusion to determine, in large part, whether users demonstrate a combination of a positive view to a new system when they consider it from the standpoint of their work. Additional support for such preparation effort comes from (Bresnahan&Brynjolfsson, 2000), who use the phrase 'complementary investment.' User training that included both technical and business processes is also helpful for firms to overcome assimilation knowledge barriers (Robey et al, 2002). Research ([Gupta, 2000], [Umble and Umble, 2002]) also sees training as one of the most important factors in ERP success. Training is also noted as an important factor by Gallivan et al. (2005) and Barker and Frolick (2003).

In the survey of Fortune 1000 CIOs, performance is a major factor in ERP success (Nah, Zuckwiler, and Lau, 2003). Quality of service is essential in ERP implementations (Siau, 2004). Usefulness is also related to performance. Perceived usefulness looks at productivity, job effectiveness, and ease of doing the job ([Segars and Grover, 1993], [Subramanian, 1994]) which could be argued as performance related variables. For example, our performance phase also looks at productivity and use of information from the ERP system by the user. Extensive research supports the notion that usefulness and ease of use are primary drivers of user intentions to adopt new technology ([Davis, 1989], [Davis et al, 1989], [Subramanian, 1994], [Venkatesh and Davis, 2000]).

The importance of transition is noted in (Al-Mashari, Al-Mudimigh, and Zairi, 2003) suggesting that it is important that an organization approaches the transition of legacy system carefully and with a comprehensive plan. Transition is a key factor in ERP implementation (Boudreau and Robey, 2005). Transition is also an important phase in the unified process model (Pressman, 2004).

The problem of maintaining integrated applications is no means a simple one and requires an interdisciplinary approach is a fact pointed out in (Mookerjee, 2005). Without the understanding of how the system is implemented, and how to maintain the efficiencies and functionality of that (ERP) system, it will be useless to the organization is noted in (Banker et al, 1988). The use of packaged software is shown to result in decreased software complexity and software enhancement effort (Banker et al, 1988) and so it is expected that ERP packages would have reduced maintenance in comparison to traditional development. So, maintenance is the final phase in ERP implementation. Figure 1 presents our ERP implementation model.

RESEARCH STUDY AND ITS FINDINGS

In our research study (Peslak et al, 2008), we conduct a confirmatory factor analysis (CFA) to test construct validity, scale reliability, and the CFA shows the existence of four phases in ERP implementation. We conduct further in-depth content analysis using qualitative interviews.

Figure 1. ERP implementation model

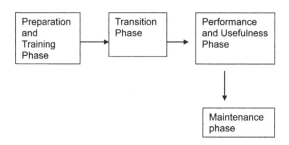

A paper based survey was prepared and administered at two divisions of a mid-size organization that had implemented an SAP R/3 ERP system. SAP is the German based, largest seller of ERP systems in the world. A cover letter and survey questionnaire were distributed to employees who were employed during the ERP implementation and also used the ERP system in their day-to-day job. Twenty-five surveys were completed in the first division and twenty-eight were completed in the second. In addition, interviews of the employees were conducted by the investigator. More details are in (Subramanian and Hoffer, 2005) and (Clayton, 2005).

In total, there were 53 valid responses to our questionnaire and the combined data set was used for the Confirmatory factor analysis (CFA). The CFA was performed on the fourteen SAP ERP implementation questions. The questions asked from the study (Peslak et al, 2008) are shown below in Table 1.

Responses to the questions were measured on a 5 point Likert scale from 1 = strongly disagree to 5 = strongly agree. The CFA extraction method was principal component analysis with Varimax rotation. Some questions were discarded after a few attempts at CFA but 10 questions remained and were found to measure four unique factors: preparation and training, transition, performance and usefulness, and maintenance. These factors are shown in Table 2. All four factors exceeded

Table 1. Survey questions

USDTY	1. I feel that I understand why our company implemented SAP as our Information System. (understand)
RECEIVED	2. I was provided with on-the-job training before we went live with SAP. (training)
PREPARED	3. On the day we went live with SAP, I felt prepared to work on SAP. (prepared to work)
TEAM	4. Everyone worked together to help the transition to SAP be successful. (team work)
SMOOTH	5. From my perspective, the transition to SAP went smoothly.(Smooth transition)
PRODUCT	6. I am able to be more productive with SAP than I was before SAP. (productivity)
ACCESS	7. I can access information easier with SAP than I could before SAP. (access information)
NEW	8. SAP provides me with information that was previously unavailable to me. (new information)
DATAENTR	9. With SAP, there is less entering of data than before SAP. (data entry)
DATE	10. With SAP, the data I use is more accurate than before SAP. (data accuracy)
EXPECT	11. I understand what is expected of me to maintain/update/confirm the information in SAP. (expectations)
RELEVANC	12. I understand how the information I input/change/confirm in SAP is relevant to our company. (relevancy)
ACCURACY	13. I feel confident that the information I input/change/confirm in SAP is accurate and correct. (accuracy)
UNDERY	14. The information I use from SAP makes sense to me. (understandability)
PREFER	15. I would rather use SAP than our previous system. (perceived use)

an eigen value of 1 which is used for acceptable cutoff (Moore, 2000). The four factors represent a very high 74% of the variance in the dependent variable, preference for the new system. In addition, scale reliability was performed on the factors and all factors were above.70, the minimum for acceptability (Nunnally, 1978). These are shown along with the factors and Varimax rotation in Table 2. Table 2 also shows the loadings of the questions on the four factors.

The research study in (Peslak et al, 2008) also showed that all these four factors had a positive effect on the preferred use of ERP. So, the use of the ERP implementation model does have a

Table 2. PCA (Principal Component Analysis): rotated component matrix

	Factor			
	Performance and Usefulness	**Preparation and training**	**Maintenance**	**Transition**
RECEIVED	-0.03985	**0.919088**	0.150648	0.077621
PREPARED	0.094718	**0.828303**	0.003379	0.275953
TEAM	0.059332	0.175064	0.076498	**0.863091**
SMOOTH	-0.00632	0.141407	0.139667	**0.830844**
PRODUCT	**0.753657**	-0.17567	-0.02085	0.270157
ACCESS	**0.826232**	-0.03514	0.170766	-0.05761
NEW	**0.884221**	0.05052	-0.07478	-0.0956
DATE	**0.603083**	0.167818	0.019928	0.031331
EXCT	0.080288	0.232754	**0.863194**	0.146275
ACCURACY	-0.00154	-0.05009	**0.910473**	0.078177
Alpha	.7969	.7674	.7354	.7314

positive impact on ERP usage. The four factors were subject to a multiple regression analysis with preferred ERP use as the dependent variable. The analysis finds that a statistically significant regression equation is formed. The R squared is relatively high.67 and shown in Table 3.

In addition to these empirical results, content analysis of interviews was conducted to provide us with solution and recommendations to apply the ERP implementation model in organizations and specifically the government sector.

CONTENT ANALYSIS: HOW IT WAS CONDUCTED

The 53 subjects in both sites of the organization were subject to a set of structured interviews about the ERP implementation. The questions were a starting point to gather as much information about the ERP implementation. The questions asked about their views on the ERP implementation process, how ERP affected their job (in both positive and negative ways), and their experience using ERP software. The users were allowed to elaborate on each of the questions and follow-up queries and details noted. Detailed notes were

taken. Then, the detailed notes were subject to content analysis.

The content analysis identified and classified the comments into the four phases: preparation and training, transition, performance and usefulness, and maintenance. If some comments are similar, we then kept track of how many users stated that comment. We looked at frequency (number of users) with comments in the four phases and calculated the percentage of the number of users at each site to see the importance of each phase as shown in Table 4 below.

Then, we grouped the comments within each phase into positive and negative comments. A further analysis and summary of the comments in each phase led us to make the solutions and recommendations we provide in the next section.

SOLUTIONS AND RECOMMENDATIONS FOR ERP IMPLEMENTATIONWITH SPECIFIC EMPHASIS ON GOVERNMENT SECTOR

When an organization considers an ERP implementation, it is imperative that the organization conduct a Strengths, Weaknesses, Opportunities

Table 3. Regression model summary

Model	R	R Square	Adjusted R Square	Std. Error of the Estimate
1	.817	.668	.637	.5955

Table 4. Content analysis distribution by ERP phases

ERP phases	Percentage of times mentioned: Site 1 (25)	Percentage of times mentioned: Site 2 (28)
Preparation and training	56%	46%
Performance and Usefulness	52%	64%
Transition	24%	17%
Maintenance	40%	38%

and Threats (SWOT) analysis as an important part of its preparation phase. The organization needs to evaluate the strengths and weaknesses in its internal value chain and business processes. Are the business processes streamlined, well defined and standardized? An ERP implementation often involves some form of business process reengineering or alignment of the current business processes with the ERP software's business process. Is the organization prepared for this change? In some cases, senior management will prefer an ERP software implementation as a means to bring in business process reengineering, especially with government.

The preparation phase needs to aim at bolstering the organization's strengths and reduce its weaknesses prior to ERP implementation. An example would be to see if a process is aligned with the ERP software and make sure that weakness is corrected. Content analysis of one of the site's interviews revealed the following comment *"Didn't have any major issues besides having some delays in shipping candy due to pipeline backup."* Another example is when a comment revealed that the ERP software was not in step with the physical system as in *"When implementing, steps were not even complete and they were continuing on to the next steps."*

Alternately, some of the strengths in the organization can be reinforced using training to explain the reengineered business process and the ERP software. Two positive comments on the use of training are reported below. *"Training was good before start-up. I was ready for implementation. Some people were not."* and *"SAP implementation went well. Up front training was a big help. More hands on training would have been beneficial."* Improper use of training could also pose problems as seen in these comments from users. *"Training wasn't as thorough as it should have been which left a lot of confusion. Supervisors and planners were unsure of the system almost as much as we were."* and *"The training (as a planner) was very brief on how to get around on*

the different screens. Theory and reasoning was almost nonexistent. The learning process after implementation was fast and furious."

Opportunities and threats associated with ERP implementation also need to be thought through during the preparation phase. Opportunities exist in having better and improved business processes and efficiencies associated with it. In evaluation of opportunities, impact on job productivity and usefulness needs to be addressed. Threats include the loss of uniqueness due to process standardization (or mechanization), loss of flexibility and a system that is not as friendly to use. Opportunities should be taken advantage of while mitigating threats. Business processes that need to be efficient and standardized need to be done through ERP software while processes that need to stay unique, flexible and easy to use need to be solved through systems other than ERP. One alternative approach to develop unique, flexible and easy to use systems is through the use of enterprise application integration by developing software and using middleware to connect them instead of using ERP systems.

The take away from the preparation and training phase is the conduct of the SWOT analysis and to effectively plan the business process changes/reengineering, identifying what business processes will be implemented using ERP and what processes will not be, align the ERP software well with business processes before implementation, and start training early and continue training through the maintenance phase. These are key recommendations for both the private and government sectors based on our study.

In the government sector, specifically, attention needs to be paid to doing a business process reengineering and process alignment with the ERP software before moving on to ERP implementation. Such a step is vital in preparation for the government to obtain successful results from ERP implementation. Training needs to be designed differently with the understanding of bureaucracy and political pressures that the use of ERP software needs to contend with.

Once preparation and training phase is planned, we are ready to move to the transition phase. Transition should be well planned, done at a steady pace so it is well assimilated and understood in the organization and contingency actions planned for any needed corrective steps. Poor execution of the transition phase is a problem highlighted in the content analysis. One of the sites had some negative comments that reflected problems in the transition phase. They are: *"As a plant we could have done more before the go-live date to help transition better instead of waiting until the last months to inform everyone," "Confused, fragmented, struggle," "Fast and furious" and "Culture shock."* However, if transition is well planned, the content analysis reveals positive feedback from users as follows. *"Implementation went pretty smooth." and "Didn't affect initially. When they implemented the purchasing module, then I started using SAP™. My transition went very well."*

One of the challenges in transition is that poor preparation or training will show up during transition and that needs to be handled. For example, if the ERP software is not aligned with the physical process well during preparation or if the process alignment is not done properly, then the content analysis shows problems that would arise from the user comments: *"Corporate had problem filling orders for customers. Lots of customer complaints. Customers dropped orders for Halloween candy. Warehouse filled up because couldn't ship. Having extra inventory sitting around upset some workers."*

Typically, transition can be accomplished in one of the following means: direct, parallel, phased or pilot. Direct is when we bring in the new system and replace the old system on an announced date. Parallel is when we keep the old and new systems together and in place for some time before we switch over completely to the new system. Phased is when we implement

different components of the new system one after the other in phases. Pilot is when the system is introduced to one area of the organization and then expanded slowly to the entire organization. For most organizations, ERP implementation is best conducted using either the phased or pilot approach. For the government sector, we would recommend using the phased and pilot approach together. The phased approach could be used to start with ERP modules with the best benefit or ease of implementation done first. As an example, the accounting or financial ERP module could be a starting module to implement in the government sector. The accounting or financial processes are well defined and easier to implement and the benefits are also much higher in terms of cost containment and efficient government. The pilot approach is important in identifying departments or units that are "tech savvy" and are interested in such technology solutions and choosing these units as the first ones to be implemented so the initial successes can help bring in ERP effectively into the entire organization. Another observation that we made from the content analysis is that one of the sites had a much more difficult transition than the other. One of the primary reasons was that the timing and pace of transition into the new system was not done effectively in the site that had more problems with the transition.

The next step in the use of ERP software is the performance and usefulness phase. In the performance and usefulness phase, the users and the organization evaluate the benefits of ERP to the job, the business processes and the organization. In evaluating the benefits, the costs involved in the use of ERP such as its difficulty in use and additional time and effort needed to learn the software is also looked at by the organization. The content analysis reveals some positive benefits seen by users as: *"SAP™ makes ordering parts easier and reduces inventory. SAP™ is light years ahead of our old system.," "SAP™ forced us to keep better inventory records, do more inventory counts, and created a couple job positions in cycle counting.," and "Process is easier, can see more information. Can find more information by using links. Easier to search the system. Do not need to go through lots of papers as we previously did. Everything is in the system and can see the changes made and who made the changes. Easier to search history. Ex. can see how much we used of a certain product last year very easily."* Some of the costs associated with the use of ERP software are revealed in these negative comments. *"More time-consuming to maintain information in system. Some processes require you to wait until certain other things are in the system due to all the checks and balances in SAP™.," "Big learning curve.," "Not as user friendly. Having to learn something new is difficult." And "It hasn't. Supervisors still give jobs without notifications or work orders."*

Two components need to be understood and assessed clearly from the performance and usefulness phase. First, the impact of the performance and usefulness on the user's job and job productivity. Using the ERP, is the user able to get his or her job done more effectively? It is shown that perceived usefulness influences the adoption of technology by users (Davis, 1989) and hence successful adoption of ERP does depend on this phase. Second, the impact of performance and usefulness of the business process also needs to be studied. If the performance and usefulness phase has a positive impact on both the job and the business process, then the users and the organization will successfully adopt the ERP technology. In spite of the positive impact, users are often concerned about the lack of ease of use of the ERP software as shown in these user comments: *"SAP™ is supposed to be a paperless system; however, I use more paper now having to print out screens," "Not as user friendly. Having to learn something new is difficult" and "User Interface is not that user friendly. The Germans do not see any drawbacks with setting up their system in 3 letter abbreviation."*

With respect to the government sector, performance and usefulness phase and its impact on the business process is more important. Business processes can be reengineered and made more effective using ERP systems and that could be a major benefit. Ease of use of the ERP software and its usefulness to the job could act either as a facilitator or inhibitor. As most government jobs tend to be unionized or in some manner protected, it is a challenge to have the users learn and effectively use the ERP software in their jobs. The reward and incentive schemes need to be designed to encourage users to use the ERP software.

The final phase is maintenance. Once the ERP software is implemented and is in use, there is constant and continuous maintenance needed. Organizations can do the ERP maintenance with in-house staff, contract the work to outside vendors or do a combination of both approaches. The content analysis of maintenance phase reveals the following positive comments: *"More precision with SAP™. Less hand written issues (legibility). Now everything is confirmed electronically. Bill of ladings are more accurate, they are all stored in system: weight, count, product.," "The warehouse management system was changed. Different actions had to be completed than before. Ex. workflow was not in previous system. SAP™ is so exact with inventory that you get errors if you don't return the exact amount of material from the floor. If material is moved, it has to match the quantity that SAP™ has in the system for it or else you get a workflow error.," and "SAP allows me to view reporting and manage spending within the same system. I can watch spending and maintenance trends without jumping through to another program."* Some of the negative comments are provided below. *"Difficult. Jobs performed twice. Vague description. Program is not user friendly. Has created chaos in performing job." and "It was frustrating at first because I felt we were unprepared. I now find it an annoyance I can live with mostly due to the improved processes."*

The maintenance phase is very important to ensure that the ERP software is running well and that the improvement in business processes is realized. If an organization has the budget, it is wise to invest in in-house staff and ERP training so that the software can be maintained in-house. External contracts are often expensive and may be selectively used in this case. However, government agencies may not desire to have a dedicated ERP staff for maintenance. Training of existing IT staff in ERP maintenance and relying mostly on external vendors for ERP software maintenance may be a better approach for government sector.

Table 5 summarizes the recommendations for government sector for the four ERP phases.

CONCLUSION

In this chapter, we first presented the literature review that led us to develop the ERP implementation model. The implementation model had four phases: Preparation and Training, Transition, Performance and Usefulness, and Maintenance phases. Each of the phases was briefly discussed followed by our research study. A survey containing questions from all these four phases and the dependent variable (preferred use of ERP) was administered at two divisions of a manufacturing organization as part of the study in (Peslak et al, 2008). The survey was accompanied by follow-up structured interviews at these divisions.

Confirmatory Factor Analysis (CFA) was conducted and the results examined and reported here from the study in (Peslak et al, 2008). The CFA findings support the existence of the four phases in our ERP implementation model. Further, regression analysis points that the ERP implementation model had a positive effect on the preferred ERP use. Additional details are available from our study in (Peslak et al, 2008).

For this chapter, we use the follow-up structured interviews to conduct a content analysis. The content analysis of the interviews was used as the basis to come up with solutions and recommendations for ERP implementation and specifically in government. Our key recommendations for the government sector include: doing a business process reengineering and process alignment with the ERP software as part of preparation phase; designing training differently with the understanding of bureaucracy and political pressures; recommending the use of the phased and pilot approach together in transition and relying mostly on external vendors for ERP software maintenance.

The implication of our findings to practitioners and researchers in the government sector is clear. If an organization wishes to have successful ERP implementation based on user perceptions, then it is important to pay additional attention to the four phases: preparation and training, performance and usefulness, transition and maintenance phases. Importantly, organizations need to manage the transition to ERP implementation well (not in a hurried manner) and carry the users with them. It is clear that the cutover to the new ERP software

Table 5. Summary of recommendations for government sector

ERP phases	Recommendations for Government Sector
Preparation and training	Attention needs to be paid to doing a business process reengineering and process alignment with the ERP software; Training needs to be designed differently with the understanding of bureaucracy and political pressures
Performance and Usefulness	Performance and usefulness phase and its impact on the business process are more important.
Transition	Recommend using the phased and pilot approach together.
Maintenance	Training of existing IT staff in ERP maintenance and relying mostly on external vendors for ERP software maintenance may be a better approach for government sector

is critical. Preparation and training of users is also a key ingredient to success. Users need to have realistic expectations of the usefulness of the software. Similarly, the maintenance workload with ERP software has to be explained to users along with the benefits of ERP software.

In addition, estimates suggest that at least 30% of all IT projects fail and it is suggested that a higher proportion of ERP projects fail, run well over budget, or fail to achieve projected cost savings and strategic advantages. This study, as noted, has prepared a model for phases of ERP implementation. We will also argue that preparation and performance are the key influences in technology adoption and acceptance of the new system. If resources and efforts are concentrated in these two phases of the ERP implementation, it is likely that costs will be reduced, projects will exhibit higher levels of success, and greater strategic advantages will be garnered.

Due to the importance of preparation stage, we recommend that organizations conduct a strengths-weaknesses-opportunity-threats (SWOT) analysis during this stage. Examining the business process and using its strengths or changing/aligning the process if it has weaknesses is a key ingredient for ERP success. Similarly, great opportunities exist in the standardization of business processes and improvement in job productivity and usefulness, especially in government, from ERP implementation. A threat to be averted in ERP software usage is the loss of uniqueness, flexibility, and ease of use of the system and business process. In the preparation phase, it is imperative that all these SWOT issues be addressed before we move to the next phase in implementation.

Future research on ERP implementation and application in government needs to look primarily at the advantages of business process improvement in government sector through the use of ERP. An additional focus could be the examination of any issues in change management and ERP implementation challenges in the government sector.

REFERENCES

Akkermans, H., & van Helden, K. (2002). Vicious and Virtuous Cycles in ERP Implementation: A Case Study of Interrelations between Critical Success Factors. *European Journal of Information Systems, 11*, 35–46. doi:10.1057/palgrave/ejis/3000418

Al-Mashari, M., Al-Mudimigh, A., & Zairi, M. (2003). ERP: A Taxonomy of Critical Factors. *European Journal of Operational Research, 146*, 352–364. doi:10.1016/S0377-2217(02)00554-4

Bagchi, S., Kanungo, S., & Dasgupta, S. (2003). Modeling use of enterprise resource planning systems: A path analytic study. *European Journal of Information Systems, 12*(2), 142. doi:10.1057/palgrave.ejis.3000453

Banker, R., Davis, G. B., & Slaughter, S. A. (1988). Software Development Practices, Software Complexity, and Software Maintenance Performance: A Field Study. *Management Science, 44*(4), 433–451. doi:10.1287/mnsc.44.4.433

Barker, T., & Frolick, M. (2003). ERP Implementation Failure: A Case Study. *Information Systems Management, 20*(4), 43–49. doi:10.1201/1078/43647.20.4.20030901/77292.7

Boudreau, M., & Robey, D. (2005). Enacting Integrated Information Technology: A Human Agency Perspective. *Organization Science, 16*(1), 3–18. doi:10.1287/orsc.1040.0103

Bresnahan, T. F., & Brynjolfsson, E. (2000). Information technology, workplace organization, and the demand for skilled labor: Firm-level evidence. *The Quarterly Journal of Economics, 117*(1), 339–376. doi:10.1162/003355302753399526

Clayton, G. E. (2005). *A Case Study and Comparison of Enterprise Resource Planning Systems: Implementation and Performance*, Master's Thesis, Penn State Harrisburg, Harrisburg, PA

Cooper, R., & Zmud, R. (1990). Information technology implementation research: a technological diffusion approach. *Management Science, 36*(2), 123–142. doi:10.1287/mnsc.36.2.123

Davenport, T. (1998). Putting the enterprise into the enterprise system. *Harvard Business Review, 76*(4), 121–131.

Davis, F. D. (1989). Perceived usefulness, perceived ease of use, and user acceptance of information technology. *Management Information Systems Quarterly, 13*(3), 319–340. doi:10.2307/249008

Davis, F. D., Bagozzi, R. P., & Warshaw, P. R. (1989). User acceptance of computer technology: A comparison of two theoretical models. *Management Science, 35*, 982–1003. doi:10.1287/mnsc.35.8.982

Gallivan, M. J., Spitler, V. K., & Koufaris, M. (2005). Does Information Technology Training Really Matter? A Social Information Processing Analysis of Coworkers' Influence on IT Usage in the Workplace. *Journal of Management Information Systems, 22*(1), 153–192.

Gattiker, T., & Goodhue, D. (2005). What happens after ERP Implementation: Understanding the Impact of Inter-Dependence and Differentiation on Plant-Level Outcomes. *Management Information Systems Quarterly, 29*(3), 559–584.

Gupta, A. (2000). Enterprise Resource Planning: The Emerging Organizational Value Systems. *Industrial Management + Data Systems. 100*, (3), 114-.

Hong, K, K. and Kim, Y. G. (2002). The Critical Success Factors for ERP Implementation: An Organizational Fit Perspective. *Information & Management, 40*(1), 25–40. doi:10.1016/S0378-7206(01)00134-3

Kwon, T., & Zmud, R. (1987). *Unifying the fragmented models of information systems implementation: Critical issues in Information Systems Research.* New York, NY: John Wiley.

Mookerjee, R. (2005, November). Maintaining Enterprise Software Applications. *Communications of the ACM, 48*(11), 75–79. doi:10.1145/1096000.1096008

Moore, J. (2000). One Road to Turnover: An Examination of Work Exhaustion in Technology Professionals. *Management Information Systems Quarterly, 24*(1), 141–168. doi:10.2307/3250982

Nah, F., Zuckweiler, K., & Lau, J. (2003). ERP Implementation: Chief Information Officers' Perceptions of Critical Success Factors. *International Journal of Human-Computer Interaction, 16*(1), 5–22. doi:10.1207/S15327590IJHC1601_2

Nunnally, J. C. (1978). *Psychometric Theory* (2nd ed.). New York: McGraw-Hill.

Parr, A., & Shanks, G. (2000). A model of ERP project implementation. *Journal of Information Technology, 15*, 289–303. doi:10.1080/02683960010009051

Peslak, A., Subramanian, G., & Clayton, G. (2008). The Phases of ERP Software Implementation and Maintenance: A Model for Predicting Preferred ERP Use. *Journal of Computer Information Systems, 48*(2), 25–33.

Pressman, R. S. (2004). *Software Engineering: A Practitioner's Approach* (6th ed.). New York: McGraw-Hill.

Rajagopal, P. (2002). An innovation—diffusion view of implementation of enterprise resource planning (ERP) systems and development of a research model. *Information & Management, 40*(2), 87–114. doi:10.1016/S0378-7206(01)00135-5

Robey, D., Ross, J. W., & Boudreau, M. C. (2002). Learning to Implement Enterprise Systems: An Exploratory Study of the Dialectics of Change. *Journal of Management Information Systems, 19*(1), 17–46.

Scott, J., & Vessey, I. (2002). Managing risks in enterprise implementations. *Communications of the ACM, 45*(4), 74–81. doi:10.1145/505248.505249

Segars, A. H., & Grover, V. (1993). Re-examining perceived ease of use and usefulness: A confirmatory factor analysis. *Management Information Systems Quarterly, 17*, 517–525. doi:10.2307/249590

Siau, K. (2004). Enterprise Resource Planning (ERP) implementation methodologies. *Journal of Database Management, 15*(1), 1–6.

Stevens, T. (1997). Kodak focuses on ERP. *Industry Week, 246*(15), 130.

Subramanian, G. H. (1994). A replication of perceived usefulness and perceived ease of use measurement. *Decision Sciences, 25*(5/6), 863–873. doi:10.1111/j.1540-5915.1994.tb01873.x

Subramanian, G. H., & Hoffer, C. (2005). An Exploratory Case Study of Enterprise Resource Planning Implementation. *International Journal of Enterprise Information Systems, 1*(1), 23–38. doi:10.4018/jeis.2005010102

Umble, E., & Umble, M. (2002). Avoiding ERP implementation failure. *Industrial Management (Des Plaines), 44*(1), 25–34.

Venkatesh, V., & Davis, F. D. (2000). A theoretical extension of the technology acceptance model: Four longitudinal field studies. *Management Science, 46*(2), 186–204. doi:10.1287/mnsc.46.2.186.11926

Yang, C., Ting, P., & Wei, C. (2006). A Study of the Factors Impacting ERP System Performance from the Users' Perspectives. *Journal of American Academy of Business, 8*(2), 161–167.

ADDITIONAL READING.

Amaoako-Gyampah, K., & Salam, A. (2004). An extension of the technology acceptance model in an ERP implementation environment. *Information & Management, 41*(6), 731–745. doi:10.1016/j.im.2003.08.010

Bajwa, D., Mooney, T., & Garcia, J. (2004). An Integrative Framework For The Assimilation Of Enterprise Resource Planning Systems: Phases, Antecedents, And Outcomes. *Journal of Computer Information Systems, 44*(3), 81–90.

Bingi, P., Sharma, M., & Godla, J. (1999). Critical Issues Affecting an ERP Implementation. *Information Systems Management, 16*(3), 7–14. doi:10.1201/1078/43197.16.3.19990601/31310.2

Brown, S., Massey, M., Montoya-Weiss, M., & Burkman, J. (2002). Do I really have to? User acceptance of mandated technology. *European Journal of Information Systems, 11*, 283–295. doi:10.1057/palgrave.ejis.3000438

Chau, P. Y. K. (2005). Influence of computer attitude and self-efficacy on IT usage behavior. *Journal of End User Computing, 13*(1), 26–40. doi:10.4018/joeuc.2001010103

Dewan, S. K., & Kraemer, S. (1998). International dimensions of the productivity paradox. *Communications of the ACM, 41*(9), 56–62. doi:10.1145/280324.280333

Fisher, D., Fisher, S., Kiang, M., & Chi, R. (2004). Evaluating Mid-Level ERP Software. *Journal of Computer Information Systems, 45*(1), 38–46.

Harel, G., & Tzafrir, S. (1999). The Effect of Human Resource Management Practices on The Perceptions of Organizational and Market Performance of the Firm. *Human Resource Management, 38*(3), 185–199. doi:10.1002/(SICI)1099-050X(199923)38:3<185::AID-HRM2>3.0.CO;2-Y

Hitt, L., Wu, D., & Zhou, X. (2002). Investment in Enterprise Resource Planning: Business Impact and Productivity Measures. *Journal of Management Information Systems, 19*(1), 71–98.

Krasner, H. (2000). Ensuring e-business success by learning from ERP failures. *IT Professional, 2*(1), 22–27. doi:10.1109/6294.819935

Nah, F., Tan, X., & The, S. (2004). An Empirical Investigation on End-Users' Acceptance of Enterprise Systems. *Information Resources Management Journal, 17*(3), 32–51. doi:10.4018/irmj.2004070103

Rajagopal, P., & Frank, T. (2000). A comparative case analysis of enterprise resource planning systems implementation and performance – SAP," *Annual Conference of Decision Sciences Institute Meeting.*

Rajagopal, P., & Frank, T. (2002). Oracle ERP and Network Computing Architecture: Implementation and Performance. *Information Systems Management, 19*(2), 53–68. doi:10.1201/1078/43200.19.2.20020228/35140.6

Soh, C., Sia, S., Boh, W., & Tang, M. (2003). Misalignments in ERP Implementation: A Dialectic Perspective. *International Journal of Human-Computer Interaction, 16*(1), 81–100. doi:10.1207/S15327590IJHC1601_6

Somers, T., & Nelson, K. (2004). A Taxonomy of Players and Activities across the ERP Project Life Cycle. *Information & Management, 41*, 257–278. doi:10.1016/S0378-7206(03)00023-5

Staehr, L., Shanks, G., & Seddon, P. (2002). Analysing ERP Use with the Structurational Model of Technology. In *Proceedings of Australasian Conference on Information Systems.*

Straub, D., Limayem, M., & Karahanna-Evaristo, E. (1995). Measuring system usage: Implications for IS theory testing. *Management Science, 41*(8), 1328–1342. doi:10.1287/mnsc.41.8.1328

Wah, L. (2000). Give ERP a chance. *Management Review, 89*(3), 20–24.

Zviran, M., Pliskin, N., & Levin, R. (2005). Measuring User Satisfaction and Perceived Usefulness in the ERP Context. *Journal of Computer Information Systems, 45*(3), 43–52.

KEY TERMS AND DEFINITIONS

Customer Relationship Management Systems: Enterprise systems that integrate all contacts with the customer and help support activities and decisions with respect to sales, marketing and customer service.

Enterprise Applications: Systems such as customer relationship management, supply chain management that can span across many functions, levels and business units and help in coordinating activities and support decisions of the firm.

Enterprise Resource Planning or ERP systems: ERP systems are integrated information systems that span the whole enterprise and coordinate key internal business processes of the firm.

Supply Chain Management Systems: Enterprise systems that integrate and support all production and operations management activities including sourcing from suppliers, planning operations, working with distribution, warehousing and retail functions.

Systems Development Lifecycle: An approach or method for developing information systems which includes analysis, design, programming and implementation.

Systems Implementation: An important stage of the systems development lifecycle where an information system is put to use.

Technology Adoption: A process by which the organization brings in and starts using a new information system.

Unified Process Model: A model developed to bring together all best practices and models used in developing information systems.

Chapter 3
E–Government
Management Practice:
Enterprise Resource Planning

John Douglas Thomson
RMIT University, Australia

ABSTRACT

E-government agencies in developed and developing countries are anticipating efficiency and effective-ness gains from the evolution of new e-business models. Such agencies are attempting to adopt and adapt the new technologies to public e-business in order to achieve the benefits being realised by entities in the private sector. The adoption of Enterprise Resource Planning (ERP) is one of these e-business models. The purpose of this chapter is to explore the adoption of ERP by the Australian Department of Defence through longitudinal action research. This development may be of interest to other public sectors wishing to avoid unnecessary expense and achieve an efficient and effective outcome in minimum time.

INTRODUCTION

Senior management in government is continuously seeking cost savings and improved effectiveness and efficiency. In this pursuit, large, medium and small governments around the world are considering Enterprise Resource Planning (ERP), and are looking for guidance as to how ERP can be used with highest amenity, lowest cost and least change. They have variously considered ERP as a pervasive government wide tool for coordinating many activities such as e-procurement, HR, project management, finance, and budgeting. This adoption has been because downsizing and outsourcing pressures to reduce costs have been and will continue to be intense. While the adoption of ERP has been viewed as a means of reducing costs, in practice such implementation often increases

DOI: 10.4018/978-1-60960-863-7.ch003

costs (Cordella and Simon, 1997. Cordella, 2006. Cordella, 2001). The ICT Development Index provides IT benchmarking information across nations indicating that 'large disparities remain among countries' (ITU, 09).

THE PURPOSE OF THIS CHAPTER

The purpose of this chapter is to examine how public e-procurement policy was translated into practice by the Australian Department of Defence and its implications for management. Contrary to senior management expectations, the implementation of this ERP pilot model did not require any expensive consultancies or any change management of existing structures, systems or processes. Its research, development and implementation was undertaken by two employees over a twelve month period. It is suggested the generic ERP model so developed may be of interest to other e-government agencies.

LITERATURE REVIEW

ERP data is often spread throughout different government functions such as accounting, project management, purchasing and procurement, and supply logistics. Wittmann & Cullen (2000) suggest that such data is a key value driver. In many government organizations it remains an untapped source of core government business data. It could be that this is because its value is not fully recognised by government managers, or that some or all of these functions have been outsourced to an external provider and so have become opaque to management. While outsourcing may seem an attractive option, outsourcing such a core function leads to dependency upon external, often rent seeking, ERP vendors. Such rent seeking can take the form of demands for system and software adoption and upgrades, specialist training for staff, ongoing license fees on a per user basis,

consultancy fees, special service fees and so on. Once committed to such ERP arrangements, it is difficult to break out of such contracts without suffering heavy penalties. But to remain in the arrangement is also very expensive (it becomes a most effective monopoly for the ERP vendor).

The benefits of ERP are that it enables masses of information, previously dispersed and fragmented, difficult and expensive to bring together manually in a timely way, to be brought together and interrogated in seconds (Wailgum, 2007). This contributes to improved e-government efficiency and effectiveness, and to a lowering of an e-government's transaction costs and environmental impacts. Because ERP can be used to collect, correlate, track and aggregate electronic transactions quickly and easily, it has the potential to become a valuable source of strategic and operational knowledge for management, with cost saving and performance management potential. For example, an ERP system enables various data from functions such as accounting, finance, logistics, e-procurement, and project management to be collected, collated, coordinated, and disseminated through active, layered, routine or special performance reports. ERP systems may be designed to record and provide data for measuring critical aspects of 'core' business operations across an organization, from strategy development, planning and execution. performance measurement and management. operations and control. An ERP system can continuously report to management the knowledge of which can be used to measure and hence evaluate organizational performance, processes and functions that were previously hidden, disparate or disjointed (Bouret, 2005). Through these means, ERP creates a single, central repository of timely, accurate data and assists in providing information so that more effective resource allocation decisions can be made by management (Business Software, 08).

ERP databases and systems are core business for any government, yet they are often outsourced to ERP vendors at considerable capital set up costs and subsequent ongoing service and maintenance costs. This outsourcing then leaves government vulnerable to activities over which management has little control (Markoff 2009a, b).

Most ERP vendor systems were initially designed to be used by discrete manufacturing companies rather than governments (Koch and Wailgum 2008). While this is changing, e-government agencies have variously struggled with different ERP vendors to modify core ERP vendor programs to their needs (Koch and Wailgum 2008). Vendors have only recently begun to offer specially tailored ERP application sets, but there is still much customization work to do (Koch and Wailgum, 2008). Packaged applications now target e-government agencies including higher education (Koch and Wailgum 2008).

It is critical for e-government agencies to determine if their way of doing business will fit a standard ERP vendor package (Koch and Wailgum 2008), before contracts are signed. There are options: public agencies can change their business structure, systems and processes to accommodate the ERP vendor software, or they can suggest modifying the ERP vendor software to fit their structure and processes (Turban 2008). ERP vendors argue that modifying their software will 'slow down the project, introduce dangerous bugs into the system and make upgrading the software to the ERP vendor's next release excruciatingly difficult because the customizations will need to be torn apart and rewritten to fit with the new version' (Koch and Wailgum 2008). It has been suggested that neglecting to map current business processes prior to starting ERP implementation is a main reason for failure of ERP projects (Brown and Vessey, 2003).

Private Sector Management Experience

In the private sector, an ERP study conducted by Lugwigshafen University of Applied Science

(Ludwigshafen University of Applied Science, 2004) surveyed 192 companies. It concluded that companies which implemented SAP's industry best practices decreased mission-critical project tasks such as configuration, documentation, testing and training.

A Meta Group (2010) (now Gartner) ERP vendor total cost of private sector ownership study investigated hardware, software, professional services and internal staff costs. Costs included initial installation and the two year period that followed. Among the 63 companies surveyed—including small, medium and large companies in a range of industries—the average total cost of ownership was US$15m (the highest was US$300m and lowest was US$400,000). This study also found that it took eight months after the new system was installed (31 months in total) to see any benefits.

Results from a 2007 Aberdeen Group survey (Jutras, 2007) of more than 1,680 manufacturing companies of all sizes found a correlation between the size of an ERP vendor deployment and the total costs. For example, a company with less than US$50m in revenue should expect to pay an average of US$384,295 in total ERP vendor costs, according to the survey results. A mid-market company with US$50m to US$100m in revenues can expect to pay (on average) just over US$1m in total costs. a much bigger mid-market company, with US$500m to US$1b in revenues, should expect to pay just over US$3m in total costs. Companies with more than US$1b in revenues can expect to pay, on average, nearly US$6m in total ERP vendor costs. Could governments with budgets of these orders expect to pay around the same amount for an ERP system to be installed and be effective?

The hidden vendor costs of ERP most likely to result in budget overrun are training (expensive). integration and testing (high risk). customization (expensive). data conversion (from old systems to new ERP vendor systems). data analysis (combined with data from external systems for analysis purposes). consultants (ad infinitum). retaining the organization's trained ERP employees. implementation (never stops). waiting for the organization's ROI. post-ERP depression. and adjusting to the new ERP vendor system.

In a Deloitte Consulting survey of 64 Fortune 500 companies (Deloitte, 2008. Khosrow-Pour, 2006. Saleh, Abdulaziz, and Alkattan, 2006), one in four admitted they suffered a drop in performance when their ERP vendor system went live—the most common reason for the performance problems was that everything looked and worked differently from the way it did before, which occurs when people can't do their jobs in the familiar way and haven't yet mastered the new way. Implementing ERP vendor systems is a difficult and costly process that has caused serious business losses because the planning, development and training necessary to re-engineer their business processes were underestimated by management. The training of end users is also a key success factor to achieving benefits.

Public Sector Management Experience

An example of a public sector education institution adopting an ERP vendor system is the Australian RMIT University, a top 200 global university in 2007 (Financial Times, 2008). The ERP vendor system was to integrate basic student administration (and related financial) tasks with Web-enrolments, the alumni system and other peripheral tasks. It went live in October 2001. According to Gray (2003), the PeopleSoft ERP implementation was subsequently the subject of a Victorian Government Auditor General's Report (Victorian Auditor General, 2003) following the ERP vendor system's failure to deliver. The problems that followed cost RMIT University more than AU$47m, or 3.7 times the original budget (Victorian Auditor General, 2003), and ultimately the resignation of the University's Vice Chancel-

lor. The structural and process changes required were underestimated, as was the time allowed for implementation. The system went live at a time when, from both a technology perspective and a business ready perspective, it wasn't ready and there wasn't a fallback position. There was an expectation that the early issues were technology problems that would be fixed fairly quickly. By the time the University realised how committed it was, it was too late to revert to its previous system.

Gray (2003) suggests that rather than trying to modify the ERP vendor software systems to suit a government's business processes, there is a need to look at ways of modifying business processes to suit the ERP vendor system. However, this may lead to other acute and expensive complications in writing software variations and revising and adjusting business structures and processes. Is this 'the tail wagging the dog'? Is an ERP system a tool of management or vice versa?

Why do ERP projects fail so often to deliver the performance promised so often? At its simplest level, Koch and Wailgum (Khosrow-Pour, 2006) suggest that ERP is a set of 'best practices' for performing different functions including e-procurement, logistics, finance, HR, and other processes. To get the most from the ERP vendor software, they argue that employees need to adopt the work methods outlined in the software. If public servants in the different government departments/agencies that will use ERP don't agree that the work methods embedded in the software are better than the ones they currently use, they will resist using the software or will want IT to change the software to match the ways they currently do things. This can be where ERP vendor projects break down. Political fights break out over how, or even whether, the ERP vendor software should be installed. IT becomes involved in long, expensive customization efforts to modify the ERP vendor software to fit the business requirements. Customizations make the software more unstable and harder to maintain when it is implemented.

Because ERP covers so much of what government does, a failure in the software can bring a government to a halt.

Every e-government agency is different, with unique work methods that an ERP vendor cannot account for when developing its software. Further, changing a public servant's work processes and habits will also create difficulties, and getting them to use the ERP vendor's software to improve the ways they do their jobs may be a harder challenge, particularly if it means that on success, many public servants will lose their jobs through 'productivity benefits and efficiency gains'. If the government organization is resistant to change, then an ERP project is more likely to fail.

So rapid have been software and hardware improvements that strategy developing and policy making senior public servants are sometimes unaware of the inherent latent usable potential available to prosecute their interests (there may also be generational issues here). In some government organizations, existing public servant ICT expertise may not be being realized or valued. Since 2000, there have been significant improvements in the computing power of generic software database tools for which there are 'at no cost' upgrades. Inexpensive training in the use of generic database software is accessible at low cost. Such may be the skill and curiosity of many public sector employees about ICT that no additional training is necessary. These ICT skills may be applicable to ICT challenges such as ERP, which function through establishing central databases. Standardization of software code makes it possible for e-government agencies to consider developing their own ERP arrangements using their own public servants who are already familiar with their government's structure, organization and culture.

Rather than outsourcing to ERP vendors, the next part of this chapter documents the Australian Department of Defence's in-house design, development and implementation of an ERP model over twelve months by two employees.

DEFENCE DEVELOPS AN ERP MODEL

The Australian Department of Defence is a complex, high tech Australian Federal Government Department of around 90,000 employees. In 2008-09 the Australian Department of Defence will spend more than $9.6 billion acquiring and sustaining military equipment and services, and will employ over 7,500 people in more than 40 locations around Australia and overseas (Department of Defence, 2009). This comprises the procurement of products (goods and services) and their support and maintenance from almost every industry sector, on a global basis. Hundreds of small to large enterprises are dependent on the Australian Department of Defence for orders through e-procurement, so whatever software is adopted by this large organization will have an impact on them also.

This action research is about the design, development and implementation of an ERP model undertaken by two Australian Department of Defence public servants networking closely with the many internal and external stakeholders. One of the employees was an experienced senior executive and project manager/engineer, the other a computer scientist/logistician. They also had the use of an administrative assistant on a part time basis. The researchers were required to keep development costs to a minimum, so the selection of Microsoft Access software was made simply because the Australian Department of Defence was already committed to generic Microsoft software as its standard (with software updates and training being virtually free). But any other database software such as IBM DB2, Oracle, Sybase, MySQL, PostgreSQL is likely to be satisfactory (Altova, 2009).

The ERP Model's Management Performance Criteria

The ERP model's design performance specification was determined through interviews and continuous contact during development with many internal and external managers. The finalised performance requirements were firstly, it had to be simple, reliable, accurate and timely and kept current with new data entry as e-procurement transactions occurred. Secondly, it had to respond to internal customer's many and varied needs on an established work priority basis but be capable of modification or adjustment should these needs change. Thirdly, it had to be user friendly, easy and intuitive to use with minimal if any training, simple to understand in concept and structure, and be perceived and accepted by authorized users as of value and not as a threat to their jobs. Finally, it needed to be developed, installed and maintained using existing data and resources at no additional resource, transaction or capital cost to the organization.

ERP Model's Management Capacity and Boundaries

To achieve the required performance criteria, the boundaries of the model were based on existing financial data for each financial year's transactions. This data was readily available, but spread throughout the Australian Department of Defence in various functional areas such as accounting, project management, procurement and supply logistics. Initial exploratory research found there were around 250,000 electronic procurement transactions per annum, around 200,000 of which were under AU\$2,000 in individual value. The ERP data for these less than AU\$2,000 commodity purchases, large in number but individually very small in value, was already available through bank card statements and could be added to the database later if necessary. Details of the remaining (approximately) 50,000 e-procurement transactions,

each above the Australian Department of Defence bank card delegation of AU\$2,000, were publicly available and formed the basis of the initial generic ERP database. These data were collected from a range of internal and external stakeholders.

Management Pursuing Simplicity: One Unique Field

For the ERP model's database development, a unique attribute common to every e-procurement transaction was necessary and was identified. This unique field, the Australian Department of Defence Purchase Order number, provided the means by which data within and across each financial year was identified. This unique attribute thus provided the basis for the individual records of related data to be selected, interrogated, dissected, grouped and extracted in many shapes and forms. A 'flat file' transparent approach made access to all data in the database easy and quick to access by authorized employees with very limited training. This approach ensured every authorized employee was able to intelligently determine the usefulness of the database to their own particular needs. Any masking of the 'flat file' data restricts and limits the usefulness of the database. Usually ERP vendors do not advocate such transparency of the entire database to all authorized users, or that a simple database such as MS Access is sufficient to cope with the challenge. It was found that the simple MS Access relational database 'flat file' structure used did not overload or make the database complicated or difficult to interrogate by users. It was very simple to interrogate and no special training was required. Relational database fields were subsequently added as 'pull down' menus, such as Zip Codes and Industry Codes (ANZIC). Pull down menus for buyer and seller attributes, such as address, contact person, email addresses, telephone numbers and so on were also added. E-procurement and supply reports were structured to meet a variety of e-government needs at the various organizational levels, for example, strategic, tactical, operational or for other specific needs. Other tailored reports were designed and developed as necessary, by the users themselves if they so desired.

Management Intuitive Use of the ERP Model

The structure of the extended relational database fields with each individual record tied to its unique Purchase Order (P/O) number was based on the chronology of Defence capability acquisition (i.e. in the order in which the processes occurred) from the Australian Department of Defence buyer to product/price to seller to delivery to final location (no changes to existing Australian Department of Defence systems or processes were required). This enabled immediate familiarity and intuitive use of the ERP model by management.

The structure included fields for the buyer's name, buyer's address and contact details, contract, contract type, account number, purchase order number and date, portfolio, department, division, branch, agency, and postcode, and details of payment arrangements and progress. product description and ANZIC industry code (Australian Bureau of Statistics, 1998), value and industry sector, seller company number, name and address, and contact details. Other data required by specialist Defence areas could be added as required. In this format, the data was able to be intuitively understood and interrogated by management, who were able to draw upon accurate and timely procurement, financial, project and supply records

continuously updated with new information at the end of each month.

Thus Defence's AU$3b to AU$4b per annum history of strategic capability acquisition over six financial years was established on a part time basis by two employees over a twelve month period. Good relations with all stakeholders were maintained during the development period, no consultants, or expensive vendor software, or special training or ongoing license fees were necessary in the development and establishment of this ERP database. And no changes to the organization's structure, systems or processes were necessary.

A Management View of the ERP Model

A management view of the ERP model's many possible fields is shown in the extract (Table 1). These fields reflect the nature of the ERP business of the Defence organization, which are largely common to most government's e-procurement activities. The chronology of the 'flat file' ERP model from buyer to supplier can be intuitively understood and rapidly interrogated by any manager to obtain desired data.

One ERP Model, Many Management Users, Many Management Uses

An important issue was the accessibility of the ERP database information to management, and the ability of management to easily interrogate the information. Many managers were already

Table 1. Some of the many database attributes (columns) and records (rows)

P/O no	Date	Value (AU$m)	A/C to date AU$m	Cost Centre	Supplies description	Qty	Supplier	Post Code
446	18Dec	9,103	8,197	DCPM	radios	20	Stanilite Electronic	2010
447	25Dec	7,557	6,000	DNSDC	Lep'c lease	1	Dan Murphy	5111
448	01Jan	6,320	0	MM	Goods	65	Disney Land	4329

familiar with MS Access and so had few diffi-culties. Others not so familiar could take a short training program with an MS Access training organization at minimum cost. The data could be made available to managers on a 'flat file' basis, that is, all attributes and individual records were made available to all authorised users all of the time. However, this approach is not one that is generally used by ERP vendors, who often wish to retain and limit such access. With 'flat file' access, the same up to date ERP information was accessible to all Defence managers. Because of this easy access to the flat file data, management could quickly and accurately answer questions however these were framed, provide formatted regular reports or develop specific reports them-selves using the one up to date information source (i.e. many users, many uses).

The ERP model was designed to be responsive, intuitive, easy to use, and adaptable (and this proved to be the outcome). For example, typical and unpredictable questions included Questions With/Without Notice from Australian Federal Parliament Government Ministers requesting advice on defence related industry located in a Minister's electorate, how much was being spent there, with which company, when, for what and so on. what spend did Defence have with a particular company or country. or what was Defence's con-tractual arrangements and their state of completion with certain suppliers. Other examples included Defence's specific exposure across a wide range of contracts to companies whose financial status was uncertain or deteriorating. In being able to access the ERP model, reports and responses to government or other stakeholder questions could be easily, quickly, consistently and accurately addressed by a few managers, thus significantly reducing the transaction costs and length of time previously associated with responding to such questions, and in particular, management coor-dination costs and time.

Management Audit to Identify Corrupt Practices

Using this ERP model, the problems associated with incomplete or corrupt e-procurement activi-ties can be reduced. With accurate management audit of historical e-procurement data over several financial years, a government is better able to select e-procurement arrangements so as to reduce the possibility of corrupt practices. It is also able to better synchronize the motivation of its agencies and its suppliers by reducing the differences of interest and information between the two, with panoptican transparency (BEN, 1985). This may reduce the opportunities for rent seeking activities by involved parties. The ERP model can imme-diately provide accurate details of each product (good or service) purchased, by whom and from which supplier in which industry, when and where, at what cost, as well as the current status of the account. This transparency in itself reduces the potential for, or possibility of, corrupt practices.

Management's Need to Know, Now: 'The Devil in the Detail'

Managers of government organizations, for a wide range of reasons, need to know with whom they are doing business, what business, and what financial exposure they have at any particular point of time. They need to know now, not in a month, or a week, or tomorrow, but now. Using this ERP model enabled Defence managers to know imme-diately the number and value of transactions, and with whom the Australian Department of Defence was doing business over the six financial years the model covered, to date.

This is demonstrated in the extract from two financial years (of six available) of the Defence ERP model (Table 2). Each of the transactions comprising the data can be individually sourced. The ERP model provided an immediate, accurate, and timely summary of such information. Without the database, it was difficult, slow and costly to obtain and coordinate current or historical data from the various Defence divisions, with doubtful accuracy.

Management Determination: Buyer Delegation Limit

Table 3 provides a typical summary extract from two financial years of the Defence ERP model. This extract demonstrates the number of notifications of value greater than the (then) Defence bank card delegation limit of AU$2,000 and the total value of the notifications in this category. This information is useful if the level of delegations is to be reconsidered, particularly as each product (good or service) comprising the data can be identified in detail. Should management wish to raise the delegation limit, how high should it be raised, in what tranches, and what will be the effect on e-procurements? These are decisions for which management needs accurate and timely e-procurement information to make (Table 3). Raising the delegation limit at each level is not only associated with a number of matters such as

management's trust of employees but also efficient organizational performance.

Management's Development of Strategic e-Procurement Policy

Major Australian Defence capability contracts, often high tech projects, were a focus of Defence's strategic management policy because of the potential for technology transfer and local high tech industry development, and the national benefits to be derived there from. The Table 4 extract summary provides an indication of whether a local high tech strategic sourcing policy was working or not. Detailed investigation of each contract from the ERP model gave information on the technology, performance, supplier details and much other information of national, strategic or operational importance. Such information gave a very good indication of the breadth and depth of high technology transfer, innovation and entrepreneurship being undertaken.

For example, in FY1, out of the total value of AU$2208.7m (of those contracts greater than

Table 2. Management's immediate access to every detail of every transaction

Value Bracket	F/Y 1: No of transactions	F/Y 1: Value AU$m	F/Y 2: No of transactions	F/Y 2: Value AU$m
$10m to $20m	18	241	12	177
$5m to $10m	28	191	28	197
$1m to $5m	193	395	253	549
$100k to $1m	2221	590	2205	583
$30k to $100k	4746	250	4410	231
$2k to $30k	43769	327	42035	309

Table 3. Determination by management of e-procurement delegation limits

Financial Year	FY1	FY2
Number of Australian Department of Defence Notifications >AU$2,000	50,989	48,995
Value of Notifications >AU$2,000 (at then year prices)	AU$3768m	AU$4054m
Value of Notifications >AU$2,000 (at constant prices)	AU$3768.06m	AU$4159m

AU$5m), AU$1074.1m was spent with Australia based suppliers. In the following F/Y, this increased to AU$1528.3m, indicating an increase of AU$454.2m in local spend with Australia based industry. This indicated that from management's perspective, strategic insourcing policies were being successfully applied. With instant access to each contract's details through the ERP model, it was also possible to confirm the nature, quality, value and content of each technology transfer.

Management's Exposure to Offshore Capability Sourcing

Defence management was interested in its offshore capability delivery vulnerability and spend. If there was a major disaster such as a tsunami, earthquake, epidemic or other global disaster such as a global financial crisis, then management needs to be quickly aware of the possible effects on its offshore suppliers. Table 5 provides an extract of aggregated data of the Country of Origin from which Defence was obtaining supplies over

one financial year (of the six available), with the specific details of each individual transaction being immediately accessible from the ERP model.

Management's Access to Comparative Business Unit Performance Data

Compilation of summary data by each of Defence's Business Unit Centres for each financial year was also easily, accurately and quickly obtained from the ERP model (Table 6). This summary extract of some of the activities being undertaken by some of the Business Units for each financial year can be used by management to review the human resources allocated to each Business Unit, its performance, commensurate with the type of procurements being undertaken, and the location. Resourcing equity across Business Units is often a key issue for management as it provides the basis for resource revision, reduction or re-allocation.

Table 4. Management's performance assessment of local e-procurement strategies

F/Y	Total value (AU$m)	Number of contracts	Value to local suppliers ($m)	Total number of contracts awarded to local suppliers
1	2208.7	60	1074.1	52
2	2382.8	52	1528.3	43

Table 5. View of management's exposure to offshore capability sourcing by F/Y

Country of Origin	F/Y: Number of suppliers	F/Y: Value
France	4	$2,603,403
Germany	3	$548,256
NZ	12	$5,196,147
Sweden	2	$1,466,168
Switzerland	6	$1,207,153
UK	33	$14,770,414
USA	126	$1,1444,801,682

Management Development of Strategic Industry Policy

Defence sources its capabilities across most UN/NATO/ANZ Industry Sectors which then provides www linkages to the UN/NATO/ANZ databases for each industry. Each e-procurement can be placed in an industry sector. In summary, Table 7 provides an extract of the principal industry sectors within which Defence has invested its sourcing activities. This information, drawn instantly from the ERP model, is valuable for a multitude of management purposes, and particularly for the development by management of strategic industry and e-procurement policy. The specific details supporting each of the contributing transactions can be made immediately available to management from the ERP model.

Management Knowledge of Top Ten Supplier Dependency

A summary of the top Australian Department of Defence suppliers by value each F/Y was also readily available from the ERP model. For the Australian Department of Defence, this management data provides defence exposure to particular companies. It is significant from industrial, national and international perspectives. An extract is given in Table 8.

Management Review of Buyer-Supplier Strategic Sourcing Relationships

The ERP model is able to be used for strategic e-procurement and supply development purposes. For example, supplier data can quickly reveal different or in some cases the same suppliers supplying the same 'off the shelf' product at significantly

Table 6. Management's access to comparative business unit performance data

Business Unit	Number of Notifications (each > AU$2,000)	Value of Notifications (AU$m)
Forces Executive	1532	40.37
Navy	6734	359.77
Army	11845	342.57
Air Force	14251	452.51
London	973	33.25
Washington	1496	72.61

Table 7. Management development of strategic industry policy

Industry Code	Industry Sector Title	No of Notifications	Value (AU$m)	% by value
15	Transport equipment	4457	1380	37
22	Construction and Construction services	4889	729	19
27	Consultancy, Property and Business services	6313	477	13
18	Computer, office Equipment and Electrical equipment not elsewhere classified	7196	422	11

Table 8. Management's knowledge of exposure to suppliers

No	Supplier	No of procurements	Value (AU$m)	% by value
1	Lockheed Martin	14	916	24
5	Raytheon	3	156	4
7	Rockwell	55	91	2
10	Shell	490	50	1
	Total top ten suppliers	2987	2046	54
	Other suppliers	48002	1723	46

different prices. This knowledge can be used to re-arrange competitive bids by fewer suppliers at better prices and so lower overall prices and transaction costs. Alternatively, because ERP data is accurate, timely and easy to access, there may be no need to limit the number of suppliers of a particular product but price setting may be to a buyer's advantage. Such technological innovation enables an organization to review, revise and renew its existing buyer-supplier strategic sourcing relationships.

CONCLUSION

This ERP model presents to management both specific and aggregate comparative micro, macro and other information about Defence e-procurement. This assisted Defence management to 'close the policy loop', that is to use quantitative and other performance measures to assist in measuring the outcomes of the various Defence industry and e-procurement management policies including the need for better e-purchasing statistics to promote improved accountability in e-purchasing (an identified major management deficiency), and effective performance measurement and resource utilisation.

No change management or adjustments to Defence organisation, structures, systems or processes were required, and there were no actual or implicit threats of job loss to employees.

Managers are encouraged by the literature to perform a thorough business process analysis before selecting an ERP vendor and undertaking ERP vendor implementation (King, 2005. Yusuf, 2004). However, such time consuming and costly analysis was found to be quite unnecessary for this ERP model. That is, the ERP model research and development team simply accepted the existing structure, processes and systems from which data was collected and did not need to interfere in any way with these arrangements, or undertake costly, time consuming detailed analysis of the existing arrangements, or engage any consultants.

The literature also suggests that ERP vendor implementation is often difficult and can be politically charged in government which is often bureaucratic and mechanistic. While Defence may also be considered by some to be bureaucratic and mechanistic, it was found that the implementation of this ERP model was not difficult nor politically charged, and complemented the existing processes, rules and semantics across the organization. No change management or business process re-engineering was necessary, with external environmental changes being reflected in and interpreted through ongoing data input.

In summary, this longitudinal action research over a twelve month period tracked the research, development and implementation of an inexpensive generic ERP model by two unremarkable public servants. The ERP model so developed did not require any study or adjustment of organization structures, systems or processes, or any additional resources, change management or special training. It did not pose a job threat to existing employees, who were involved in its development and was accepted by them. It is suggested that the strategic ERP model so developed may be of interest to other managers of e-government agencies.

REFERENCES

Altova, F. (2009), 'Database mapping. Altova (http://www.altova.com/ products/mapforce/ xml_to_db_ database _mapping.html accessed March 2009. Bouret, R., (2005), XML and Databases, XML Guild, September, file://C:\ TEMP\3EERCYBR.html accessed March 2009.

Brown, C., and I. Vessey, (2003) Managing the Next Wave of Enterprise Systems: Leveraging Lessons from ERP, MIS Quarterly Executive, 2(1).

Business Software, (2008), Top 10 ERP Vendors – 2008 Profiles of the Leading Vendors, Business Software.com.

Cordella, A. (2001), *Does Information Technology Always Lead to Lower Transaction Costs?* The 9th European Conference on Information Systems, Bled, Slovenia, June 27-29.

Cordella, A. (2006). Transaction costs and information systems: does IT add up? *Journal of Information Technology, 21*, 195–202. doi:10.1057/palgrave.jit.2000066

Cordella, A., & Simon, K. A. (1997), *The Impact of Information Technology on Transaction and Coordination Cost*, Conference on Information Systems Research in Scandinavia (IRIS 20), Oslo, Norway, August 9-12.

Deloitte (2008). *In fighting shape?*. 2008 survey of cost-improvement trends in the Fortune 500', Deloitte.

Department of Defense. (2009). *Defense Materiel Organization*. Australian Government.

Financial Times Higher Education Supplement. (2008). *University Rankings, Financial Times Higher Education Supplement*. New York, NY: Financial Times.

Gray, P. (2003). *In depth: RMIT's PeopleSoft disaster*. Australia: ZDNet.

Jutras, C. (2007, July). *The Total Cost of ERP Ownership in Mid Sized Companies*. Boston, MA: Aberdeen Group.

Khosrow-Pour, M. (2006). Emerging Trends and Challenges in Information Technology Management, *Information Management Association*, International Conference, Idea Group Inc.

King, W. (2005). *Ensuring ERP implementation success. Information Systems Management*. Hershey, PA: IGI Global.

Koch, C., & Wailgum, T. (2008). *ERP Definitions and Solutions*. CIO.

Ludwigshafen University Of Applied Sciences. (2004). *Enhanced Project Success Through SAP Best Practices*. Germany: International Benchmarking Study, Ludwigshafen University.

Markoff, J. (2009a). *Worm Infects Millions of Computers Worldwide*. New York, NY: The New York Times.

Meta Group. (2010). Longhaus. Retrieved from http://www.longhaus.com/ research/naked-chief-blog-link/tags /META-Group/

Saleh, K., Abdulaziz, A., & Alkattan, I. (2006). A Services – Oriented Approach to Developing Security Policies for Trustworthy Systems. In *Emerging Trends and Challenges in IT Management*. Hershey, PA: IGI Global.

Turban, A. (2008). *Information Technology for Management, Transforming Organizations in the Digital Economy*. New York: John Wiley & Sons.

Victorian Auditor General. (2003). *Report of the Auditor General on RMIT's Finances*. Australia: June, State Government of Victoria.

Wailgum, T. (2007). *ERP Definitions and Solutions*. CIO.

Williamson, O. E. (2002a). *The Lens of Contract: Private Ordering*. Berkeley: University of California.

Wittmann, C., & Cullen, M. (2000). *B2B Internet*. First Union Securities.

Yusuf, Y., Gunasekaran, A., & Abthorpe, M. (2004, February). Enterprise Information Systems Project Implementation: A Case Study of ERP in Rolls-Royce. *International Journal of Production Economics, 87*(3). doi:10.1016/j.ijpe.2003.10.004

ADDITIONAL READING

Al-Fawaz, K., Zahran, A., & Tillal, E. (2008), Critical Success Factors in ERP Implementation: a Review, European and Mediterranean Conference on Information Systems, May 25-26.

Australian Bureau Of Statistics. (1998). *1291.0 - A Guide to Major ABS Classifications*. Canberra: Commonwealth of Australia.

Bentham, J. (1785), *The Panopticon Writings*. Ed. Miran Bozovic (London: Verso, 1995). p. 29-95

Carayannis, Eg., & Popescu, D. (2005). Profiling a methodology for economic growth and convergence: Learning from the EU e-procurement experience for central and eastern European countries. *Technovation*, 1–14. doi:10.1016/S0166-4972(03)00071-3

Centre For Environment and Sustainability. (2002). Technology and Policy for Sustainable Development. *Chalmers University of Technology and the Göteborg University, 5*(February), 4.

Daneva, M., & Wieringa, R. (2008). *Requirements Engineering for Cross-organizational ERP Implementation: Undocumented Assumptions and Potential Mismatches*. University of Twente.

Dehning, B., & Stratopolous, T. (2003). 'Determinants of a Sustainable Competitive Advantage Due to an IT-enabled Strategy. *The Journal of Strategic Information Systems, 12*, 2003. doi:10.1016/S0963-8687(02)00035-5

Esteves, J., & Pastor, J. (2004). Enterprise Resource Planning Systems Research: An Annotated Bibliography. *Communications of AIS, 7*(8), 2–54.

Finkle, J., & Chernikoff, H. (2008). *Waste Management sues SAP over software quality*. London, UK: Reuters.

Fukuyama, F. (1999). *The Great Disruption*. London, UK: St Edmundsbury Press.

Head, B., (2003, April). *Exchange of Pace*. The Age.

International Association For Impact Assessment, (1999). *Principle of Environmental Impact Assessment Best*. Practice, European Union.

ITU. (2009). *Measuring the Information Society: The ICT Development Index*. Geneva, Switzerland: International Telecommunication Union.

Lee, Sm., Tan, & Trimi, S. (2005). Current practices of leading e-government Countries. *Communications of the ACM*, (10): 99–104. doi:10.1145/1089107.1089112

Markoff, J. (2009b), 'Vast Spy System Loots Computers in 103 countries. New York, NY: The New York Times.

Moe, C. E. (2004). *Public e-procurement – Determinants of Attitudes Towards Adoption*, Electronic Government, In Proceedings. *Lecture Notes in Computer Science*, 278–282. doi:10.1007/978-3-540-30078-6_46

Monk, E., & Wagner, B. (2009). *Concepts in Enterprise Resource Planning" 3rd*. Boston, MA: Course Technology Cengage Learning.

Petts, J. (Ed.). (1999). *Handbook of Environmental Impact Assessment*. Oxford, UK: Blackwell.

Porter, M. E. (2008). *On Competition*. Cambridge, MA: Harvard Business School Publishing Corporation.

Post, A. (2003), Business Magazine, Australia Post http://www1.auspost.com.au/priority/index.asp?issue_id=30&area=features&article_id=632 accessed March 2009.

Puschmann T and Alt R, (2005), *Successful use of e-procurement in supply chains, Supply Chain Management: an International Journal*, (2), 122-133.

Selsky, J., Goes, & Oguz, B. (2007). Contrasting Perspectives of Strategy Making: Applications in 'Hyper' Environments. *Organization Studies*, *28*(1), 71–94. doi:10.1177/0170840607067681

Thompson, G., Frances, J., Levačić, R., & Mitchell, J. (1991). *Markets, hierarchies and networks: the coordination of social life*. Thousand Oaks, CA: Sage.

Williamson, O. E. (1991a). Comparative Economic Organization: The Analysis of Discrete Structural Alternatives. *Administrative Science Quarterly*, *36*(June), 269–296. doi:10.2307/2393356

Williamson, O. E. (1991b). Economic Institutions: Spontaneous and Intentional Governance. *Journal of Law Economics and Organization*, *7*(Special Issue), 159–187.

Williamson, O. E. (1996). *The Mechanisms of Governance*. New York, NY: Oxford University Press.

Williamson, O. E. (2002b). *The Theory of the Firm as Governance Structure: from Choice to Contract*. Berkley, California: University of California.

Williamson, O. E. (2002c). *Empirical Microeconomics: Another Perspective* in Mie Augier and James March, eds. The Economics of Choice, Change and Organization, Brookfield, VT. Edward Elgar.

Chapter 4

How ERP Systems are Centralizing and Standardizing the Accounting Function in Public Organizations for Better and Worse

Catherine Equey Balzli
University of Applied Sciences, Switzerland

Emmanuel Fragnière
University of Applied Sciences, Switzerland

ABSTRACT

We have conducted research in an attempt to understand why the accounting function of a Swiss public administration has significantly changed following the implementation of an ERP system. To study this social phenomenon, an ethnography research strategy was followed. This approach is well suited for situations facing deep structural changes such as the transformation of a profession. The sample consisted primarily of accountants, accounting managers, and related professions. We have structured the analysis around the 3 following axes: 1. organizational structure changes, 2. standardization and centralization processes, and 3. centralization's effect on accounting tasks. Research findings and analyses indicate that the power of each public administration department under review is very strong to the point that it has negatively impacted the necessary standardization imposed by an ERP system implementation. So, the full potential of the ERP is not exploited at all. However, the financial statements can now comply with international standards such as International Public Sector Accounting Standards (IPSAS). Consequently, our case study shows that an ERP implementation project cannot be managed in the same manner as those realized in the private sector.

DOI: 10.4018/978-1-60960-863-7.ch004

INTRODUCTION

Due to the new IT in general and to ERP in particular, the organizational changes are very well described in the literature. Authors agree that the ERP systems impose "generic processes" and are supposed to provide the business with "best practices" (Davenport, 1998, p. 123-125). Moreover, academic research points out that some ERP's characteristics, such as the integration of business processes and data, standardization of work, and centralization of internal services allowed the transformation of the management accounting function (Scapens & Jazayeri, 2003). Information technology and organizational changes seem to be the two most important change drivers in management accounting practices (Yazdifar & Tsamenyi, 2005). The impact of ERP system implementation on employees' work in general (Kumar et al., 2002; Arnold, 2006), and on accountants' tasks in particular (Burns & Vaivio, 2001), is also largely described.

The public sector is also very well studied by academic researchers. A recent study by Rosacker and Olson (2008) indicates that IT investments increased, and predicted IT's expenses for state and local governments (in the USA) would be around USD 72 billion by 2011. It is generally acknowledged that the public sector is considered to be a very promising market for IT development. Indeed, several studies have advocated that the public sector must face great challenges and reforms. The public sector has to modernize its way of serving citizens and improving accounting transparency. ERP system implementation is a way to address these challenges (Deloitte, 2006; Cacciaguidi-Fahy et al., 2002).

Despite the fact that ERPs in the public sector are also largely studied (Chang, 2000; Gulledge & Sommer; 2003, Wagner & Lederer; 2004, Raymond et al., 2005; Rosacker & Olson, 2008) the evolution of the accounting function following ERP implementation is, to our knowledge, not addressed in research. Consequently, the aim

of this chapter is to examine the impact of ERP implementation on accounting service organizations. The research question of this study is to determine how the accounting and finance professional functions change when implementing an Integrated Financial System (i.e. the finance modules of an ERP system).

This chapter is organized as follows: The Literature Review section inventories research findings related to ERP implementation's impact on an organization as well as on employee tasks. The Research Design section presents the ethno-methodology approach that was employed in our study to investigate the ERP impact on the accounting function in a public administration. The Case Study section details the context of the ERP implementation in a Swiss public administration. The Results and Discussion section provides a synthesis of our fieldwork as well as the concluding remarks.

LITERATURE REVIEW

ERP and Organizational and Structural Changes

As described in the Introduction, one of the major contributions of ERP system implementation is the integration of all (or at least, several) functions of the organization in a single system. Rikhardsson and Kræmmergaard (2006) have provided a good description of the "integration effect" (p. 43) due to the implementation of an ERP system, as well as the difficulties it creates. Integration in this study refers to the "integration of business processes" (Ibid). Respondents in their study have emphasized that ERP implementation did not match properly with the company's processes. However, the change in business processes is perceived by managers as "a chance to modernize the organization business processes" (p. 44), as well as a chance to create a strong business standardization that has "employee resistance and obstruction" (Ibid). The fact that employees now must comply with procedures has led to significant changes in the behaviors and attitudes of employees.

Rikhardsson and Kræmmergaard (2006) have qualified Enterprise Systems (ES) as "an actor in the organization defining possibilities, costs, benefits, behavior, integration and the relation between other organizational actors." They explained that an ES implementation is not a simple "system implementation project" but "an organizational development journey" (p. 46). This is due to the fact that: ES supports processes and not functions, processes are integrated into a single database and data structure; standard processes must be adopted on a company-wide basis and will therefore have an impact on the company's organization, and the technical aspects of implementation are less important than organizational and business process issues.

It must be noted that the necessity of standardization is often imposed from a group in order to control its subsidiaries (Yamin et al., 2007; Quattrone et al., 2005). Another issue about organizational change is revealed by Scapens and Jazayeri (2003), cited in Arnold (2006). The researchers distinguished three levels of organizational impacts of change in an ERP system implementation: "upper management, mid-level management, and operational activities" (p. 10). They go on to point out that these organizational impacts vary, depending on the "hierarchical" level at which the change arises. It also seems that change is less visible at the upper management levels than in the operational activities. Grandlund and Malmi (2002) also outlined that organizational independence and (hierarchical) responsibilities changes take place following ERP implementation. Finally, Caglio (2003) quoted several authors' perspectives and affirmed that "IT is an external force influencing the definition of organizational structures, but its impact is mediated and moderated by human agents, and by their habits, their communication and cognitive schemas, as well as their behavioral norms" (p. 126).

ERP and Organizational Changes in Accounting Services

ERP system implementation regarding organizational changes is also seen as the "creation of a new organizational division" (Granlund & Malmi, 2002) or even as a decentralization of services (Velcu, 2007). According to Scapens and Jazayeri (2003), the organization of management accounting is deeply modified following an ERP implementation. In their case study, they noticed the development of a center of "shared services" (p. 212) for accounting tasks (i.e. centralization of accounts payable and receivable).

In a study supported by the Association of Chartered Certified Accountants (UK) concerning "the Financial Shared Services Centres," Cacciaguidi-Fahy et al. (2002) consider the ERP system to be an "enabling" (p. 17) technology (between others) by allowing the creation of "Shared Services Centres" (p. 37) in private and public organizations. In particular, they indicate that ERP systems provide a unique software platform for multiple sites. These authors, for example, advocated that "payroll, disbursements and routine data transaction as well as more complex functions such as accounting, legal counsel and human resources" (p. 73) could be shared and would bring "standardization, cohesion, [and] efficiency" (Ibid). The creation of "a Financial Shared Service" is an important organizational change, and is often linked to the ERP system implementation.

ERP and Accounting Professions and Practices Changes

A case study conducted by Caglio (2003) revealed that the ERP project was an "occasion for 'structuring'... a new and desirable 'way of working',... 'a unique opportunity to revise processes' and to 'integrate financial accounting with management accounting.'" The decision to implement an ERP system was not presented to the staff as an

IT project but rather as a reorganization project which was "an essential option for the firm's success" (p. 135). As did Scapens and Jazayeri (2003), Caglio (2003) also pointed out three categories of "structurational characteristics" that entailed changes in accountants' practices and positions: standardization of accounting practices, integration and interfunctional collaboration, and leadership of the accounting department in the management of the new ERP system. Caglio (2003) also notes that the impact on accountants' practices and positions depends on the number of modules that are implemented.

Scapens and Jazayeri (2003) reveal that SAP implementation played an important role as a "change driver" (p. 204) but did not lead to the use of new accounting techniques or methods. Booth et al. (2000), like Scapens and Jazayeri (2003), argues that "ERP... have little influence on the use of new accounting practices" (p. 4). However, Scapens and Jazayeri (2003) state that the use of an ERP system involves new roles for the accountants' line managers.

Academic literature primarily indicates that the accounting profession has evolved from being primarily technical (bookkeeping), to increasingly managerial (project management, strategy). In other words, the field has gone "from 'controller' or 'score-keeper' to 'business support' or 'internal business consultant'" (Burns and Vaivio, 2001, p. 390). Velcu (2007) points out significant business process changes, mainly in accounting functions such as new tasks, reassignment or decentralization of the financial management tasks, and the real-time follow-up of business. Regarding the benefits of the use of an ERP system, Velcu (2007) argued that ERP allows: a "better account receivables management," "more flexible invoicing," improved "cash management" and improved "service time in accounting tasks," "improved access to information," and improved "customer service" (p. 1324).

The reduction of "routine work" is also considered a change that is a result of the use of ERP systems (Grandlund & Malmi, 2002; Scapens & Jazayeri, 2003). Scapens and Jazayeri (2003) noticed that, with an ERP system, entries in the accounting records are made automatically (coming from other modules used by other departments). In the firm studied by Caglio (2003), it is observed that "accountants have lost some discretion in applying the procedures for the collection, elaboration and provision of information" (p. 141). Caglio (2003) also pointed out that ERP systems imply "work uniformity" (p. 136).

Grandlund and Malmi (2002) have solely identified a limited impact of an ERP system on management accounting. Their study of ten large Finnish companies revealed that ERP systems do not have a major impact on certain activities such as cost accounting, balanced scorecards systems, or budgets because these are frequently kept outside of ERP systems (generally using spreadsheets). Complexity was the main reason cited for not using ERP systems for certain tasks. On the other hand, Scapens and Jazayeri (2003) mention better financial forecasting and talked about a change of "culture" (p. 221).

Another transformation of management accounting due to the use of ERP systems has to do with the ease of access to information. Previously, only accounting managers had access to accounting information (reporting). Rikhardsson and Kraemmergaard (2006) define the notion of "monopoly on access" which is disappearing rapidly. They argue that "accounting department(s) had to change and find other ways to service decision makers and the organization at large." New activities provided by accountants include "data analysis, scenario building, and new ways of delivering valuable information to decision makers..." (p. 43). According to Caglio (2003), Management Accountants also must support other departments with information interpretation.

ERP System Implementation in the Public Sector

A study of ERP system implementations in UK public sector institutions (universities) indicated that ERP projects "reinforce cultural change" by using private sector practices to favor "process to fit ERP" (Allen et al., 2002, p. 5). This study also notes that new technologies "enforced the adoption of centrally designed practices and procedures" (p. 6). It is interesting to note that implementation is less problematic in a university that is already managed as a private sector organization.

The same idea is developed by Gulledge and Sommer (2003), who studied "new ways of managing public enterprises" (p. 482) in the United States Department of Defense. They describe the public sector's business process as being old-fashioned, "top-down and hierarchical" (p. 473). They advocate that the use of "process-aligned standard software solutions" in the private sector will allow for the modernization of public sector management. It must be said that the findings of this study are based on the authors' personal experiences, not on scientific results, and therefore, should be considered with precaution.

The accounting functions in public administrations that have not been particularly subject to specific research. On the other hand, academic and professional studies clearly point out the differences between the two sectors (private and public), confirming the need for further research in this field. For instance, Chang et al. (2002) insist that the notion of "ERP knowledge management" is problematical in governmental contexts. Cacciaguidi-Fahy et al. (2002) indicated that work changes are particularly tedious to foster in public administrations. Such changes must be typically supported by unions of state employees. Gulledge and Sommer (2003) observed that incentives and performance indicators might differ between private and public administrations. "There is nothing special about the management of public organizations that precludes them from implementing modern private sector management practices and integrated information systems." Gulledge and Sommer (2003) conclude that it is crucial that we manage to obtain comparable information from both the public and private organizations.

We could nevertheless hypothesize that findings obtained from the research about ERP implementations in the private sector could be sufficient to draw conclusions for the public administrations. However, we believe that there are too many discrepancies between the two sectors to do so. Actually, Wagner and Lederer (2004) state that public administrations have far less practice and use in terms of ERP deployment than do private ones. However, as Raymond et al. (2005) mentioned that ERP systems are of growing importance for public administration, they also confirm the need for more academic studies on this topic. Bajjaly (1999), quoted in Rosacker and Olson (2008), pointed out that public administrations are at risk when implementing an ERP system, because research is deficient in this field.

The literature review revealed that an ERP system implementation was not only a question of "technical criteria" (p. 128) but one of strategic and organizational issues (Davenport, 1998). Organizational and structural changes impact everyone's work, including that of accounting employees. Therefore, we advocate that all these changes affect the organization of the accounting services and, therefore, the tasks performed by accountants.

ERP implementation is clearly described by academic authors as a change driver. The impact of this new technology on accountants' job in the private sector is largely studied in the literature but is less considered in the public sector. In particular, the accounting function in a public administration has not been subject to specific research. To our knowledge, the changes in the accounting professions of the Swiss public sector have never been studied.

RESEARCH DESIGN

Research Methodology

We have adopted a qualitative research approach. The data collection essentially comes from semi-structured interviews with employees of a Swiss public administration. We asked respondents to describe their accounting tasks before and after the ERP implementation. The data sample consisted of sixteen semi-directed interviews that were conducted between June and October 2009. The transcripts were written directly after the interviews and went through validation by the respondents less than a week afterwards. Schedules with interviews have been conducted in a timely manner with respondents being very cooperative during the entire process. Moreover, the interviewees seemed happy to describe their job or the tasks they performed.

This research approach adopts the philosophy of "interpretivism," which we believe to be appropriate for this kind of study. The main objective of this study is to understand how accounting tasks change following the implementation of an ERP system in a public administration. We followed the ethnography research strategy: "its purpose is to describe and explain the social world that the research subjects inhabit in the way in which they would describe and explain it. It is a very appropriate strategy in business, if the researcher wishes to gain insights about a particular context and better understand and interpret it from the perspectives of those involved" (Saunders et. al., 2007). This approach is well suited for situations facing deep structural changes such as the implementation of integrated IT tools.

A qualitative approach like the one employed in this study is typically useful in tackling "questions about people's experiences" (Patton, 2002, p. 33) and "is particularly oriented toward exploration, discovery, and inductive logic" (p.

55). The methodology employed to study the gathered information is based on a "cross-case" (p. 57) scheme.

Questionnaire and Interviews

The questionnaire was structured as follows: general respondent information (e.g., name, position, and department); description of changes in accountants' roles; profiles, and job duties; description of changes in the organizational structure; and evaluation of the ERP system and implementation project. We do not use the answers to the last part for the analysis presented in this chapter.

We selected respondents based on the following hierarchical levels: the ERP project leader, the finance managers, the ERP end users (the bookkeepers or accountants), the human resources managers, the IT managers, and external consultants. Even though the questionnaire structure was used each time, we had open discussions with our respondents. Our goal was to make them as comfortable as possible in order to obtain any unusual information from them. We generally encouraged them to communicate their views regarding accountants' tasks and the organization changes of their service and department after the ERP implementation in a free manner. We have also requested documentations from our respondents such as job descriptions and project paperwork. These documents were not easy to obtain, so we agreed not to incorporate them in our examination.

Population

In order to make our convenience sample more effective, we decided to concentrate on the three departments that played a major role in the ERP deployment:

- The Department of Finance, which was in command of the implementation project.

- The Department of Education, which is by far the largest department, as shown in Table 1, and appeared to be very dominant in the overall decision making process associated with the ERP implementation.
- The Department of Construction and Information Technologies, which was responsible for the IT infrastructure and maintenance of the ERP project.

Then, for each retained department, we selected respondents in the following hierarchical levels:

- The ERP project leader
- Finance managers
- The ERP end users (bookkeepers/accountants)
- Human resources managers
- IT managers
- External consultants

In each of the three retained departments, we interviewed two finance managers, at least one of which was from the centralized finance service. The selection of the finance managers was aided by the Project Leader. We have preferred key actors of the ERP implementation as well as very implicated staff. We included two HR managers who occupied their job position prior to the ERP implementation in our sample. Via finance managers' recommendations, we were able to interview three IT managers and three ERP end users (one per department). Evidently, the Project Leader of the finance department was part of the sample. His views were very important since he had successfully supervised the ERP project. We also interviewed the manager of the external consultants. Consequently, sixteen interviews were conducted during the field work. The goal of this varied convenience sample was to determine whether and how the perceptions of each function and job would compare.

CASE STUDY

Governmental Organization

The public administration that was studied is organized into seven agencies, which are subject to the "Conseil d'État" (the State Council, or the executive body) and the "Grand Conseil" (the Main Council, the lawmakers). The departments written in bold in Figure 1 were chosen for interviews. These bodies are audited by the "Cour des Comptes" (the Committee of Auditors) and are supported by the "Chancellerie d'État" (the State Chancellery). The law power is assured by the "Pouvoir Judiciaire" (Judiciary Power) as an independent body. The organizational chart in Figure 1 displays the complex configuration of the public administration that was under review.

Government Agency Organization

It is relevant to note that prior to the ERP project all departments presented a different organizational chart. In 2006, the new State Councilors enacted a "Plan de mesures" (list of measures) to enhance the performance and the quality of services that were provided their administration. One of these measures recommended standardizing the organizational charts of all agencies in order to reduce the number and size of hierarchical positions. These charts are currently shown in Figure 2.

Each department is directed by a State Councilor. A general staff member, "Secrétariat Général" (Corporate Secretary), who is directly attached to the State Councilor, supervises centralized services of finance, logistic, information systems, human resources, and internal control (a new service); as well as a "Bureau" or General Managements (3 to 9 depending on the department) which accomplishes the department's missions. Conversely, the organization of financial services in each "Bureau" or General Management is different from one to the other as confirmed by the results of our analysis.

Figure 1. 2008's organizational chart of the cantonal government (constructed by authors from Internet sites information)

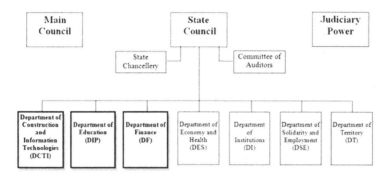

Figure 2. 2008 general standardized organization of each department: upper level (constructed by authors from Internet sites information)

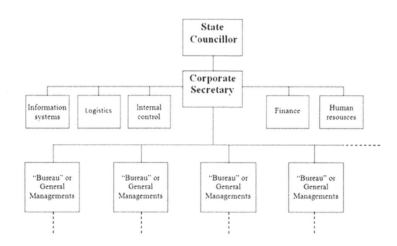

This new and very structured organization does not result from the ERP implementation but is clearly defined in the trend by the new government to improve the quality of work and services of the Cantonal administration. However, these organizational changes were made at the same time as the ERP implementation and our hypothesis is that it was not left to chance. Another point that is relevant to our study is the significant differences between the departments in terms of size and mission (see Table 1 for the size differences of each finance service). The distinctness of each department makes it very difficult to compare them and to generalize the results.

An analysis of Table 1 revealed that the Department of Construction and Information Technologies (DCTI) and the Department of Finance (DF) have more accounting and finance employees than the other departments. This is very understandable since they are "Financial Shared Services" for the entire government. In contrast, the differences among the other departments are significant and reveal the freedom of each department to organize their services and, a priori, there is no uniformity in work and processes. Even if the general organizational chart of each department were standardized, the organization of each department still varies. We postulate that the

Table 1. Size of finance services: comparison among departments—2008

	DCTI	DF	DIP	DI	DES	DSE	DT	Total
Global budget of the department (in million CHF)	1,195	1,461	1,874	547	1,031	1,543	359	8,010
Total of employees of the department (full-time equivalent)	1,082	672	7,384	2,555	207	654	479	13,033
Employees of the centralized finance service of the department (full-time equivalent)	31	15	18	7	4	5	9	89
Employees of the centralized finance service of the department (in % of the total of employees)	2.9%	2.2%	0.2%	0.3%	1.9%	0.8%	1.9%	0.7%
Users of ERP (in number of people)								
Entry & Consultation	336	291	597	269	80	101	101	1,775*
Users of ERP (in % of the total of employees)								
Entry & Consultation	31.1%	43.3%	8.1%	10.5%	38.6%	15.4%	21.1%	13.6%

* 354 further users have access to the application (ERP) but are outside of the cited departments

Source: Director of Information Systems of the Finance Department

power of each department is very strong, and this is certainly the main issue in our case study because it has had a negative impact on the necessary standardization required for the ERP system implementation.

Description of the ERP Project

Observing the evolution of the Information Systems in the public administration studied, we noticed that the first implemented systems would systematically pursue specific goals. At the end of the 1990s, many IS accounting applications had no real overall consistency. At that time, the accounting workforce would spend most of their energy "consolidating" the information to produce financial reports.

As such, a 1998 inventory of IT systems includes the following:

- One accounting system used by the DIP
- One accounting system used by the DCTI

- One accounting system used by "the Chancellerie," the finance department, and all other departments. This accounting system was also used for consolidation purposes
- One information system used by the central purchasing department;
- One budget system for the DIP
- One budget system for all agencies
- Over one hundred "business solutions" often interfaced with accounting systems.

This inventory explains the motivation for a new integrated system. The first initiative for a centralized and unified system started around 2000. This initiative had the merit to consider the accounting function in an integrated and coherent manner for a large and complex state. Moreover, the intent was also to improve the governmental decision-making process. As such, this integrated system should give the deputies and the cabinet an overall overview of the Cantonal state finances.

Another goal of this project was related to operations management. Indeed, a consistent part of the project was devoted to the identification of operations redundancies as well as to the establishment of unified work procedures for every state department. Operations would therefore be improved and enable the different services and departments to meet mandatory deadlines. In all, the new accounting system should provide better cash and treasury management. The new Integrated Financial System should ultimately enable the Finance Department to produce more reliable and transparent financial reporting. Indeed, the accounting process needed to be more rigorous and efficient, and produced in due time. The new ERP implementation was chosen to meet all the above mentioned goals that could not have been fulfilled previously.

The Scope of the ERP Project

An action plan was created in March 2000 to implement the following modules:

- General Ledger
- Accounts Receivable
- Accounts Payable (with engagements)
- Purchase Orders
- Inventory, Fixed Assets
- Budget and Financial Planning/Forecasting
- Administrative Processes
- Cash Management and Forecasting
- Counter/Box Office
- Document Management/Filing and Business Intelligence.

It also included specific interfaces for payroll, human resources, and business systems. Following the 2000 implementation plan, additional modules have been incorporated, including project management, school supplies management, simulation of salaries and decentralized cash account management. Beginning in April 2009, each module has been available and fully functioning in the seven

departments. The state is dealing with a growing number of accounting information; this means 300,000 accounts, 2.5 million accounting entries, and 200,000 invoices (accounts payable) per year. Therefore, it is evident that such an integrated accounting system is unavoidable. However, the system has not deployed all its benefits.

The "Human" Resources Involved in the ERP Project

The Directorate General for Economic and Financial Affairs (DGFE) part of the Department of Finance has initially been in charge of ERP project management. The CTI (Center for Information Technology of the State) was particularly involved in the resolution of technical issues related to IT implementation. A group varying between 30 and 130 full-time employees (state workforce and consultants) has been engaged in the implementation of the ERP since the beginning of the project. On the whole, the project managers have stated that a total of 39,000 man-days have been required so far, which corresponds to a sizable project management in terms of workforce. Today, there are approximately 2000 ERP users.

Organization after the ERP Implementation Project

Near the end of 2000, we counted almost 25 finance services and 300 employees devoted to accounting and finance functions. There is also a significant variety of financial functions: accountant, bookkeeper, accounting secretary, accounting manager, cash accountant, financial assistant, and chief financial officer. The main change in the finance functions attribution is the will to centralize accounting and finance competencies and tasks in the Finance Department and the Department of Construction and Information Technologies, which means more responsibilities for these departments. Despite this centralization, there are always enough finance and accounting people in the departments, and the number of employees of the finance services of each department is not homogenous, as described in Table 1.

RESULTS AND DISCUSSION

Structural Changes

In the finance department and during the ERP implementation, two services were "reorganized." As described below:

Because of the missing accounting set of skills, two services have exploded: the cash management service and the central purchasing. The reorganization of these two services was not planed but this change was done because these services were under the control of the Finance Department. The same changes were not done in the other departments because they do not have the volition to change. (ERP Project Leader, personal communication, June 22, 2009).

In fact, the problem with these services was that the employees did not have the necessary set of skills to work with the new IT tools. Therefore, the employees had to be fired and replaced, which is unusual in a state organization. According to the project leader, this "reorganization" was performed in the services of the finance department because they were hierarchically dependent. What is more interesting is that the same "reorganization" was also necessary in other departments but was not completed. As described by the ERP project leader, it created quality and efficiency issues with regard to ERP implementation and, finally, in the accounting work. It was a critical issue in the ERP implementation under review from the government. We advocate that it was necessary for the finance department to have a hierarchical relation (with authority) on all the finance services of the entire government. This condition is vital

to the success of ERP implementation. Another respondent also complained about the excessive power of each department and revealed that this is a significant difference in the private sector and a problem in a governmental context:

The other departments don't want reorganization or centralization. Their hierarchical power is strong and the DCTI and the DF can't impose their way to do. We have to consult and to accept their points of view. This is a great difference with the private sector, where the finance department has generally more weight and where a CEO could impose the decisions. (CFO, personal communication, July 16, 2009).

So, obviously there was a problem when considering both the functional and hierarchical structures of the overall organization of the state studied. The match between the two does not work properly; this is the consequence of a lack of a clear central authoritative power inside the administration.

Centralization Processes

Concerning the (re)organization, one of the main aims of the ERP implementation is to centralize the finance services of the entire government. The most astounding comment received in our interviews was the explanation given by an accountant regarding the difficulty in centralizing the accounting functions:

Centralization is not possible because we have seven departments with seven different ways to work. (Accountant, personal communication, September 16, 2009).

It is simply unthinkable that this accountant could not even imagine that the objective was to standardize the accounting work. Again, this phenomenon is linked to the lack of central hierarchy.

The centralization of this public administration was quite complicated, despite several attempts. First of all, the Accounts Payable (AP) accounting was centralized in the Finance department. Accountants from other departments moved to this department but continued to deal with the AP from their previous divisions. This centralization failed to meet expectations because currently, only AP are centralized in the finance department, accountants do the same work as before (in fact, they only moved their workplace), the AP processing was not shared among accountants, and the goal to reduce accounting staff failed. Indeed, the number of employees of the concerned service increased to thirty (compared to seven before the ERP implementation), and only eight accountants were transferred.

Second, the accounting of fixed assets was centralized in the Department of Construction and Information Technologies. For this purpose, no staff members were moved but new employees (with better accounting qualifications) were hired. Finally, the accounting and finance functions were also centralized in each department. The role of each finance service (of the departments) differs from for each department. However, the new, generic roles of these centralized finance services are: budget preparation, controlling and checking, and analyses and forecasts. Accounts Receivable accounting was maintained in the "Bureau" or General Management of each department.

It is interesting to note that, prior to the ERP implementation, an accounting manager complained that the ERP project was presented as a decentralization tool. In fact, after this implementation, he found it to be a centralization tool with a loss of autonomy for his service:

The ERP project was presented to us as a decentralization tool which must allow us to be more independent. In fact, we assist to a centralization of the finance functions. Furthermore, second wave of centralization is expected with a bigger risk

to lose our independence. (Accounting manager, personal communication, September 7, 2009).

One HR Manager qualified the centralization and decentralization as a "going or moving back and forth" process, with hesitations between centralization and decentralization. The answer of another CFO is particularly appropriate. He pointed out that the necessity to centralize or to decentralize depends on the kind of tasks performed:

The centralization of the accounts payable, investments, and litigation management is indispensable, but the accounts receivable management must be done in the specific services as they have the necessary information and knowledge of the "customer-citizen." Centralization seems to be most efficient when specialized (accounting) knowledge is required. Moreover, the right question is not about centralization or decentralization but about the good knowledge and accurate analysis of the business processes. (CFO, personal communication, July 16, 2009).

Centralization's Effect on Accounting Tasks

During the interviews, we intended to obtain information about accountants' tasks. We asked and inventoried the types of tasks performed by accountants and accounting managers, and we also described the elements of perception regarding those tasks. Tables 2-4 provide summaries of participant answers and are categorized according to respondent functions.

It is relevant to note that accountant and accountant managers' perceptions seem to be very similar. Furthermore, IT and HR managers did not discuss accounting tasks and therefore their answers are not included in the above tables. This is not surprising as accounting is not part of their usual skill set.

Table 2. Summary of tasks analysis of accounting staff categorized by respondents' functions: book-keepers and accountants

	Before ERP	After ERP	Ideal
Accountants kind of tasks	• Accounting data entries • Reverses entries and corrections • Controlling of balance sheet accounts	• Payments of Accounts Payable • Internal entries • Less reporting tasks • Less information to give to colleagues because they have access directly to the system	No answer
Perception / Evaluation of tasks	• Accounting was more simple • More freedom • Better global view of the business • Tasks more varied	• Less work, as certain data entries are automatics. More work, for instance, to follow Accounts Receivable • Feeling to be obeying orders and to be less of an actor • More information to enter into the system • More standardization (processes and rules to follow up) • Change of work corresponding as a change of job • Tasks less varied • More work • Follow up of work is more difficult • The global structure is less comprehensible • Work is more varied • Borrowing tasks, as accruals, are automatic	No answer

Source: Participant interviews

Our findings confirmed the changes in accountants' tasks and jobs. A bookkeeper mentioned that the change of her work was so immense that she felt like it was a complete job change. The answers concerning accountants' work highlighted the fact that their roles seem to be limited to entries concerning accounts payable, accounts receivable, or cash accounts. Furthermore, year-end operations or cash management were, after the ERP system implementation, not part of their responsibilities. They also pointed out a loss of "freedom" due to standardization, rules, and processes. Standardization is in line with the literature (Rikhardsson & Kraemmergaard, 2006; Scapens & Jazayeri, 2003), but changes for accounting staff and their feelings toward losing control upon the tasks were strongly perceived during the interviews.

The second main issue was about the professionalization in government accounting. The use of international standards (IPSAS), the improvement of cash management, and the use of accrual basis accounting and of a unique system (rather than three different ones) were the main enhancements pointed out during the interviews. Respondents mentioned that these changes were possible due to the implementation of a new Integrated Financial System, which is a "change driver" (Scapens & Jazayeri, 2003, p. 229). But the Integrated Financial System was not the main reason for the change; new laws and political willingness were clearly the motivations for these changes.

Accounting managers' tasks also changed, but in an opposite way than that of bookkeepers or accountants. However, they also "lost" certain tasks such as year-end closing and, in some departments, they lost supervision tasks because staff moved to the "Financial Shared Service Center" of the Finance department. Conversely, accountant managers' tasks were enhanced as they were primarily in charge of analysis, reporting, and controlling. Again, this is consistent with previous literature (Caglio, 2003). It is relevant to note that the only task that seems not to have changed is drawing up

Table 3. Summary of tasks analysis of accounting staff classified by respondents' functions: accountant managers

	Before ERP	**After ERP**	**Ideal**
Bookkeepers' kind of tasks	• Accounting data entries • Cash accounts management (with an Excel spreadsheet) • Accounts Receivable (invoices made with a word processor)	• Purchase orders • Cash entries • Accounts receivable • Procurements and purchases	• Cash accounts management • Invoice (Accounts Payable and Investments) issues and checks • VAT entries • Stock entries • Estimated liability (provision)
Accountants' kind of tasks	• Coaching of Bookkeeper	No answer	• Control and check • VAT breakdown • Closing entries (estimated liability or provision and accrual) • Internal entries • Accounting codification management
Accountant managers' kind of tasks	• Supervision • End of year closing • Reconciliation • Salaries management • Subvention management • Analysis • Drawing up the budget	• Budget and reporting • Analysis and controlling • Validation of order, purchase, and personal expenses	• Supervision and controlling • Check of investments and depreciations • Inventories • Approval of Accounts Payable
Perception / Evaluation of tasks	• Accounting was more simple (no accrual basis accounting, amortization deferred) • Accounting entries made in two different systems	• Use of accounting standards (IPSAS) • Centralization of Accounts Payable accounting • Centralization of Investments accounting (centralized Share Service) • Improving of cash management • Change in the way to work • Sophistication of work • No more double entries • No more control on the whole accounting process (year-end entries done twice, entries done by the Department of Finance without explanation) • Purchase order are more long and complex • More information could be entered into the system (cost management information) • More possibilities of reporting and request	No answer

Source: Participant interviews

the budget, which is certainly the most important task of the finance service of a public government.

Discussion

The findings of our research provide evidence of structural changes in accounting tasks. These modifications indicate that a completely "new job"

determines the current role of accountants and accounting managers. Interestingly, the two main changes brought to light during our interviews were completely different. First of all, the main issue concerning accounting tasks is clearly an impoverishment of their day-to-day work. We found that prior to the ERP System implementation; they had some tasks of actual "accounting" and are now

Table 4. Summary of tasks analysis of accounting people classified by respondents' functions: project leader

	Before ERP	After ERP	Ideal
Kind of tasks	• Cash management done with an Excel spreadsheet (no forecasting possible) • Filling authorization request (codification of accounting information on invoice)	• Internal control • Reporting with end of month clothing	No answer
Perception / Evaluation of task	No answer	• Professionalization of cash management (with forecast) • Professionalization of accountants' work • Change of kind of job for accounting manager	No answer

Source: Participant interviews

more like "keyboarders." Accountants also pointed out a loss of "freedom" due to standardization, rules, and processes. The second important finding addresses the professionalization of accounting that had an implication on accounting managers' tasks. Their job also changed, but in the opposite way than that of bookkeepers or accountants. Indeed, it seems that accounting managers' tasks are enhanced because they are increasingly in charge of analysis, reporting, and controlling tasks. We therefore observe that the implementation of ERP systems in public administrations is deeply changing accounting professions and roles. This phenomenon is certainly less visible in today's overreliance on computer screens and keyboards. Nevertheless, it transforms the accounting function into a more centralized and standardized manner than it was in the past.

ERP system promoters in public administrations usually invoke new financial capabilities like the performance of calculations or the optimization of limited resources. We also concluded this with our research of the professionalization of accounting. This means than an administration could be more efficiently managed. However, the notion of performance is often not properly defined when producing "public services." So, on the macro-organization level, while the overview should theoretically be improved, the primary role

of accounting in a public administration might be neglected. (Is tax money payer reliably spent? Or are the public services performing well? These are completely different questions).

At the micro-level, two kinds of accountants are emerging, the bright ones who use the system for analytical purposes, and the less talented ones who simply input figures through the keyboard. Standardization, division of work, specialization, and centralization should enable the administration to accomplish the accounting function in a more cost-effective manner. The reality that we have observed in our case study is different. The accounting production is becoming increasingly complex and is not as effective as expected. Many reasons for this could be suggested. The first reason is the very strong hierarchical power of each department over its finance service. Departments of different sizes and functions are leaving a "battlefield" that is not prone to the standardization and centralization of accounting activities. Second, the monotony is even greater for a profession that is not known to be very elite. Additionally, individual autonomy is reduced; it is surprising to observe the lack of clear understanding of the objectives of an ERP system during the interviews.

We recall that this research is based on exploratory approach, which means that our goal is to obtain new research hypotheses. So the main limitation of our work is that, even though the fieldwork is grounded on a systematic and rigorous approach, our hypotheses are still not validated. In subsequent research, we intend to validate them through quantitative surveys. Results must be corroborated before they can be generalized into other business contexts. Nevertheless, and to our knowledge, this research is the first to highlight the fact that ERP implementation in the public sector provokes profound changes in organizational structure, standardization and centralization processes, and centralization's effect on accounting tasks. Consequently, we believe that this topic should attract further research.

CONCLUSION

We have studied the implementation of the finance modules of an ERP in a public organization in an effort to understand why the accounting function of a Swiss public administration has significantly changed following the implementation of an ERP system. To study this social phenomenon, an ethnography research strategy was followed. Our findings indicate that the benefits of an ERP system implementation in the public sector are not as worthwhile as in the private sector, and that it is mainly due to the "power game" among departments. To the contrary, the transformation of the accounting profession seems to be very similar to that of the private sector. We are currently studying the impact of the ERP implementation on the concerned Public administration regarding the development of new risk management and Internal Control System (ICS) functions, which is in the trend of all measures taken to improve the efficiency of the public administrations.

ACKNOWLEDGMENT

The authors thank Maud Maréchal and Loïc Marchand for their valuable contributions.

REFERENCES

Allen, D., Kern, T., & Havenhand, M. (2002). ERP critical success factors: An exploration of the contextual factors in public sector institutions. Paper presented at the *Proceedings of the 35th Hawaii International Conference on System Sciences*, Hawaii.

Arnold, V. (2006). Behavorial research opportunities: Understanding the impact of enterprise systems. *International Journal of Accounting Information Systems*, *7*, 7–17. doi:10.1016/j.accinf.2006.02.001

Bajjaly, S. T. (1999). Managing emerging information systems in the public sector. *Public Productivity and Management Review*, *23*, 40–47. doi:10.2307/3380791

Booth, P., Matolcsy, Z., & Wieder, B. (2000). The impacts of enterprise resource planning systems on accounting practice. *The Australian experience. Australian Accounting Review*, *16*, 4–18. doi:10.1111/j.1835-2561.2000.tb00066.x

Burns, J., & Vaivio, J. (2001). Management accounting change. *Management Accounting Research*, *12*, 389–402. doi:10.1006/mare.2001.0178

Cacciaguidi-Fahy, S., Currie, J., & Fahy, M. (2002). Financial Shared Services Centres: Opportunities and Challenges for the Accounting Profession. *ACCA Research Report, 79*.

Caglio, A. (2003). Enterprise Resource Planning systems and accountants: towards hybridization? *European Accounting Review*, *12*, 123–153. doi:10.1080/0963818031000087853

Chang, S.-I., Gable, G., Smythe, E., & Timbrell, G. (2000). A Delphi examination of public sector ERP implementation issues. Paper presented at the *Proceedings of the 21st International Conference on Information Systems*, Brisbane, Queensland, Australia.

Davenport, T. H. (1998). Putting the enterprise into the enterprise system. *Harvard Business Review*, *76*(July-August), 123–131.

Deloitte Research Study. (2002). *The keys to smart enterprise transformation for the public sector.* Retrieved from http://www.deloitte.com/assets /DcomGlobal/Local%20Assets /Documents/ DTT_DR_keyspublicsector.pdf

Granlund, M., & Malmi, T. (2002). Moderate impact of ERPs on management accounting: a lag or permanent outcome? *Management Accounting Research*, *13*, 299–321. doi:10.1006/ mare.2002.0189

Gulledge, T., & Sommer, R. (2003). Public sector enterprise resource planning. *Industrial Management & Data Systems*, *103*(7), 471–483. doi:10.1108/02635570310489179

Kumar, V., Maheshwari, B., & Kumar, U. (2002). ERP systems implementation: Best practices in Canadian government organizations. *Government Information Quarterly*, *19*, 147–172. doi:10.1016/ S0740-624X(02)00092-8

Patton, M. Q. (2002). *Qualitative Evaluation & Research Methods* (3rd ed.). Thousand Oaks, CA: Sage Publications.

Quattrone, P., & Hopper, T. (2005). A time–space odyssey: management control systems in two multinational organisations. *Accounting, Organizations and Society*, *30*, 735–764. doi:10.1016/j. aos.2003.10.006

Raymond, L., Uwizeyemungu, S., & Bergeron, F. (2005). ERP Adoption for E-Government: an Analysis of Motivations. Paper presented at the *Proceedings of the E-Government Workshop 2005*, West London, UK, Brunel University.

Rikhardsson, P., & Kræmmergaard, P. (2006). Identifying the impacts of enterprise system implementation and use: Examples from Denmark. *International Journal of Accounting Information Systems*, *7*, 36–49. doi:10.1016/j. accinf.2005.12.001

Rosacker, M., & Olson, L. (2008). Public sector information system critical success factors. *Transforming government: People, Process and Policy*, 60-70.

Saunders, M., Lewis, P., & Thornhill, A. (2007). *Research Methods for Business Students* (4th ed.). Upper Saddle River, NJ: Pearson.

Scapens, R. W., & Jazayeri, M. (2003). ERP systems and management accounting change: Opportunities or impacts? *European Accounting Review*, *12*, 201–233. doi:10.1080/0963818031000087907

Velcu, O. (2007). Exploring the effects of ERP systems on organizational performance: Evidence from Finnish companies. *Emerald Group Publishing Limited*, *107*(9), 1316–1334.

Wagner, W., & Lederer, Y. (2004). An Analysis of the Imagine PA Public Sector ERP Project. *Paper presented at the Proceedings of the 37th Hawaii International Conference on System Sciences*, Big Island, Hawaii.

Yamin, M., & Sinkovics, R. R. (2007). ICT and MNE reorganisation: the paradox of control. *International Business Review*, *3*, 322–336.

Yazdifar, H., & Tsamenyi, M. (2005). Management accounting change and the changing roles of management accountants: A comparative analysis between dependent and independent organizations. *Journal of Accounting & Organizational Change*, *1*, 180–198. doi:10.1108/18325910510635353

KEY TERMS AND DEFINITIONS

Accounting Tasks: The work performed by financial and accounting employees in order to establish financial statements.

Centralization: The fact of grouping tasks and functions from different departments in one service.

ERP: A package of software applications which integrates all functions in order to manage the resources of the organization using the best business practices.

Financial Shared Services: Unique and centralized finance division.

Integrated Financial System: The finance modules of an ERP system.

Public Administration: An organization that depends on a government.

Standardization: The use of uniform processes.

Chapter 5
The Didactic Approach to Manage Strategic Inconsistencies in ERP:
An E-Initiative

Sangeeta Sharma
University of Rajasthan, India

ABSTRACT

This chapter addresses the fundamental question of how the didactic approach can help in managing the impediments and fallouts in the formulation, implementation and evaluation of ERP especially for the societal progress. Further the role of e-initiative is inbuilt in its advocacy for effective delivery. The building blocks of any institution are individuals who must have training in ethics and morality. This is a normative and idealistic analysis but predestined due to continually changing socio-economic dynamics of complex society in modern times. It proposes ERP III with moral epicentre assuming that humanity can be attained if individuals are trained in the moralistic values which eventually redefine the entrepreneurial goals such that it adopts befitting approach in pursuing the specific targets. It includes three sub-areas first focusing on conceptual prologue of ERP, introductory note about didactic approach to see how it directly affects the existing schemes of individuals in the organization; second the major strategic inconsistencies along with finding out the reasons for these irregular variations; and third deals with the e-solutions managing these inconsistencies by designing and planning for institutions in a prudent manner. Precisely, this chapter highlights concept, strategic paradoxes, rebuilding through didactic approach by e-initiative and prognostic strategy for ERP III.

DOI: 10.4018/978-1-60960-863-7.ch005

INTRODUCTION

The decade of nineties infused some neologism in the domain of management. The Enterprise Resource Planning often referred, as ERP is one such concept. Research and Analysis firm Gartner Group initiated it in 1990 to represent a more coherent strategy to ease the flow of comprehensive information between different units of functionaries in any organization. Thus it includes activities like delivery, production, quality management, cataloguing, sales and billing. The concept, which initially emerged for business organization, may also be applied to the system of governance with appropriate alterations. The ERP systems are cross-functional having wider periphery that embraces e-government besides e-commerce. The recent advancement in this field, which refers to ERP II a term in existence since 2000 is inclusive of web-based accessibility to all information in relation to various functional realms of the institutions, may it be it private or public.

The concept of ERP is an evolutionary concept focusing on strategic designs having compatibility with the mission, vision, operability and resource mobilization. It also implicit the process of formulation, evaluation and responses to changes. This in turn entails the attainment of objectives by confirming effective value moulds to ensure the satisfaction of larger section of users. In the institutions of public governance the strategic failures are more frequently visible as several paradoxical situations arise due to political or social or economical or international or moral compulsions. These dilemmas cumulatively result into strategic inconsistencies.

Further, mostly the ERP solutions follow the economic track of enhancing profits by providing professional guidelines for introducing appropriate interventions at each level rather than addressing issue from the perspective of social impacts and morality. This presumption is the core discussion of this chapter. Any profiteering enterprise without ascertaining its social responsibility is more damaging as it advocates the concept of wealth accumulation by individual entrepreneurs making them richer at the cost of mankind. Therefore the whole perspective needs to be re-looked keeping in view the consequences of excessive usages of excavated resources for human and ecological environment. Any solution that promotes callous use of resource inputs for profiteering gains cannot be considered an appropriate one, as it might have latent and graver repercussions in general. The unsustainable utilization of resources has already added to more problems; see for instance the man-created damages to the surroundings. All philosophical dicta have time and again emphasised on indulging into such activities, which are harmless and are for the purpose of perpetuating humanity.

BACKGROUND

The didactic approach having lineage to Greek word '*didaktikos*' means apt at teaching, which is morally instructive, hence refers to the teaching of moralistic lessons to people. This approach strongly relies on 'content-based approach (Widdowson, 1979). It has been applied to various domains of studies varying from mathematics to behavioural to social to psychological fields. Though it is deterministic in its orientations but behavioural movement has also influenced the conventional approaches towards learning. The external environment affects all behaviour and learning focuses on acquisition of knowledge which is incremental (Kohn, 1999).Integrating didactic principles in an e-learning environment, several steps have been identified such as creating learning path; adding the assessors; activating learning paths; solving package; monitoring the progress and grading (Caniels, 2004). A parallel has been drawn between organizational models and didactic architectures adhered by businesses and to manage internal training such as web-based training, e-learning through online distribution of autonomously used learning materials in user-generating content that facilitates the sharing of knowledge (Gonella and Pento, 2005). Trentin's classification (Trentin, 2001) defines didactic model as 'peer to peer' aimed at creating collaborative groups, which share knowledge and experience to enable whole group to grow. Siemens coined the term 'connectivism' to define new ways of learning (Siemens 2005). Precisely this refers to the system of learning in moralistic teachings through web-based approach. Recently the importance of this approach has been revived at creative platforms where an integrated learning is facilitated by sharing through 3D cases which are learning exercises where simultaneous use of brain, body and attitude constitutes a 3D access to learning based on parallel thinking, task focus and no judgment (Byrge & Hanson, 2009).

The ERP initially focused on Inventory Manufacturing Requirement Planning in 1960s has evolved since then as a concept, which is more elastic and focuses on client service. A historical view can trace out its pedigree to various forms, for instance in 1970s it was identified as Material Requirement Planning, a software basically designed for completion of production and operational aspects; in 1980s it turned out to be Manufacturing Requirement Planning a software for applications of coordinating manufacturing process from product planning to product distribution (Bruce Zhang, 2005); in 1990s it referred to the integration of business activities across functional departments and more recently ERP II has become the web-based programming of activities related to the entire gamut of entrepreneurial tasks.

In this chapter an effort has been made to suggest a value-pronged *e-designing* with the basic objective of realigning the thought process of individuals imbued in morality and ethics with the patterns of entrepreneurial activities. This takes a pedigree into the assumption that unison of evolved mind and humane action is helpful in managing the inconsistencies in a more consistent manner. This can be further supported by an argument that by aligning attitudes around ethical axis, a fundamental change in individual's approach to define actions is possible which gets manifested in all entrepreneurial activities. Moreover the enterprises are composite structures of human, for human and therefore need to be humanity inclined.

This presentation is in the arena of normative research intertwined with philosophical arguments and mathematical logistics. Incidentally this also suggests the practical ways of implementing conceptual construct and proposes a mechanism of finding out more accurate and quantified measurement of real change at the cognitive level to deal with the inconsistencies. The need is felt more today than at any other time as negative postures of life styles are profoundly prevalent and ridiculing the social existence. The erosion of moral values has multiplied the problems; hence the thesis that adoption of corrosive policy measures will only lead to the depletion of resources seems to have some logic. It takes the pretext that without changing the microcosmic configuration of individual as person no real change in the outer sphere will occur.

Additionally this chapter discusses possibilities of introducing change in cognitive learning if trained in Indian theological writings about '*Aishvaryas*' (i.e. eight principles of attainment of higher salvation). This might reorient the attitudes of individuals who plan the ERP solutions through didactic approach, which inoculates moralistic values. In didactic approach this forgotten path has been retraced to put forth an argument that strategic inconsistencies in ERP can be dealt with, if people know how to manage their 'inner-self' by imbibing humanitarian values based on morality as mentioned in these eight principles. The e-initiatives can be powerful instruments to disseminate the positive dimensions of our innate properties in ensuring the strategic consistency.

The literary metamorphoses of this concept till recent times indicate that the prime mover for resource planning in the enterprises is the optimization of profit but this presentation takes a slightly deviant position by arguing that if solutions permeate moralistic internalization in ethics, then it will shift the onus from profiteering to humanity. This shift will be in the interest of larger section of mankind.

The discussion builds up around identifying the reasons for strategic inconsistencies followed by presentation of solutions based on the premises of '*Aishvaryas*' with vector logistics to compute the morality scores of employees in any governmental or private entrepreneurial entity. The prognostic standpoint in this chapter is suggestive trajectory in the form of ethically driven ERP III model, which proposes solution for government and private to plan activities by including moralistic values.

STRATEGIC INCONSISTENCIES

The paradoxical situations in planning are attributed to the opacity of ideas Thus confusions at subliminal level make the situation more critical due to inability to set goals especially for resource utilization in the right perspective. The desires attached to final output of decision impede the path of growth and is compendious to the principles enshrined in dicta. By further probing we may find that the common reasons for such imperious actions lies in the multiplicity of thought originating from the confused state of mind and to the externality of factors. Assuming that the internal state of mind and external peripheral conditions control the dilemmas some peculiar paradoxical situations emerge which may inhibit strategic decisions.

More specifically, fearfulness; impurities of mind; self-sensuality; undisciplined behavior; insincerity; violence of thoughts; calumny; covetousness and impatience lead to conceited actions. The conceited actions which form nebula around choosing the conscientiously between right and wrong eventually converts into inconsistent self-driven predicaments. This impasse once created

fails to relate mind with situations thus brings in paradoxes, which lead to strategic inconsistencies.

The reasons for commonly observed strategic inconsistencies are elucidated below:

- Situational Speciousness: The inability of an individual to adjudge the situation in right perspective due to internally disturbed state of mind at subconscious level will lead to illogical validations of decisions made under such state of mind. This permeates close-mindedness thus blocking the process of assessing situations in its entirety. The illogical justifications further complicate the process of applying the privilege of right choice to decide in the interest of the common person. It might affect the strategic inputs for decisions due to befuddled understanding and irrationally justifying one's own position despite knowing the fact that these are contrary to truth.

- Deeply Deluded Egocentric Individuals: The adherence to false beliefs inflicted with self-serving aspiration creates closed ego as an icon on the altar of yearning for power amongst individuals. Hence this myopic vision cannot understand the pure reality thus gives away scope for advancing their hypocritical portrayal of righteousness and concealing the hidden motives behind any action. This leads to the act of deception in any enterprise, which not only impairs the strategic formulations but also erodes the trust of stakeholders. The short-sighted policies do not benefit any one in long term.

- Inhibited Intellectuality: The duality at subliminal level inhibits the intellectual capability of an individual to analyse the latent aspects of decisions. Consequently, with this limited capability the truth cannot be perceived and it is most likely that in absence of truth a decision loses its sanctity. The captivity of dualism may deform the personalities manning the enterprises, which could subsequently turn out to be catastrophic due to the state of indecisiveness. The multiple polarized variations on account of inhibited intellectuality result into making of obscure strategies that are devoid of ethical-rationality.

• Knowledge as Under-Utilised Instrument: As depicted in Indian epical source that the knower, the knowledge and known constitute the triune stimulus to action (Verse 18 of Geeta). Viewed from this standpoint the under-utilised knowledge will not generate the sufficient stimulus for knower to incite appropriate decision. Furthermore the ponderous of improper and lopsided knowledge do not help the strategist to take a holistic perspective, failing in which may be detrimental for the enterprise.

These reasons innately lead to strategic inconsistencies varying from the linguistic ambiguity to behavioural aberration ultimately leading to dissuaded action. It will be pertinent to address the types of strategic inconsistencies arising thereafter so that decision to design rational strategic interventions can be taken.

The important types of strategic inconsistencies can be categorized into four types:

• Textual Inconsistency: The indistinct usage of words and incorrect sentence formation inflicted with jargonised expressions makes the entire content ambiguous. Any ambiguity at the level of the content inclusion of strategy in turn makes the subject matter incommunicable. It may have larger hidden intentional strategic purposes to convey different connotations to different people thus keeping enough space for the strategist to change interpretations as per the situational convenience suitable to one's personal preferences. This is highly

unconstitutional way of formatting the contents of strategy, which also reflects the depletion of ethical values. The possibilities of allowing misinterpretations furthermore indicate grave violation of norms that constitute an enterprise. In terms of resources planning odious agendas are conveyed to different target groups. This kind of inconsistency is not only lethal but carries the divisive intonations that might impinge on the basic societal fabric of communion.

• Perceptive Inconsistencies: The textual non-clarity affects the perception in two ways. In one way it increases the gap between what is formatted and what is conveyed and in another way it causes fissure between perception and expectation on account of indistinctness of the subject matter. In both ways failures are due to incorrect perceptions about strategies. This type of inconsistency may extrapolate the entire course of action at a different perceptive level hence deteriorating the outcome of the action.

• Subliminal Inconsistencies: The inherent confusions at the level of subconscious mind generally get converted into complexes thus affecting the ability to take right decisions. The individual are thus plagued by the self-doubts creating more delusions. Hence the uncertainties that sneaks through due to this confusion lead to persistent malfunctioning of the system. The dilemma-inflicted strategies can create the environment of distrust for the employees themselves and for the users outside the enterprise.

• Segmental Inconsistencies: The self-driven motive behind constructing a strategy cannot cut across the concept of 'whole.' A relational matrix will not emerge without understanding the symbiotic need to survive collectively. The concept of building individual entrepreneurial empires has done more harm by disallowing to draw consensus on the issues that might affect the larger sections of the mankind. This is the defiance of the natural laws of existence which otherwise perpetuates the causes of buoyant collaboration.

These inconsistencies bring out tangible effects in terms of credibility; misappropriation of resources; displacement of entrepreneurial position; deep conflicts; affecting the biodiversity and perpetuate money-happiness fallacy.

Thus there is a need to go back to the basics of productive altruistic alliances between various components of ecosystem with more comprehensive ERP to induce morality amongst the employees so that confusions can be managed at the subliminal level itself. The parochial entrepreneurial policies are defeating the existence of humanity. The proposed ERP model suggests for working out more cohesive and complete plans to attain the universal harmony by defying the materialistic propagation. One of the greatest Saints propounded that, possessions of material riches without inner peace is like dying of thirst while bathing in a lake, it is spiritual poverty not materialistic lack that lies at the core of all human sufferings. Further built-up the belief that the materialistic scientist uses the force of nature to make the environment of man better and more comfortable, the spiritual scientist uses mind-power to enlighten the soul (Paramhansa Yogananda, 1946, Kriyananda, 2006, p.1).

The deeper problems are overtly or covertly linked to the strategic failures of enterprises in not working with this simple innate aim at the larger co-existential plateau. The enterprises have to be instrumental in merging the ethics with practicality such that each reinforces the other. It is the time to transform the life in general by rejuvenating the ethics in government and corporate world. The modern world is adopting this strategy but in a scattered way at various platforms by disseminating the reading and training materials world over

to inspire leaders to increase personal effectiveness, creativity and team building capabilities. Individual entrepreneurs, small businesses, international corporations, governmental departments are now rediscovering the path of serenity shown by our great masters, and this has brought a new wave of developing a communion with inner self and outer society. Swami Kriyananda offers a constructive alternative to contemporary education which emphasizes rote learning and technological competence at the expense of spiritual values and personal maturation (Kriyananda, 2006, p.230).

The proposed ERP III model basically extends the alchemy of materialistic riches with inner peace, the only path to strategize in a more meaningful manner. This model therefore applies the didactic mode of reprogramming the 'thought-seeds' to look beyond moneymaking activity in individuals who are carriers and makers of the environment in enterprises. A proper human resource management inoculated with high morals and effective planning to train them into this kind of moulds would inevitably redefine the goals of entrepreneurial activity. Apparently seen in the larger perspective this might cause successive changes in the other enterprises. The proposed model assumes that basic reformation at the attitudinal level will provide vital inputs to the enterprises to change the milieu. All enterprises are minute droplets into the ocean of humanity capable of social emancipation by setting goals of covenanting bond of compassion. This forms the core of proposed model.

DIDACTIC APPROACH

The theoretical frame of reference which can be used for moralistic teachings include 'cognitivism' dealing with the learning approaches related to thought process and 'constructivism' referring to the active interactive reinforcement by constructing new materials (Scotti & Sica, 2007). The didactic approach through moralistic instructive measures needs to inculcate values to manage inconsistencies at the initial stage. The induced inconsistencies are manageable up to the level it remains within the reversible mode by refurbishing moralistic values through didactic teaching in enterprises. The didactic approach which focuses on ethics building through moralistic training removes deeply rooted confusions and dilemmas that often lie in the mind of employees regarding the right or wrong facets of any actions. Thus the early-referred reasons of strategic inconsistencies can be dealt in a more insightful manner.

The demarcation between morality and immorality is very flimsy and the change over from moral to immoral act is possible at any moment of time in a person whose base is not strong enough to uphold virtuous undercurrents. The element of relativity would eventually decline with didactic purification at the level of enterprises because it will carry the cascading effect for its stakeholders. The predictive value would be more morally value oriented if trained in ethics.

The concept of ERP in enterprises needs to address to the cause of humanitarianism, which is attainable by changing the mindsets of those who are in the process of planning and implementation. More particularly the governmental domain relates to common person hence more inclusive strategic designs are needed. The computation of profit in terms of absolute money gains will have to be replaced by mechanism of computing relative valuations in terms of damages done to the society at large in the process of making money. Hence goal structure based on humanitarian will redefine the concept of 'enterprise' in all realms be it private or governmental. This approach will help in reorienting the concept at the levels of goal, resource management and activity design by liberating enterprises from materialistic inclinations. This can be depicted as Figure 1.

The didactic approach prepares enterprise as an individual entity permeating humanistic ethical based values within its periphery but eventually generating a 'moral field,' which might replicate these alterations into others. The entrepreneurial activity thus needs to look into the individual contribution in maintaining general humanitarian index at the world stage. The postmodern era has registered enormous growth of enterprises focusing on moneymaking role (Sangeeta, 2010). However this has promoted the unhealthy competition and resulted into ruthless mobilization of resources rallied for maintaining the top position.

The strategic interventions have also supported this point of view. This has further been given extra leverage by strategic interventions that have been worked out in a uni-pronged manner by focusing only on using the available resources for profit. Additionally, immorally designed strategies are now leading to disastrous end. The man-created disasters are more clearly noticeable in modern era than any other time. Amongst many contributing factors greed to earn more can be singled out as

Figure 1. The didactic effect

Level	Attributes	Effects
Goal	Pervasive; ecumenical; foreseeable, humanitarian	Conscience driven
Resource	Responsible sharing; constructive utilization, eco-friendly	Collaborative ownership
Activity	Selfless; human sensitivities; conscientious and inclusive	Crusading humanity

(Source: Sangeeta, 2010)

the crucial mind-set with which enterprises set their working terrain. To change the direction it is essential for the enterprises to realize the truths in scriptures, which are the vast ocean of purely synchronized ideas, malleable to humanity. The *'ecohumanism'* which means partnership-based cooperation for the common good of all people, their descendents and natural environment commonly supported by science and high technology (Leslaw Mechnowski, 2008).

The brief review of present situation markedly points towards revision of strategies so far adopted by the enterprises. The reasons of strategic inconsistencies conferred earlier and the discussion regarding managing these inconsistencies would be seen in the same context at the conjecture that moralistic teachings can induce major changes in perceptions which may reorient the entire process of cognition. The philosophical dictums are of great help to deal with the deeply fossilized and regimented perspicacity of attaining happiness through money. The discussion is based on the following premises:

1. The entrepreneurial activities have to reset the goals to achieve the higher objectives of collaborative existence by shifting the thrust from 'earning more money' to 'championing humanity.'
2. The restructuring of goals will demand the major change in resource mobilization from single pronged analysis to multi pronged analysis. The cost has to be ascertained in terms of damage incurred to the 'whole' while excavating resources.
3. The social responsibility of enterprises will have to be decided by two way intercession, one from where the resources have come and another how responsibly products have served the socially deprived.
4. The unplanned and digressive mode of planning have to be replaced by progressive planning which takes into account the

self-corrective measures to reassure the prosperity of mankind.

The premises are based on an intrinsic assumption that morally driven strategies are capable of delivering more humanitarian end-products which in longer run might create a more sustainable, safe, and serene enterprise contributing to humane society. But this requires a basic turn around in de-linking money with achievement in terms of money gains only at the goal setting level. The core idea of ERP so far has been towards profiteering of enterprises, without taking into account the aspirations of the marginalized sections of the society. However concept of making more money needs to shift towards attainment of happiness for the larger mankind. Hence the proposed ERP III model approach is based on building up of enterprises with human capital trained in upholding purity of mind through generic planning in nurturing values. This in turn stabilizes the minds of employees in serenity capable of initiating actions that are in the interest of humankind in general.

The focus of teaching has to on awakening; an awakened person can recycle human resource in any enterprise to direct them to work conscientiously. The philosophical guidance can help in understanding the whole mechanism of creating an environment, which is self-magnetic and perpetual to deal with the situation of duality. The moralistic teaching and training empowers the enterprises to manage four kinds of strategic inconsistencies by refining the perception and developing deeper understanding. A clear textual content of strategy and conscious mind streamlined with ethics will design strategies conscientiously.

The eight elemental principles referred in great epic Geeta, *anima, mahima, laghima, garima, parapti, vashitva, prakamya and Isha* though relates to the attainment of divine powers. The perceptions will be through intuition; inter-planetary and inter-astral movements. (Sri Sri Paramhansa Yogananda, 2002, p.736) The context is of highest virtue but these can be reiterated in to the realm of entrepreneurial management for attaining clairvoyance where the strategic interventions designs can help in managing the inconsistencies:

1. *Anima* is as small as desired, which may be manifested in the enterprises in the form of sub-activity
2. *Mahima*, large as desired, which may be viewed in the context of enterprises as conglomeration of sub-activities to larger entrepreneurial goals.
3. *Laghima* is as lightweight as desired, which may be viewed as the desire to make contribution to the circle of its own kind of enterprises.
4. *Garima*, as heavy weight as desired, may mean to the enterprises as the desire to make contribution to the humankind.
5. *Parapti* is to obtain anything as desired may be viewed as the entrepreneurial attainment in terms of fulfillment of its mission.
6. *Vashitva* is to bring anything in His control may be viewed as the urge of enterprise to control all actions.
7. *Prakamya* satisfies all desires as His will may be viewed as the accomplishment of larger goal.
8. *Isha* is to become like Him, may be viewed as the role enterprises can play as saviors and crusaders of humanity.

The above discourse taken from Indian epical source can be divided into three functional domains when applied to the enterprises- goal, positional-relativity and action. The desires will conclude the goal of any enterprise, the respective contribution made by an enterprise to its specific field and general field will determine the relative weight it carries and activities designed to accomplish the goals enshrined constitute the action. The interesting aspect of this analysis is that these are not hierarchical but cyclic thereby reinforcing each domain and developing a pattern. Furthermore each pattern generates particular

experience, which gets percolated both at the micro and macro levels. The change at any level may induce subsequent changes in any of these domains. To explain it further, for instance by molding the desires instant or distant goals can be set and reset. This changes the relative positions of enterprises within their limited or unlimited periphery. The relative positional changes may bring out subsequent alterations in the action plan. So whenever a change is introduced in any of these functional domains, it sets the motion of subsequent changes in others as depicted in Figure 2.

The figure illustrates a cyclic relationship between three functional domains of enterprises. The outer circle (i-i-i) depicts the profit enhancing activity that has remained the thrust area of ERP models developed so far. However the inner circle (ii-ii-ii) focuses on the activities of enterprises, which concentrate more on the human aspect hence converging into surmise of universal ethics. This needs didactic interventions to prepare human resource for ethical commitment.

The revelations in *Geeta* are in the context of having communion with *supreme will* from lower to highest desires. However in the enterprise's milieu the concept can be applied to see individual enterprise as the composite of certain activities attuned to the specific objective (*Anima*) and in the larger context as the part of humanity in general (*Isha*). This entrepreneurial metamorphosis for discharging 'selfless role' from 'self-satisfying role' is possible when right perspective is internalized through teachings in morality. The ERP solutions since inception have focused on improvisation of various activities varying from inventory to production and reinforcing human resource to attune to the increase in the level of performance.

The suggested ERP III model provides solution in the reverse sequential order of actions focusing on preparing individuals to absorb high moral ethical values among human resource in different enterprises even facilitating enterprises to attain

Figure 2. Reinforcement

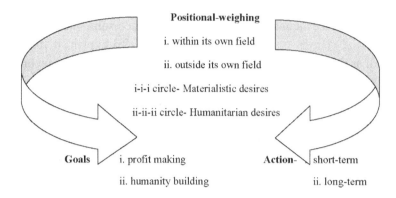

Source: Sangeeta,2010

humane objectives with fine moral perfection. This will have cyclic and resultant effects to bring out changes at the subliminal level by inducing ethical and moralistic sensitivities amongst people in general. The presumption that ethically driven people in general will make institutions ethically functional holds true in this situation as institution reflects the values prevalent in the functional arena. Further ethics also reinforces the comprehensible vision and sharpens the acumen for perceiving the affecting factors significantly. Consequently people are equipped to work better in harmony pertaining to higher causes thus making it easier for enterprises to change patterns by becoming more socially responsible.

ERP III SOLUTIONS

The ethical-value laded ERP solution induces in-built self-corrective measures by focusing on the restoration of right values and training people to live up to higher aspirations at the cognitive and constructive framework,(Scotti & Sica, 2007). A more capable mind can address the impediments of inconsistencies that might be inhibiting the process of strategic designs, as it will develop finer coordination with the goal of enterprises but within the humanitarian value frame. The four types of strategic inconsistencies viz., textual, perspective, subliminal and segmental can be dealt effectively because didactic approach induces changes in the pattern of cognitive formation with subsequent modifications in the habits of individuals. A person attuned with high moralistic value has deeper and calm mind capable of understanding situations in the subterranean context of human development. The thought variations are controllable, vision is specific and actions are in consonance with the larger goals. The logistics for managing inconsistencies is as under:

1. The moralistic teachings will lead to the textual-content-designs rich in humanly activities.
2. The humane rich text content will inculcate selfless perspective leading to broader viewpoint.
3. The wider and humane perspective releases person from dualism at the subliminal level by resolving contradictions in mind.

4. An evolved mind capable of managing duality and multiplicity can change the ambience of enterprise.

Thus, 1 leads to 2 leads to 3 leads to 4 and hence enterprises can contribute to maintenance of universal altruism.

Binary Programming for ERP III Solutions

The steps include:

a. *Human Resource Assessment*
    Number of employees = N
    The identification of two polarized categories of traits = X and Y
    Grouping together the virtuous values prevalent in employees= $x_1, x_2, x_3 \ldots x_n$
    Grouping together the vicious values prevalent in employees= $y_1, y_2, y_3 \ldots y_n$
b. *Transformational Assessment*
    Grouping virtuous values in totality into Strong = X_s; compassion, brotherhood
    Grouping virtuous values in totality into Mild= X_m ; realism
    Grouping vicious values in totality into Strong= Y_s ; hatred, envious
    Grouping vicious values in totality into Mild= Y_m ; exuberant materialistic desires
c. *Convertibility Assessment*
    Conversion of X_m into X_s Probability is high
    Conversion of Y_m into X_s Probability is high
    Conversion of Y_s into X_s Probability is low
d. *Risk Assessment*
    Risk factor $\int$ confused goals, digital apathy, less efforts, indifference.

Convertibility α Risk Factor

Thus the conversion is subject to risk factor. For instance confused goals, digital apathy, lesser efforts and indifference will slower the process due to opacity, whereas clear goals, digital savvy, rigorous efforts and concern will expedite the process of conversion due to clarity.

E-INITIATIVES

The digital revolution is the biggest contribution in the post- modern era that had a major and penetrative impact on civilization. The world has initiated the change by preparing e- educative modules and e-courses, which have compiled detail information on various aspects of human dynamics (see for instance www.Teach12.com, 2010). The e-initiatives are driven by ecological factors such as political, administrative, economical, societal, cultural, and psychological (Sangeeta, 2006). The didactic approach is now a practical package; hence the need is to introduce values at the entrepreneurial level through e-initiatives. The need for content based syllabus started when the relevance of teaching the language discipline was highlighted as the opportunity to teach the linguistic text in meaningful and purposeful manner was felt (Mohen, 1986; Brinton Snow and Wesche, 1989). The didactic approaches have been meeting out the pedagogic demands of inculcating morality through on-line learning modulations. Various e-learning modules are constructed to provide web-based training in different areas, the popular ones are *e-learning 1.0*; *e-learning 2.0* (Downes, 2005; Siemens, 2005). Many professional e-solutions like *Epicor* Software Solutions are delivering solutions to different businesses to prepare them to take maximum mileage of the changing economic tide.

The philosophical anecdotes are available on web into easily accessible e-packages. This verifies the fact that detail information is available on related dimensions of moralistic values and ethics on websites. However the process of excavating preferred moralistic values and converting into specific value moulds as per the entrepreneurial requirements needs more attention. This can be done in the format of binary programming at three levels viz., goal setting; human resource management and relative weight attached to the individual enterprise. It can identify all qualities, which are to be measured for an enterprise and can be demonstrated in the vector form as under:

Say there are 'N' qualities in combination of 'virtuous' and 'vicious'

$[Q_1 \ldots \ldots \ldots Q_n]$ Vector of qualities of individual employee.

Subsequently each quality can be given weight in terms of most positive to most negative.

So, $[W_1 \ldots \ldots \ldots W_n]$ Vector of weights of individual qualities.

Thus in any enterprise each quality can be assigned weight and measurement of Quality in employee can be computed as

$[X_1 \ldots \ldots \ldots X_n]$,

Thus per employee variation scale on the basis of weight for quality can be computed.

n

Therefore, Morality Score $= \sum W_i X_i$

i=1

$\longrightarrow \longrightarrow$

In Vector form $= W \times X$

The steps are,

- Identify the qualities of interest and put them in a Quality matrix;
- Assign weight to these qualities as per the humanitarian preferences of an enterprise.
- Measure these qualities in each employee and arrange these measurements in a matrix called 'Quality Measurement Matrix'
- Identify the qualities on the measured scale where didactic interventions are required.

The individual employee scores in the enterprise can be plotted and it is very likely that direction of morality scores of the total employees can be computed thus helping the enterprise to find out which qualities are the causes of strategic inconsistency. Once this identification is made the didactic approach can now be designed in the form of software.

On the basis of this the ERP III solution for morality score in any enterprise can be depicted by plotting positive qualities and negative quali-

Figure 3. Datasheet for morality score

M＼N	X1	X2	X3	X4	X5	Y1	Y2	Y3	Y4	Y5
E1										
E2										
E3										
En										

(Source- Sangeeta, 2010)

ties amongst 'n' number of employees in Figure 3. For the convenience of the enterprise X and Y can be depicted as positive and negative qualities respectively. Data can be generated into following respective quality domain to facilitate the conversion of Low Morality Score into High Morality Score along with the interdependent dynamics in enterprise:

1. Demographic domain-gender, education and position
2. Ideal value domain- having highest positive value
3. Positive value domain- compassion, honesty, responsibility, truthfulness, impartiality.(X)
4. Negative value domain- biased, envious, insensitive, deceitful, destructive.(Y)
5. Conversion domain- the individual score and enterprise score
6. Didactic domain- the areas where moralistic teaching need is highest and areas where moralistic teaching need is least. This means,

EMS = IMS – EmMS

Whereas, EMS—Enterprise Morality Score; IMS—Ideal Morality Score; EmMS—Employee Morality Score. The scores are on 1-10 grading scale (Figure 3).

Additionally value variations in respect to the gender, education and position can give the finer contours of direction and further making it possible to find out the locus of change incessantly required.

The data collected in the domains can be computed for finding out the morality level of individual employees in any enterprise. Whereas total sum of the positive and negative qualities of all employees will give the score of morality at the Enterprise level. A comparative scale can be constructed by setting up the Ideal level of Morality Score and the Existent level of Morality Score in any enterprise. The larger is the difference lesser would be the concern for humanitarian activities. This computation will also help in getting data on value variation with respect to gender, education and position. This model comprehensively computes morality score for individual, enterprise and how much is the visible variation in males and females; more educated or less educated and lower or higher position held by the employees in the enterprise.

The didactic modules will be designed by keeping in view the relationship as:

1. The value of least difference between the Existent level of Morality Score and Ideal level of Morality Score.
2. The value of the highest difference between the Existent level of Morality Score and Ideal level of Morality Score.
3. The qualities in which the variation is maximum.
4. The didactic moralistic training modes to be designed for the maximum value variation in the quality.
5. The general morality modules for enterprises with exclusively materialistic ambitions can be designed by computing common collective scores in this format and can be perpetuated by e-didactic training designs.

The entire analysis is based on the underlying assumption that the reasons for conflicting dilemmas, which are responsible for formulating anti-humankind strategies, can be identified scientifically and consequently through moralistic training in '*Aishvaryas*' principles. It is possible to remove the blockades from the path of designing strategies, which have more humanitarian focus. The effect of this in managing the strategic inconsistencies is measurable by finding out the qualitative change in strategic designs.

THE PROBLEM AREAS

The discussion follows line of normative-idealizations. The basic questions that might ignite further dialoguing and empiricism may include:

a. Is metamorphosis of any profit making enterprise to humanity driven enterprise possible?
b. Is idealization more rational and less pragmatic?
c. Is it possible to control conditioning factors such as politico-social configuration of societies at the mega level?
d. Is alteration at subliminal level workable to restructure the habit formations?
e. Is there anything like humanity being approachable?

These inquisitive queries sublimate problem areas basically in regards to empiricism. The realism does have seeds sown in idealism. The idealizations are forces of transformation and the movement from complexity to simplicity is possible by changing the viewpoints of people through proper maneuvering into ethics. The argument that normative propositions cannot lead to change is a one-sided advocacy. The fundamental problem pointers indicate areas such as, ideological frames, economical situations, social norms, cultural lineages political structures and bureaucratic legacies, which need serious attention. But a more penetrative support comes from the presumption that change in psyche is within one's own realm. Value inculcations are subject to inner strengths and externalities can only be inlets for facilitating the process of ethics formations.

There is a need to move from social ontological and ideological bases by considering how to understand the idea of social responsibility (Ari-Veikko, 2008). The two extreme theories that can give us some support in this direction are economic responsibility theory and ethical responsibility theory (Windsor, 2006). Within the business ethics the concept of corporate social responsibility

is defined as a continuum from immortal action to mortal action. The four-fold scheme of corporate responsibility viz., economic responsibility; legal responsibility; ethical responsibility and philanthropic responsibility explains that how a moral enterprise should make the profit within law and still remains ethical and citizen centric (Caroll, 1991).

Every act of individual or institution is an add-on act in contribution that is made in the process of upholding humanity, which can be attained through more cohesive actions. Making a dedicated effort to look beyond the profit-making objective can reinforce the dynamics of humanity. The results get reciprocated so inconsistencies can be dealt at the mind altitude through teachings. The suggested ERP III model on morality is only a step in the direction of redefining the notion of entrepreneurial goals. The goals in the redefined frame of discussion will include resource mobilization in terms of providing safety to environment; enterprise social responsibility; enterprise morality score and didactic interventions required. The strategic designs when build with more clear vision of achieving universal peace will indubitably take care of misjudgments.

The scriptural truths must be realized and incorporated into entrepreneurial functioning. The moralistic values thus acquired will facilitate ERP at all levels be it inventory or performance or human. The planned activity at individual level can be manifested as a cosmic underpinning uniting the composites into uniformed system of enterprising.

FUTURE RESEARCH DIRECTIONS

This model re-deciphers the elemental purpose of ERP in the context of any entrepreneurial activity be it governmental or any other. In modern times as indicated earlier that mere confession about existence of problem is not going to resolve the problem, rather there is a need to make a conscientious action plan to deliver the reverential goods. The attainment of materialistic desires is not the inner nature of man, rather the postulates of contemporary theory of competition relating it with more earning, more money, subjugation of others and eventually are driven by the urge of outgrowing rest of the fellow-beings. This leads to dehumanization and desensitization at a macro level. The line between morality and immorality is very fragile and any immoral act may bring down the efficiency of a system despite the best planning, formulation and strategy designs. The immorality sneaked into the system as a result of this must be defied completely with unsullied understanding, interpretation and designing strategies, which can bring about changes at subliminal level. The digital devices can be instrumental in changing the ambience and mindsets.

Veiled during the materialistic eras the indestructible passion for humanity is to be revived through technological devices. The need is to create Enterprises with Welfare Responsibility with clearly defined perspective of being instruments of buoyant transformation. Recently most of the corporate houses have started taking up responsibility through various drives to render their services for important sectors of human development such as education, health, poverty and rehabilitation. The profit earned is now getting newer outlets of achieving humanitarian objectives, for instance Microsoft, Goggle, Tata etc to name very few are at the pedestal of extending more generic services. The parallel activities that are undertaken with amalgamation of profiteering and social arenas need a different ERP to deliver the output. It needs to incorporate wider standpoint with selfless motives into entrepreneurial arena and this construct sets some futuristic direction as ERP III. The potential research can test the conceptual construct to validate the construction.

CONCLUSION

The inconsistencies of any kind can be managed through clairvoyance. The opaque ideas may develop amorphous mass of indecisiveness. Any entrepreneurial activity can deal with the state of opacity by restructuring the perceptions which sediment at the subliminal level. This model provides solutions to enterprises to transact with the problem of depletion of morality and evasion of ethics by identifying the receptors of humanitarian action. Certain realms of individuals are very tender; fragile and are grooming grounds for seeds of thoughts. These are the right areas where restructuring can have undeviating effects. For any enterprises incumbents are the right targets to initiate the moralistic upbringing. The didactic approach helps at two distinct levels one before and other after individual ingresses the enterprise.

At the elemental socialization stage of any individual some simple value moulds in narrative forms can be prepared to train tender minds in virtues. The earlier value formations at tender stage may build strong virtuous convictions, which are more likely to be carried forward by an individual at the later stage. Similarly at the entrepreneurial stage these evolved trained minds can formulate strategies which more likely to increase the weight of such enterprises in humane periphery. Such larger weighed enterprises may magnetize other enterprises to work for the same cause as theirs and subsequently can increase the circumference of humanitarian tasks undertaken.

The value moulds can be constructed on the basis of the combination of existent level of ethical capabilities and the required level of ethical capabilities. For more precise computations, a comparative score with ideal score can be calculated through ERP III for enterprises. The enterprises must be transformed into the hermitages of conscientious activities wherein individuals can strive for congenial environment to attain universal peace.

This ERP III model of morality provides solutions for removing the mental obstructions that cause confusions and illusions in the minds, which eventually lead to inconsistencies, through didactic approach. The multiplicity of thought can ricochet at the goal setting stage of enterprises as the materialistic endeavor. To completely disown the materialistic desires will be a utopia but keeping such desires harmless is attainable. In the times when simplicity is overshadowed by exuberant desires of entrepreneurs to earn massive profit margins are structuring enterprises through earlier ERPs in a manner that is actually costing universe more pain. The goals of enterprises must be compatible with the fulfillment of serving the humankind. The nature is beyond mathematics and warning is alarming. All activities individually or collectively must converge into composite act of conscience. The solutions are available but willingness has mellowed down. The two way responsibility has to be ascertained, first the damage incurred in terms of unsustainable utilization of these resources for the larger sections of the people and second replacing the goal of incurring massive profit with humanity. The enterprises are not different from the human conglomerations and hence moral fabric is the best knitting ingredient to deliver the solace and serenity.

REFERENCES

Anttiroiko, A.-V. (2008). Social responsibility: Structure, content and process. In Sharma, S. (Ed.), *Transformative Pathways: Attainable Utopia* (pp. 52–81). Jaipur: Pratiksha Publications.

Bonaiuti G. (2006). *E-Learning 2.0 futuro dell'appren dimento in rele tra formale e- informale.* Trento: Erickson.

Byrge, C. & Hansen. (2009). The Creative platform: A didactic approach for unlimited application of knowledge in interdisciplinary and intercultural groups. *European Journal of Engineering Education, 34*(3), 235–250. doi:10.1080/03043790902902914

Caniel, M. C. J. (2004). Teaching competencies efficiently through Internet: A practical example. *European Journal of Vocational Training, 34,* 40–48.

Carroll, A. B. (1991). The pyramid of corporate social responsibility: Toward the moral management of organizational stakeholders," *Business Horizon,* July-August 1991. RetrievedonJune26,2010,fromhttp://www.rohan.edsu.edu/faculty / dunnweb/rprnts.pyramidofcsr.pdf.

Cornell, J., Ferres, N., & Traveglione, T. (2003). Engendering trust in manager-subordinate relationships: Predictors and outcomes. *Personnel Review, 32*(5), 569–587. doi:10.1108/00483480310488342

Corner, M. L. (2007). *Informal learning.* Retrieved on May 13, 2010 from http//: agelesslearner.com/ intros/informal.html.

Downes, S. (2005). E-learning 2.0. *Elearn magazine,* October 17, 2005. Retrieved on June 20, 2010 from http://www.elearnmag.or /subpage.cfm.

Gonella, L., & Panto, E. (2005). *Didactic architecture and organization models; A process of mutual adaptation.* Retrieved on June 20, 2010 from www.elearningeuropa.info /files/media.

Gyorgy, M., & Szeged, Z. D. M. (2003). Didactic approach for teaching non-determinism in automata theory. *Analysis, 35*(2), 48–61.

Kohn, A. (1999). Getting back to basics: Unlearn how to learn. *Washington Post,* October 10, 1999. Retrieved on June 26, 2010 from www.alfiekohn. org/teaching /alagbtb.htm

Michnowski, L. (2008). Ecohumanism as a developing crossing. In Sharma, S. (Ed.), *Transformative Pathways: Attainable Utopia* (pp. 107–136). Jaipur, India: Pratiksha Publications.

Nadler, L. (1984). *The handbook of HRD.* New York, NY: John Wiley and Sons.

Nonaka, I., & Takeuchi, H. (1995). *The knowledge creating company: How Japanese company create the dynamics of innovations*. Oxford, UK: Oxford University Press.

Scotti, E., & Sica, R. (2007). *Community management*. Milan, Italy: Apogeo.

Sharma, S. (2006). Ecology of e-Governance. In Antorioko, A. V. (Ed.), *Encyclopaedia of digital government* (pp. 431–436). Hershey, PA: IGI Publications. doi:10.4018/978-1-59140-789-8.ch065

Sharma, S. (2010). Breaking mind inertia for humane business through ICT. In Chhabra, S. (Ed.), *Integrated e-models for government solutions: Citizen-centric service oriented methodologies and processes* (pp. 179–194). Pennsylvania: IGI Global Publications.

Siemens, G. (2003). *Learning ecology, communities and network extending the classroom*. Retrived on June 2, 2010 from http//: www.elearnspace. org/articles /learning communities.htm.

Sri Sri Paramhansa Yogananda. (2002). *The bhagavad gita: The immortal dialogue between soul and spirit a new translation and commentary*. Kolkata: Publication of Yogoda Satsanga Society of India.

Tansley, C., Newell, S., & Williams, H. (2001). Effecting HRM-stage practices through integrated human resource information in system. *Personnel Review, 30*(3), 351–371. doi:10.1108/00483480110385870

Trenti, G. (2001). *Dalla formazione a distaza all' apprendimento in rete*. Milan, Italy: Franco Angelle.

Widdowson, H. G. (1979). *Explorations in applied linguistics*. Oxford, UK: Oxford University Press.

Windsor, D. (2006). Corporate social responsibility: Three key approaches. *Journal of Management Studies, 43*(1). Retrieved on May 23, 2010, from http://www.blackwell-synergy.com /doi/pdf.

KEY TERMS AND DEFINITIONS

Didactic Approach: The didactic approach having lineage to Greek word '*didaktikos*' means apt at teaching, which is morally instructive, hence refers to the teaching of moralistic lessons to people.

e-Learning: The e-learning comprises all forms of electronically supported learning and teaching. The Information and Communications systems whether networked or not, serve as specific media to implement the learning process.

e-Learning 2.0: The e- learning 2.0 refers to a second phase of e- learning based on web 2.0 and emerging trends in arena.

ERPIII: The ERP III model is based on building up of enterprises with human capital trained in upholding conscience through generic planning in nurturing values. This in turn stabilizes the minds of employees in serenity capable of initiating actions that are in the interest of humankind in general.

Morality Score: The morality score in any enterprise can be depicted by plotting positive qualities and negative qualities amongst 'n' number of employees on the table as proposed in ERP III morality data sheet.

Chapter 6
E–Government Citizen Centric Framework at District Level in India:
A Case Study

Susheel Chhabra
Lal Bahadur Shastri Institute of Management, India

D. N. Gupta
Government of Orissa, India

ABSTRACT

This chapter evaluates service quality, and suggests E-Government Citizen Centric Framework for Citizen Service Centers (CSC) of Haryana State in India. Citizen Centric framework is suggested by using responses collected from 300 users of five (5) E-Government citizen service centers. This framework can be used in other similar E-Government citizen service centers to evaluate service quality.

INTRODUCTION

It is widely acknowledged that Information and Communication Technologies (ICTs) are effective tools in bridging service quality gaps and can play important role in accelerating economic growth. Specifically, to realize tangible advantages, E-Government offers big opportunity for government to provide services efficiently, empowerment of people, and to usher in knowledge-based economy. It offers the scope for transformation of apparatus of Government. In the last one decade, E-Government has heralded a new chapter in the public service delivery. Several E-Government projects have been initiated by the state governments across the country in India. The launch of

DOI: 10.4018/978-1-60960-863-7.ch006

National e-Governance Programme (NeGP), with a specific objective to add one Lakh Common Service Centers (CSCs) in rural areas has provided a fillip to the efforts under E-Government.

Haryana is one of the most progressive states in India. The capital of Haryana is Chandigarh, which is administered as a union territory and is also the capital of Punjab state in India. It has an area of 44,212 Sq. Kms. The state is divided into four divisions for administrative purposes - Ambala, Rohtak, Gurgaon, and Hisar. There are 20 districts, 47 sub-divisions, 67 tehsils, 45 sub-tehsils, and 116 blocks in Haryana. (http://en.wikipedia.org/wiki/Haryana). More than 70% of the population is dependent on agriculture for their livelihood. People speak several similar sounding dialects of Hindi. The tele-density registered in urban areas was 16.5 as compared to rural areas (2.3) as on 31 March, 2003 (BIH, n.d.).

The information technology policy of the state government provides for improvement in the quality of delivery of public services. It proposes to establish electronic delivery of services in the public domain in its departments, boards and corporations using state-of-the-art technology. The state government is committed to provide better services to its citizens through E-Government, which is efficient, speedy, simple and cost effective. Such delivery of services has been planned and being implemented through e-DISHA, which includes information kiosks, interactive voice response systems, etc.

The government has established e-DISHA Citizen Service Centers (CSC) in 8 out of 20 districts of Haryana (http://haryana.gov.in/e-disha.htm) under the preview of New Agent of Information—District Level Integrated E-Government Services of Haryana for All (NAI-DISHA). The E-Government services provided at these Centers include forms & procedures, birth & death certificates, house tax collection, water billing, social welfare schemes, caste & residence certificates, passport applications, arms license, learner &

permanent driving license, vehicle registrations, pension distribution, complaints, and revenue records, etc. (http://gurgaon.nic.in/edisha.htm).

The objectives of these e-DISHA centers are to provide longer hours of service delivery, easy, improved quality of service, transparent, efficient & effective delivery at the citizens doorsteps, reliable & real-time services, effective dissemination under single roof, reduced delivery and opportunity costs, elimination of 'touts' and exploitation, citizen friendly environment, quick redressal of citizen grievances, strengthening the back office operations for timely availability of information, consolidated information for effective decision making, integration of databases of government departments and organizations, and creation of knowledge based jobs in the district. These centers have been established as front-end interfaces of Haryana government departments to provide E-Government services.

The feed back of citizens in terms of evaluating quality of services received at citizen service centers from the Government is important. An understanding of citizens' perspective of service quality helps the governments to plan and execute E-Government services efficiently and effectively. The objective of this chapter is to develop E-Government service quality framework for Citizen Service Centers named as e-DISHA in Haryana as a case study.

BACKGROUND

Undoubtedly, E-Government offers big opportunity for the government to transform, and the scale of transformation is huge. It can be immensely useful in raising the efficiency of government functioning and improving public service delivery, as also in bridging geographical divide. However, it is widely acknowledged that e-governance projects are usually complex, people-oriented, and have long gestation period. Several studies on E-Government (Bhatnagar, Subhash, 2003; Singh, Amar, 2005) in India have indicated salient findings such as:

- Inadequate Number of services at e-Kiosks: The services provided (through e-Governance projects) at Tehsil are only a few (like Driving License, Caste or Income certificates; in some cases Registration of sale deeds). Only, some E-Government projects like e-SEVA and e-Lokmitra that provide services for collection of user charges (electricity, water, etc.) are successful, as these involve very small processes. But, the services (a large number of them) that have large processes or require decision-making at various levels are not delivered efficiently.
- Poor Performance Level: The reduction in time and cost (in terms of travelling) of availing services has not reduced in many cases, though there is some improvement in the case of e-kiosks (Citizen Service Centers) in towns / cities.
- Lack of usage of e-Kiosks: As the number of services provided is very small and there is very little improvement in performance level, so users are not very much inclined to use e-kiosks

The scholars in general have practiced service quality all over the world in various contexts (Parasuraman et al., 1988; Zeithaml et al., 1996; Carman, 1990; Cronin and Taylor, 1992 to name a few). The SERVQUAL instrument, as suggested by Parasuraman, a 22-item scale that measures service quality along five factors - tangibility, reliability, assurance, responsiveness, and empathy, forms the cornerstone on which all other works have been built.

According to Cronin and Taylor (1992), it is only by evaluating the end performance of service that customer's perception of service quality can best be evaluated. Based on this rationale, they later developed their own service quality measurement model, SERVPERF that evaluates service quality on the basis of customer's perception of performance on the five quality dimensions of SERVQUAL.

The SERVPERF scale has been mostly used as a summed index in the literature. However, some researchers have noted that overall consumer satisfaction is a function of attribute-level evaluations of product performance (LaTour & Peat, 1979; Mittal et al., 1999). The premise is that attribute-level evaluations can capture a significant amount of variation in overall satisfaction. Further, Zhou (2004) has also advocated use of multidimensional SERVPERF scale as opposed to summed index for the purpose of strategic significance for managing service quality.

RESEARCH HYPOTHESES AND PROPOSED MODEL

This section proposes an E-Government service quality framework (Figure 1 and Figure 2). The framework is suggested using selected E-Government citizen service Centers established by Government of Haryana. The service quality serves as the criterion variable that contributes to quality of services provided at citizen service Centers (e-DISHA). The dependent variable on the other hand is the overall service quality. The overall service quality is measured using five dimensions which include tangibles, reliability, assurance, empathy, and responsiveness. The log linear regression analysis is used to suggest the framework.

The null hypotheses stated in this study are:

A. For testing existing service quality of E-Government citizen service Centers.
    H1: Service quality of E-Government citizen service Centers is satisfactory-> tangibles

Figure 1. E-Government services quality framework

The proposed model

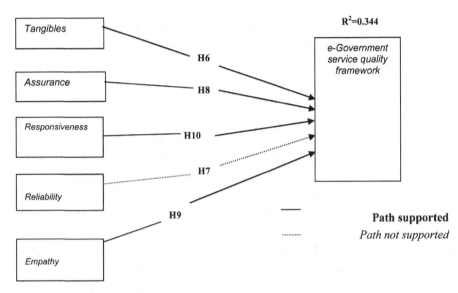

Figure 2. Conceptual diagram of E-Government services quality framework

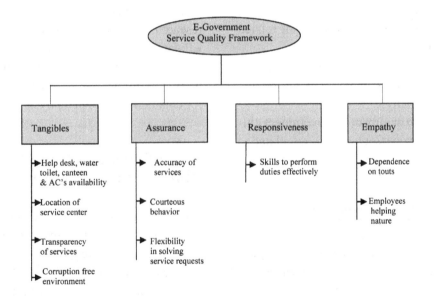

H2: Service quality of E-Government citizen service Centers is satisfactory -> reliability

H3: Service quality of E-Government citizen service Centers is satisfactory -> assurance

H4: Service quality of E-Government citizen service Centers is satisfactory ->empathy

H5: Service quality of E-Government citizen service Centers is satisfactory -> responsiveness

B. For testing the relationship of individual attributes of service quality with overall service quality.

H6: Service quality of E-Government citizen service Centers -> is not related to tangibles

H7: Service quality of E-Government citizen service Centers -> is not related to reliability

H8: Service quality of E-Government citizen service Centers -> is not related to assurance

H9: Service quality of E-Government citizen service Centers -> is not related to empathy

H10: Service quality of E-Government citizen service Centers -> is not related to responsiveness

RESEARCH METHODOLOGY

The research objective is to suggest service quality framework for E-Government citizen service Centers of selected districts of government of Haryana. The framework led to design of questionnaire for the citizens. The citizens involved in receiving E-Government services from citizen service Centers were called 'Citizens' for the purpose of the study.

At the time of conducting the survey eight (8) E-Government citizen service centers were operational out of 20 districts in Haryana. These districts were Panipat, Gurgaon, Karnal, Kaithal, Ambala, Hisar, Jind, and Panchkula. Based on geographic and demographic attributes five (5) districts, namely Panipat, Gurgaon, Karnal, Kaithal, and Ambala were selected for the study representing the four (4) divisions Ambala, Rohtak, Gurgaon, and Hisar.

Sixty (60) citizens were selected randomly based on various services they are receiving from 5 citizen service Centers in each of the 5 districts. The sample size was 60 X 5 = 300. The respondents involved in receiving services from these Centers were mostly from nearby villages, local shopkeepers, and employees.

The responses for questionnaires were obtained on a seven-point Likert scale, 1 being strongly disagree, and 7 strongly agree (1-Strongly disagree, 2-Disagree, 3-Somewhat disagree, 4-Neutral, 5-Somewhat agree, 6-Agree, and 7-Strongly agree).

In order to analyze the data accrued from this research, factor analysis was used to identify and validate the factor structure and the log linear regression analysis was used to design the framework. The application software (SPSS) was used for data tabulation and analysis.

E-GOVERNMENT SERVICE QUALITY FRAMEWORK

Factor analysis was conducted to identify factors (dimensions) using a sample size of 300. Factor analyzed a set of 14 items from the E-Government services user questionnaire (Q. 7 – Q.20, Table 1, results Table 2) to test priori assumptions about the underlying factor structure. As a result 14 items were clubbed together in 5 dimensions: tangibles, reliability, assurance, empathy, and responsiveness (Table 3). The items in respective dimensions are placed in descending order of their factor loadings.

Instruments Reliability and Testing of Hypothesis

Before suggesting E-Government service quality framework, it is pertinent to test existing service quality of citizen service Centers. The five (5) service quality dimensions were tested for statistical significance. The instruments reliability and testing of hypothesis is given in Table 3.

The reliability of instruments of all the dimensions (H1-H5) is acceptable for this type of research, which ranges from .58 to .73. The table also shows significance of all hypotheses at 5% level. Hence the entire hypotheses are rejected. Therefore, it can be concluded that there is a need to improve service quality of E-Government citizen service Centers.

Framework Summary

A log linear regression analysis was conducted to design the service quality framework based on predictor's variables (dimensions). Table 4 summarizes the framework.

Relationship of Individual Dimensions to the Overall Service Quality: Testing of Hypothesis

Table 5 illustrates the relationships among the various dimensions to the overall service quality; 'Critical Ratio' was calculated for each relation along with the findings. 'Critical Ratio' (CR) was calculated using the formulae "critical ratio = estimate / standard errors." The CR values greater than 1.96 and 2.32 are known to be statistically significant at 0.05 and 0.01 levels, respectively.

Hypothesis H6 and H8-H10 are rejected at .01 and .05 levels of significance. Hypothesis H7 was not found significant at .01 or .05 levels. Hence, relationship of reliability has not been established in this case. Therefore, reliability dimension can be excluded from the framework.

The contribution of each factor to the service quality is summarized in Table 6.

Table 1. Service quality items of e-government citizen service centers

Service quality items
Q.7 Employee's solved your service request in a single time frame.
Q.8 When you faced your service problem, employee's solved your problem as per designated time frame.
Q.9 The location of service center is convenient.
Q.10 Corruption has been reduced due to services provided at this centre.
Q.11 Availability of employee's is in accordance with service timings.
Q.12 Employees know how to perform their duties satisfactorily.
Q.13 Employees do not put their designated jobs to other employees.
Q.14 Services provided are fully transparent in nature.
Q.15 Services provided are correct in nature.
Q.16 You do not believe in getting work done from touts.
Q.17 The services timings are convenient
Q.18 Employees use soft language in dealing with citizens.
Q.19 Employees use flexible approach in solving service problems.
Q.20 Help desk, water, toilet, canteen, and air conditioning services are Satisfactory

Table 2. Result of factor analysis

Item (s)	Factor-1	Factor-2	Factor-3	Factor-4	Factor-5
Tangibles					
Q.20 Help desk, water, toilet, canteen, & air conditioning services are satisfactory	**0.76**	-0.01	0.17	0.09	0.08
Q.9 The location of service center is convenient.	**0.69**	0.02	-0.10	-0.10	-0.28
Q.14 Services provided are fully transparent.	**0.63**	0.29	0.41	0.15	-0.24
Q.10 Corruption has been reduced due to services provided by this Centre.	**0.56**	0.34	-0.17	0.08	0.13
Reliability					
Q.17 The services timings are convenient	-0.05	**0.78**	0.22	0.13	-0.35
Q.8 When you faced your services problem, employee's solved your problem as per designated time frame.	0.33	**0.77**	-0.12	-0.04	0.19
Q.11 Availability of employee's is in accordance with service timings.	0.08	**0.64**	-0.11	-0.21	0.24
Q.7 Employee's solved your service request in a single time frame.	0.64	**0.54**	0.08	0.03	0.17
Assurance					
Q.15 Services provided are correct in nature.	-0.27	-0.03	**0.82**	0.18	0.06
Q.18 Employees use soft language in service dealing.	0.21	-0.13	**0.75**	0.06	-0.24
Q.19 Employees use flexible approach in solving your service problems.	0.47	0.21	**0.61**	-0.24	0.33
Empathy					
Q.16 You do not believe in getting work done from touts.	-0.04	-0.12	0.01	**0.90**	-0.19
Q.13 Employees do not put their designated jobs to other employees.	0.39	0.11	0.44	**0.66**	0.19
Responsiveness					
Q.12 Employees know how to perform their duties satisfactorily.	-0.05	0.12	-0.04	-0.09	**0.86**

Note: a. Extraction Method: Principal Component Analysis

b. Rotation Method: Varimax with Kaiser Normalization.

c. Rotation converged in 9 iterations.

The overall service quality explained by external factors is 0.344 (34.40%). The tangibles have gained highest contribution (0.308) to the service quality, followed by assurance (0.288), responsiveness (0.210), reliability (0.001), and empathy (-0.149).

E-Government Service Quality Framework

The framework is shown in Figure 3 along with the path coefficients. Figure 4 presents a conceptual diagram of this framework.

The study has given an empirically validated service quality framework for E-Government citizen service Centers: service quality is explained 34.40% by the external variables, which includes tangibles, assurance, responsiveness, reliability, and empathy.

RECOMMENDATIONS

The model suggests various items related to four dimensions of service quality. Under tangibles, the e-DISHA service centers need to address service problems related to help desk, water, toilet

Table 3. Instruments reliability and testing of hypothesis

Null Hypothesis	Reliability-Alpha	Test Value = 5 (Somewhat Agree)		Mean	Sig. (2-tailed)	Mean Difference	95% Confidence Interval of the Difference		Decision
		#	t value				Lower	Upper	
Service quality of E-Government citizen service Centers is satisfactory -> tangibles	.68	H6	-15.55*	3.93	0.00	1.08	1.21	0.94	Rejected
Service quality of E-Government citizen service Centers is satisfactory -> reliability	.73	H7	-12.43*	4.16	0.00	0.84	0.97	0.71	Rejected
Service quality of E-Government citizen service Centers is satisfactory -> assurance	.63	H8	-4.90*	4.75	0.00	0.25	0.35	0.15	Rejected
Service quality of E-Government citizen service Centers is satisfactory -> empathy	.58	H9	-2.82*	4.80	0.01	0.20	0.35	0.06	Rejected
Service quality of E-Government citizen service Centers is satisfactory -> responsiveness	.70	H10	-4.83*	4.61	0.00	0.39	0.54	0.23	Rejected

Note: df = 299, * Significant at 5% level

Table 4. Framework summary

R	R Square	Adjusted R Square	Std. Error of the Estimate	Change Statistics				
				R Square Change	F Change	df1	df2	Sig. F Change
0.586	0.344	0.332	0.204	0.344	30.819*	5	294	0

Note: Predictors variables: (Constant), tangibles, reliability, assurance, empathy, and responsiveness.

The F value is significant at 1% level of significance at (5/294) degree of freedom. The R square value (.344) indicates the overall contribution of service quality (34.40%).

Table 5. Testing of hypothesis (path coefficients)

Null Hypothesis		Un-standardized Coefficients		Critical Ratio (t)	Sig.	Findings
		B	Std. Error			
(Constant)	#	0.483	0.123	3.930	0.000	
Service quality of E-Government citizen Centers is not related to -> tangibles	H6	0.308	0.038	8.151*	0.000	Rejected
Service quality of E-Government citizen Centers is not related to -> reliability	H7	0.001	0.044	0.014	0.989	Accepted
Service quality of E-Government citizen Centers is not related to -> assurance	H8	0.288	0.060	4.830*	0.000	Rejected
Service quality of E-Government citizen Centers is not related to -> empathy	H9	-0.149	0.048	-3.074**	0.002	Rejected
Service quality of E-Government citizen Centers is not related to -> responsiveness	H10	0.210	0.036	5.786*	0.000	Rejected

Note: Dependent Variable: Q21Y (Overall service quality)

* Significant at p<0.01 level, ** Significant at p<0.05 level

Table 6. Results of factor contributions

Construct	No. of Items	B values
Overall service quality of citizen service Centers (R Square)		0.344
Tangibles	4	0.308
Assurance	3	0.288
Responsiveness	1	0.210
Reliability	4	0.001
Empathy	2	-0.149

& AC availability. These service centers should provide assurance to citizens in terms of accuracy of services, courteous behaviors and flexibility in solving service requests of citizens. There is a need to improve skills of service level executives to enhance responsiveness to customers. The study shows that the citizens depend on touts to get their work done in these service centers. The empathy dimension requires that the employees working

Figure 3. E-Government services quality framework

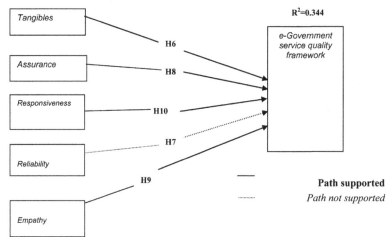

Figure 4. Conceptual diagram of e-government services quality framework

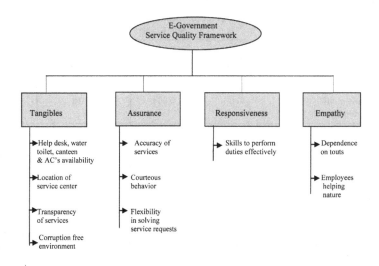

in these centers should always be ready to help citizens to provide various government services.

FUTURE RESEARCH DIRECTIONS

Due to financial and time constraints, the research has been conducted in a limited domain covering only Government Departments and citizen service Centers located in Haryana. The study can be conducted in a larger domain by involving significant sample of Government Departments and citizen service Centers all over India. The cost-benefit analysis involving various E-Government services including additional private services, which can be started at E-Government citizen service Centers can be taken as an agenda for future research.

CONCLUSION

The structure of this model can be used as a reference point to suggest similar other models for the E-Government. The chapter has suggested service quality framework of e-DISHA citizen service Centers for Government of Haryana. Other Governments can use this suggested model to leverage strategic advantage.

REFERENCES

Bhatnagar, S. (2003). Administrative Corruption: How Does E-Government Help? In *Proceedings of Global Corruption Report 2003*, Transparency International. Retrieved June 30, 2007 from http://www.gipi.az/ssi_eng /egov/20030324.pdf.

BIH. (n.d.). *Business in Haryana*. Retrieved June 23, 2006 from http://www.haryana-online.com / business.htm.

Carman, J. H. (1990). Consumer perceptions of service quality: an assessment of the SERVQUAL dimensions. *Journal of Retailing, 66*(1), 33–55.

Cronin, J. J., & Taylor, S. A. (1992). Measuring service quality: a re-examination and extension. *Journal of Marketing, 56*(July), 55–68. doi:10.2307/1252296

LaTour, S. A., & Peat, N. C. (1979). Conceptual and methodological issues in consumer satisfaction research. Wilkie, W.F. (Ed.), *Advances in Consumer Research, 6*, Association for Consumer Research, Ann Arbor, Ml, 431-437.

Mittal, V., Kumar, P., & Tsiros, M. (1999). Attribute-level performance, satisfaction and behavioral intentions over time: a consumption-system approach. *Journal of Marketing, 63*(April), 88–101. doi:10.2307/1251947

Parasuraman, A., Zeithaml, V. A., & Berry, L. L. (1988). SERVQUAL: a multiple-item scale for measuring customer perceptions of service quality. *Journal of Retailing, 64*(Spring), 12–40.

Singh, A. (2005). *Sidestepping Pitfalls. Data-Quest*, May 21, 2005. Retrieved May 29, 2006 from http://www.dqindia.com /content/egovernance /2005/105052101.asp.

Zeithaml, V. A., Berry, L. L., & Parasuraman, A. (1996). The behavioral consequences of service quality. *Journal of Marketing, 60*(April), 31–46. doi:10.2307/1251929

Zhou, L. (2004). A dimension-specific analysis of performance-only measurement of service quality and satisfaction in China's retail banking. *Journal of Services Marketing, 18*(6/7), 534–546. doi:10.1108/08876040410561866

KEY TERMS AND DEFINITIONS

Citizen Service Centers (CSC): The Citizen Service Centers (CSCs) are envisioned as the Single window service delivery physical channels for Government to Citizen (G2C) & Government to Business (G2B) services for ensuring accessibility, convenience, transparency and timeliness in service delivery.

Critical Ratio: The ratio of a particular deviation from the mean value to the standard deviation.

E-Government: "E-Government" refers to the use by government agencies of information technologies that have the ability to transform relations with citizens, businesses, and other arms of government. Traditionally, the interaction between a citizen or business and a government agency took place in a government office. With emerging information and communication technologies it is possible to locate service centers closer to the clients. Such centers may consist of an unattended kiosk in the government agency, a service kiosk located close to the client, or the use of a personal computer in the home or office.

Log Linear Regression Analysis: Log Linear regression analysis is used to describe the pattern of data in a contingency table. A model is constructed to predict the natural log of the frequency of each cell in the contingency table.

Service Quality: Service quality is a focused evaluation that reflects the customer's perception of specific dimensions of service: reliability, responsiveness, assurance, Empathy, tangibles.

SERVPERF Scale: Various definitions of the term 'service quality' have been proposed in the past and, based on different definitions, different scales for measuring service quality have been put forward. SERVQUAL and SERVPERF constitute two major service quality measurement scales. SERVPERF being a variant of the SERVQUAL scale and containing perceived performance component alone, 'performance only' scale is comprised of only 22 items. A higher perceived performance implies higher service quality.

Section 2
ERP Processes and Applications
for E-Government

Chapter 7
Architecture for ERP System Integration with Heterogeneous E–Government Modules[1]

Lars Frank
Copenhagen Business School, Denmark

ABSTRACT

ERP (Enterprise Resource Planning) systems consist normally of ERP modules managing sale, production and procurement in private businesses. ERP systems may also have modules for special lines of business or modules for the different sectors of E-Government. However, the ERP systems of today use a common database and therefore, it is normally only possible to use modules supported by the ERP supplier. This limits the possibilities for special lines of business like the different sectors of E-Government. It is normally not possible to use the traditional ACID (Atomicity, Consistency, Isolation and Durability) properties across heterogeneous ERP modules and therefore, it is not possible to integrate such modules without inconsistency and anomaly problems. That is, the users cannot trust the data they are reading and even worse they can undermine the validity of the databases if they update the databases by using such invalid information. However, it is possible to use so called relaxed ACID properties. That is, it should, from a user point of view, look as if the traditional ACID properties were implemented, and therefore, the users can trust the data they are reading and cannot do anything wrong by using this data.

INTRODUCTION

In this chapter, we will describe how the architecture of a distributed modular ERP system can be used to integrate ERP Systems with heterogeneous modules specialized for E-Government

DOI: 10.4018/978-1-60960-863-7.ch007

A *distributed modular ERP system* is a set of ERP systems/modules that may operate in different locations where each ERP module can use the resources of the other ERP modules in its own or in other ERP locations (Frank, 2008). In a distributed modular ERP system, the ACID properties must be relaxed both across locations and across modules in the same location. That is within a module the traditional ACID properties of a DBMS may be used while relaxed ACID properties are implemented by the modules themselves for all accesses/updates across modules. Each ERP module has full autonomy over its own resources/tables. That is its tables may be recovered independently from the tables owned by other ERP modules.

In a distributed modular ERP system, it is easier to integrate special line of business ERP modules as the modules may be heterogeneous and have different suppliers.

In the extended transaction model used in this chapter the relaxed ACID properties are implemented in the following way: The global atomicity property is implemented by using compensatable, pivot and retriable subtransactions in that order. The global consistency and isolation properties are managed by using countermeasures (Frank and Zahle, 1998), and the global durability property is implemented by using the durability property of the local DBMS (Data Base Management System) systems.

Applications with relaxed ACID properties function from a user point of view as if the traditional ACID properties were implemented by the underlying DBMS systems. However, in reality the relaxed ACID properties are implemented as an integrated part of the applications. Therefore, it does not matter whether all the different ERP modules use the same DBMS system or not.

The chapter is organized as follows: First, we will describe the transaction model used in this chapter. Next, we will describe the properties of a distributed modular ERP system that are necessary for integrating heterogeneous ERP modules. This is illustrated by a description of how to integrate E-Government modules in a business oriented ERP system. Finally, we have future work and conclusions.

Related Research: The transaction model described in section 2 is *the countermeasure transaction model* (Frank and Zahle, 1998 and Frank,

2010). This model owes many of its properties to (Garcia-Molina and Salem, 1987; Mehrotra et al., 1992; Weikum and Schek, 1992 and Zhang, 1994). The architecture of a distributed modular ERP system was first described in Frank, 2008. However, this description focused on migrating ERP systems and not in integrating traditional ERP modules and E-Government modules. Frank and Munck, 2008, describes how it is possible to integrate electronic health records from different hospitals by using relaxed ACID properties and Frank and Andersen, 2010, describes how it is possible to solve/reduce the problems in integrating incompatible tables used by heterogeneous modules.

THE TRANSACTION MODEL

A *multidatabase* is a union of local autonomous databases. *Global transactions* (Gray and Reuter, 1993) access data located in more than one local database. In recent years, many transaction models have been designed to integrate local databases without using a distributed DBMS. The countermeasure transaction model (Frank and Zahle, 1998) has, among other things, selected and integrated properties from these transaction models to reduce the problems caused by the missing ACID properties in a distributed database that is not managed by a distributed DBMS. In the countermeasure transaction model, a global transaction involves a *root transaction* (client transaction) and several single site *subtransactions* (server transactions). Subtransactions may be nested transactions (i.e. a subtransaction may be a *parent transaction* for other subtransactions). All communication with the user is managed from the root transaction, and all data is accessed through subtransactions. The following subsections will give a broad outline of how relaxed ACID properties are implemented.

The Atomicity Property

An updating transaction has the *atomicity property* and is called *atomic* if either all or none of its updates are executed. The atomicity property is important as it makes it possible to restart a failed transaction without making special programming to repair the database. If short duration locking is used, only the subtransactions of a global transaction are recovered in an atomic way (i.e. some subtransactions may be committed and some may be aborted or not executed). This is not acceptable and therefore, in the countermeasure transaction model, the global transaction is partitioned into the following types of subtransactions that may be executed in different locations:

- The *pivot* subtransaction managing the commitment of the global transaction. The global transaction is committed when the pivot subtransaction is committed locally. If the pivot subtransaction aborts, all the updates of the other subtransactions must be compensated.
- The *compensatable* subtransactions, all of which may be compensated. Compensatable subtransactions must always be executed before the pivot subtransaction is executed to make it possible to compensate them if the pivot subtransaction cannot be committed. A compensatable subtransaction may be compensated by executing a *compensating* subtransaction that removes the updates of the compensatable subtransaction.
- The *retriable* subtransactions designed in such a way that the execution is guaranteed to commit locally (sooner or later) if the pivot subtransaction has been committed.

The global atomicity property is implemented by executing the compensatable, pivot and retriable subtransactions of a global transaction in that order. For example, if the global transaction fails before the pivot has been committed, it is possible to remove the updates of the global transaction by compensation. If the global transaction fails after the pivot has been committed, the remaining retriable subtransactions will be (re)executed automatically until all the updates of the global transaction have been committed. However, the order of execution described above may sometimes be bypassed as a retriable subtransaction can be executed before the pivot subtransaction if the retriable subtransaction more or less compensates a compensatable subtransaction executed earlier. For example, in e-commerce all the order lines may be created by compensatable subtransactions. At any time before the pivot is executed, a retriable subtransaction may reduce the amount ordered by a compensatable subtransaction. If the amount ordered in an order line is reduced to zero, the compensatable subtransaction should be fully compensated by deleting the order line.

RPCs and transaction messages can be used to call/start the compensatable subtransactions and the pivot subtransaction because the execution of these subtransactions is not mandatory from a global atomicity point of view. If any problems occur before the pivot commit, it is possible to compensate the first part of the global transaction.

After the commit decision of the global transaction has been made, all the remaining updates are mandatory. Therefore, update propagations (UPs) are always used to execute the retriable subtransactions, which always are executed after the global commitment.

If the pivot fails or cannot be executed, the execution of all the compensating subtransactions is mandatory. Therefore, UPs are always used to execute the retriable compensating subtransactions.

Example

Let us suppose that an amount of money has to be moved from an account in one location to an account in another location. In such a case, the global transaction may be designed as a root transaction that calls a compensatable withdrawal subtransaction and a retriable deposit subtransaction. Since there is no inherent pivot subtransaction, the withdrawal subtransaction may be chosen as pivot. In other words, the root transaction executed at the user's PC may call a pivot subtransaction executed at the user's bank, which has a UP that "initiates" the retriable deposit subtransaction.

If the pivot withdrawal is committed, the retriable deposit subtransaction will automatically be executed and committed later. If the pivot subtransaction fails, it will be backed out by the local DBMS. In such a situation, the retriable deposit subtransaction will not be executed.

The Consistency Property

A database is *consistent* if its data complies with the consistency rules of the database. If the database is consistent both when a transaction starts and when it has been completed and committed, the execution has the *consistency property*. Transaction *consistency rules* may be implemented as a control program that rejects the commitment of transactions, which do not comply with the consistency rules.

The above definition of the consistency property is not useful in distributed databases with relaxed ACID properties because such a database is almost always inconsistent. However, a distributed database with relaxed ACID properties should have *asymptotic consistency* (i.e. the database should converge towards a consistent state when all active transactions have been committed/compensated). Therefore, the following property is essential in distributed databases with relaxed ACID properties:

If the database is asymptotically consistent when a transaction starts and also when it has been committed, the execution has the *relaxed consistency property*.

The Isolation Property

The isolation property is normally implemented by using *long duration locks*, which are locks that are held until the global transaction has been committed (Frank and Zahle, 1998). In the countermeasure transaction model, long duration locks cannot instigate isolated global execution as retriable subtransactions may be executed after the global transaction has been committed in the pivot location. Therefore, *short duration locks* are used (i.e. locks that are released immediately after a subtransaction has been committed/aborted locally). To ensure high availability in locked data, short duration locks should also be used in compensatable subtransactions, just as locks should be released before interaction with a user. This is not a problem in the countermeasure transaction model as the traditional isolation property in retriable subtransactions is lost anyway. If only short duration locks are used, it is impossible to block data. (Data is *blocked* if it is locked by a subtransaction that loses the connection to the "coordinator" (the pivot subtransaction) managing the global commit/abort decision). When transactions are executed without isolation, the so-called *isolation anomalies* may occur. In the countermeasure transaction model, relaxed isolation can be implemented by using countermeasures against the isolation anomalies. If there is no isolation and the atomicity property is implemented, the following isolation anomalies may occur (Berenson et al., 1995 and Breibart, 1992):

The lost update anomaly is by definition a situation where a first transaction reads a record for update without using locks. Subsequently, the record is updated by another transaction. Later, the update is overwritten by the first transaction. In extended transaction models, the lost update anomaly may be prevented, if the first transaction reads and updates the record in the same subtransaction using local ACID properties. Unfortunately, the read and the update are often executed in different subtransactions belonging to the same parent transaction. In such a situation, a second transaction may update the record between the read and the update of the first transaction. The following important example illustrates the situation: In an updating dialog a user often wants to see the old data before they are changed. In order to prevent locking the data across a dialog with the user the data must be read in one subtransaction before the dialog, and later updated by another subtransaction. The so-called "Reread Countermeasure" may be used in both central and distributed databases to prevent the lost update anomaly as it is possible to compensate a transaction if it rereads a record for update and detects that the record has been changed since it was first read.

The dirty read anomaly is by definition a situation where a first transaction updates a record without committing the update. Subsequently, a second transaction reads the record. Later, the first update is aborted (or committed) (i.e. the second transaction may have read a non-existing version of the record). In extended transaction models, this may happen when the first transaction updates a record by using a compensatable subtransaction and later aborts the update by using a compensating subtransaction. If a second transaction reads the record before it has been compensated, the data read will be "dirty." *The Pessimistic View Countermeasure* reduces or eliminates the dirty read anomaly and/or the non-repeatable read anomaly by giving the users a pessimistic view of the situation. In other words, the user cannot misuse the information. The purpose is to eliminate the risk involved in using data where long duration locks should have been used. The pessimistic view countermeasure may be implemented by using the pivot or compensatable subtransactions for updates that "limit" the users' options. That is, concurrent transactions cannot use resources that are reserved for the compensatable/pivot subtransaction.

The pivot or retriable subtransactions should be used for updates that "increase" the users' options. That is, concurrent transactions can only

use increased resources after the increase has been committed.

Example

When updating stocks, accounts, vacant passenger capacity, etc. it is possible to reduce the risk of reading non-available stock values. These pessimistic stock values will automatically be obtained if the transactions updating the stocks are designed in such a way that compensatable subtransactions (or the pivot transaction) are used to reduce the stocks and retriable subtransactions (or the pivot transaction) are used to increase the stocks. That is, for attributes with stock like values the compensatable subtransactions that reduce the stock may be used to "limit" the users' options and the retriable subtransactions that increase the stock may be used to "increase" the users' options.

The non-repeatable read anomaly or *fuzzy read* is by definition a situation where a first transaction reads a record without using locks. Later, the record is updated and committed by a second transaction before the first transaction has been committed. In other words, it is not possible to rely on the data that have been read. In extended transaction models, this may happen when the first transaction reads a record that later is updated by a second transaction, which commits the update locally before the first transaction commits globally.

The phantom anomaly is by definition a situation where a first transaction reads some records by using a search condition. Subsequently, a second transaction updates the database in such a way that the result of the search condition is changed. In other words, the first transaction cannot repeat the search without changing the result. Using a data warehouse may often solve the problems of this anomaly (Frank, 2010).

Above we have described countermeasures that are later used in this chapter. However many more countermeasures exists. Frank (2010) has a detailed description of how to use countermeasures to reduce the problems of the isolation anomalies.

The Durability Property

Updates of transactions are said to be *durable* if they are stored in a stable manner and secured by a log recovery system. In case a global transaction has the atomicity property (or relaxed atomicity), the global durability property (or relaxed durability property) will automatically be implemented, as it is ensured by the log-system of the local DBMS systems (Breibart et al., 1992).

E-GOVERNMENT INTEGRATION BY USING AN ERP ACCOUNTING MODULE WITH RELAXED ACID PRPOERTIES

A traditional ERP system consists of modules like Sale, Production, Procurement, Accounting, CRM, HRM, etc. with the applications that are common for most types of industry. These modules may be extended with specific line of business modules (e.g. the hospital sector, the transport sector, and all the different sectors of E-Government) in order to make it possible for the ERP system to function as an integrated system that support all the administrative functions of a specialized organization. In a traditional ERP system, the whole database is common for all the modules of the ERP system. That is the applications of the ERP system have full ACID properties. We define a distributed modular ERP system as an ERP system where each module has full autonomy over its own database tables and applications. The applications of a module may access the tables of its module directly. However, when an application in one module needs data from another module it must use (e.g. SOA services) where data managed by the other module is not accessed directly but only through applications. In the case of SOA, access to data managed by another module is

offered through web services. Applications that only use data owned by their module may have full ACID properties. The applications of a module that use services from another module can only have relaxed ACID properties because the services of a module must only use short duration locks, where no data is locked across the boundaries of the module. Therefore, it is only possible to have relaxed ACID properties between the different possible heterogeneous databases that are used by the different modules.

An application module with relaxed ACID properties has full autonomy over its tables. Therefore, its tables may be recovered independently from the tables owned by other application modules with relaxed ACID properties. By using this property, it should be possible to build ERP applications in the same way as package-deal houses by using different standard components / modules that may be delivered by different suppliers and in the case of software modules, these may in turn use different databases.

However, in order to implement the properties described above, the following rules must be followed.

- Read requests from other modules must only use short duration locks, and therefore, countermeasures against the isolation anomalies should normally be used in such situations.
- In order to make the modules as autonomous as possible, the pivot subtransactions of the applications of a module should always be executed in the location of the module. That is, all modules must only offer read only, compensatable, and retriable services to be used from other modules.

Suppose the Accounting module of an ERP system owns the Department, Account and Account item tables and offer read only, compensatable and retriable application services to be used by other application modules. This is illustrated in the right part of the ER-diagram of Figure 1. The left part of the figure illustrates how traditional E- government application modules may be integrated with the tables of the accounting module.

The E- Government module may (e.g. deal Tax cases where some of the Case items may involve tax payments). When a payment is received by the Tax system a compensatable subtransaction should debit the Account of the Citizen and a retriable subtransaction should credit the Account of the tax department. That is the pessimistic view countermeasure is used against the dirty read anomaly. In a similar way, the Fine system of police authorities may receive fines from the convicted citizens. In Social cases, the Citizens may receive payments from social authorities. In this situation, a compensatable subtransaction should first debit the Account of the social authorities. Next, a retriable subtransaction should credit the Account of the Citizen. In a similar way, other payments from E-government systems like Salary systems may take place. In Figure 1, the reread countermeasure may be used if one of the E-Government modules wants to change the attributes of a Department record belonging to the accounting module.

The different types of E-Government modules may be integrated with each other by using relaxed ACID properties in the same way as the integration with the accounting module. The ERP modules may be distributed. For example, the accounting module may be common for several different government sectors with different specialized ERP modules in different locations.

FUTURE RESEARCH DIRECTIONS

The description of this chapter may be much more detailed as we did not illustrate how different heterogeneous E-Government systems may be integrated without using an accounting module. However, in Frank and Munck, 2008, and Frank and Andersen, 2010 it is described how different heterogeneous health records from different hospitals may be integrated by using relaxed ACID properties. In the same way, other types of industry may in our view benefit by using the integration theory described in this chapter. Therefore, it is our objective in the future to analyze and describe more of these possibilities.

CONCLUSION

In this chapter, we have described an architecture for integrating E-Government systems with the accounting module of a modular ERP system. The integration theory described in this chapter makes it is possible to integrate different heterogeneous application modules by using relaxed ACID properties across the different modules.

Figure 1. Illustration of the integration of the accounting tables with some e-government module

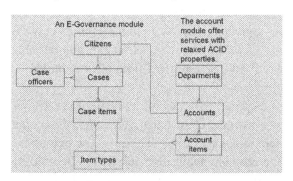

REFERENCES

Berenson, H., Bernstein, P., Gray, J., Melton, J., O'Neil, E., & O'Neil, P. (1995). A Critique of ANSI SQL Isolation Levels. In *Proc ACM SIGMOD Conf.*, pp. 1-10.

Breibart, Y., Garcia-Molina, H., & Silberschatz, A. (1992). Overview of Multidatabase Transaction Management. *The VLDB Journal, 2*, 181–239. doi:10.1007/BF01231700

Frank, L. (2008). Smooth and Flexible ERP Migration between both Homogeneous and Heterogeneous ERP Systems/ERP Modules. In *Proc of the 2ⁿᵈ Workshop on 3ʳᵈ Generation Enterprise Resource Planning Systems*, Copenhagen business School.

Frank, L., & Susanne Munck. (2008). An Overview of Architectures for Integrating Distributed Electronic Health Records. In *Proceeding of the 7th International Conference on Applications and Principles of Information Science* (APIS2008), 297-300.

Frank, L. (2010). *Design of Distributed Integrated Heterogeneous or Mobile Databases*. Saarbrücken, Germany: LAP LAMBERT Academic Publishing AG & Co. KG, Germany, 1-157.

Frank, L., & Andersen, S. K. (2010). Evaluation of Different Database Designs for Integration of Heterogeneous Distributed Electronic Health Records. In *Proc. of the International Conference on Complex Medical Engineering* (CME2010), IEEE Computer Society.

Frank, L., & Zahle, T. (1998). Semantic ACID Properties in Multidatabases Using Remote Procedure Calls and Update Propagations. *Software, Practice & Experience, 28*, 77–98. doi:10.1002/(SICI)1097-024X(199801)28:1<77::AID-SPE148>3.0.CO;2-R

Garcia-Molina, H., & Polyzois, C. (1990). *Issues in disaster recovery. IEEE Compcon*. New York, NY: IEEE.

Garcia-Molina, H., & Salem, K. (1987). *Sagas*. In *Proceeding of the ACM SIGMOD Conf*, pp 249-259.

Gray, J., & Reuter, A. (1993). *Transaction Processing*. San Francisco, CA: Morgan Kaufman.

Mehrotra, S., Rastogi, R., Korth, H., & Silberschatz, A. (1992). A transaction model for multi-database systems. In *Proc International Conference on Distributed Computing Systems*, pp. 56-63.

Polyzois, C., & Garcia-Molina, H. (1994). Evaluation of Remote Backup Algorithms for Transaction-Processing Systems. *ACM TODS, 19*(3), 423–449. doi:10.1145/185827.185836

Weikum, G., & Schek, H. (1992). Concepts and Applications of Multilevel Transactions and Open Nested Transactions, A. Elmagarmid (ed.), *Database Transaction Models for Advanced Applications*. San Francisco, CA: Morgan Kaufmann.

Zhang, A., Nodine, M., Bhargava, B., & Bukhres, O. (1994). *Ensuring Relaxed Atomicity for Flexible Transactions in Multidatabase Systems*, Proc ACM SIGMOD Conf, pp 67-78.

ADDITIONAL READING

Frank, L. (2010). *Design of Distributed Integrated Heterogeneous or Mobile Databases*. Saarbrücken, Germany: LAP LAMBERT Academic Publishing.

Frank, L., & Andersen, S. K. (2010). Evaluation of Different Database Designs for Integration of Heterogeneous Distributed Electronic Health Records. In *Proceedings of the International Conference on Complex Medical Engineering* (CME2010), IEEE Computer Society.

Frank, L., & Munck, S. (2008). *An Overview of Architectures for Integrating Distributed Electronic Health Records*. In *Proceeding of the 7th International Conference on Applications and Principles of Information Science* (APIS2008), 297-300.

KEY TERMS AND DEFINITIONS

ACID Properties: The properties imply that a transaction is *Atomic*, transforms the database from one *Consistent* state to another consistent state, is executed as if it were *Isolated* from other concurrent transactions, and is *Durable* after it has been committed.

Atomic Transaction: A transaction which either performs all the updates or removes them (the "A" in the ACID properties). The atomicity property makes it easier to do database recovery.

Isolation Anomalies: Inconsistencies that occur when transactions are executed without the isolation property (the "I" in the ACID properties).

Relaxed ACID Properties: Application implemented properties that from a user point of view simulates that the traditional ACID properties are implemented.

SOA (Service Orientated Architecture): SOA is special way to call a remote application/service without knowing its internet IP address. This gives flexibility as the IP address of an application/service may change in case of a major site failure.

System Integration: The property that data or applications from one system can be used by another system without manual intervention.

Transaction Abort: Removal of the updates of a transaction. Transaction aborts are normally executed by a DBMS (Data Base Management System).

Transaction Compensation: Removal of the updates of a transaction. Transaction compensation is normally executed by an application program in order to simulate the atomicity property in relaxed ACID properties.

ENDNOTE

[1]   This research is partly funded by the 'Danish Foundation of Advanced Technology Research' as part of the 'Third Generation Enterprise Resource Planning Systems' (3gERP) project, a collaborative project between Department of Informatics at Copenhagen Business School, Department of Computer Science at Copenhagen University, and Microsoft Business Systems.

Chapter 8
Customer Relationship Management Adoption in Local Governments in the United States

Christopher G. Reddick
The University of Texas, USA

ABSTRACT

Customer Relationship Management (CRM) is part of the use of Enterprise Resource Planning (ERP) systems to transform government. This chapter examines the common characteristics of the New Public Management (NPM) and e-government models applying them to CRM adoption in local governments in the United States. Both of these models are commonly cited in the public administration literature as drivers of organizational reform and change. Some of the common characteristics of the NPM and e-government are examined with data from a survey of local government chief administrators. The results of this chapter indicated that more of the characteristics identified in the e-government literature were exemplified in CRM adoption in local governments. In addition, local governments that used more advanced CRM technology were more likely to report organizational changes from these models. The implications of these findings are that researchers should understand both the NPM and e-government principles as important for understanding organizational change.

DOI: 10.4018/978-1-60960-863-7.ch008

INTRODUCTION AND BACKGROUND

In the public sector Customer Relationship Management (CRM) technology has the potential to transform governments (King, 2007). This technology enables citizens to contact government using different channels such as the phone, email, web, and over the counter with a request for a service or information (Schellong, 2008). CRM can be integrated, meaning that the different contact channels use the same database, and through centralization this relieves the burdens of customer service from departments. CRM has the potential to create a seamless contact experience for citizens with their government, increasing citizens' satisfaction with government is a result of this technology (West, 2004; Welch, Hinnant, & Moon 2004). Essentially, CRM can create organizational change in public sector organizations. The transformation of government is part of the greater movement of e-governance to reform public sector institutions.

CRM systems are part of the larger area of research on Enterprise Resource Planning (ERP), which are integrated enterprise computing systems, providing seamless integration of all the information flowing through an organization (Kumar, Maheshwari, & Kumar, 2002). An ERP software suite like CRM uses an application to integrate processes across department or agencies and links them to a common data repository. Government organizations are increasingly adopting ERP systems for benefits such as integrated real-time information, better administration, and result-based management (Ward, 2006). However, public sector organizations, due to their social obligations, higher legislative and public accountability, face unique challenges in the transition to enterprise systems that the private sector (Kumar, Maheshwari, & Kumar, 2002). In the private sector, ERP has been adopted to achieve greater competitive advantage and profitability for the firms, which are much different

incentives than the public sector. Research shows that ERP systems have not been able to deliver what vendors have promised, but they have been able to transform government by lowering costs, increasing performance, and improving customer service (Miranda & Kavanagh, 2005; Raymond, Uwizeyemungu, & Bergeron, 2006). Gulledge and Sommer (2003) applied private sector principles of ERP adoption to the public sector and found that these approaches worked. Other authors believe that there are similarities between the public and private sector in the implementation of ERP systems, but there are some critical success factors are different in the private sector (Frye, Gulledge, Leary, Sommer, & Vincent, 2007). Research shows that organizational culture, constructions of past technological implementations, relationship and knowledge management, and the existing power structures within the organization are key issues that the public sector must contend with in ERP adoption (Allen, Kern, & Havenhand, 2002). Research also shows that management support is important for successful ERP adoption in the public sector; therefore, organizational factors are vital to the adoption of ERP system (Crisostomo, 2008). Essentially, CRM is an important component of ERP systems and the movement of transforming government through e-governance.

This chapter examines CRM technology in local governments in the United States. Local governments' were chosen since they are an ideal case study of the adoption of this technology because citizens' initiate much of their contact with this level of government (Thomas & Streib, 2003). They might, for instance, contact local government to get information on office hours or conduct more advanced functions such as renewing a vehicle registration online. This chapter explores through survey evidence the impact of CRM on local governments, examining two common organizational change models noted in the public administration literature (Dunleavy, Margetts, Bastow, & Tinkler, 2006).

The first model examined is the New Public Management (NPM) model, which has its roots dating over twenty years with the movement of reforming government using business principles (Dunleavy & Hood, 1994; Hood & Peters, 2004). The focus of NPM was on improving performance of the organization by being responsive to the needs of citizens, essentially treating them as customers (Reschenthaler & Thompson, 1996). In the late 1990s, with the rise of the Internet as a popular tool for citizens to initiate contact with government, e-government model began to blossom (Milward & Snyder, 1996; Chadwick & May, 2003). Unlike NPM with its focuses on decentralized and entrepreneurial government, e-government scholars advocated for the centralization and consolidation of information in government through Information Technology (IT) (Grant & Chau, 2005). The Internet became an ideal platform to centralize information delivery more efficiently to citizens (Ebrahim & Irani, 2005). This chapter examines both models to determine their relevance for implementing change as a result of CRM technology. The research question of this chapter, *does CRM technology adoption in local governments possess more of the characteristics of the NPM and/or the e-government models*?

In order to examine the relevance of the NPM and e-government models to CRM adoption this chapter is divided into several key sections. There following section examines the key differences in the NPM and e-government models. This is followed by a section that examines CRM technology and some of the factors noted in the literature that are expected to impact adoption of this technology. There is a discussion of the research methods of collecting survey evidence on CRM adoption and the findings from the survey are presented showing the influence of the NPM and e-government models. The final section provides a conclusion that discusses the implications of the survey findings.

DIFFERENCES BETWEEN NEW PUBLIC MANAGEMENT AND E-GOVERNMENT MODELS

NPM and e-government have many important differences as shown in the five characteristics in Table 1. Each of these characteristics indicates differences in structure, actors, and process which impacts information system development (Torres, Pina, & Royo, 2005; Dunleavy, Margetts, Bastow, & Tinkler, 2006; Homburg, 2008; Fountain, 2009). When comparing the two models, one can see the importance of CRM in the e-government model, as it is able to integrate the organization and create an enterprise approach to governance (Fjermestad & Romano, 2003; Ebrahim & Irani, 2005). This model and its five characteristics are examined in the remainder of this chapter to determine the influence of CRM adoption in local governments in the United States.

In regards to the role of actors, NPM provides an emphasis on being responsive to citizens (Reschenthaler & Thompson, 1996; Denhardt & Denhardt, 2000). Citizens in this model, as previously noted, are similar to customers in the private sector. Governments provide services in response to the needs of their customers. There is a one-way interaction with government and customers in the NPM model (Chadwick & May, 2003). While in the e-government model, citizens are not viewed as customers, but partners in the collaborative process of governance. There is more of a two-way interaction with citizens and government in the e-government model (Ho, 2002; Dunleavy, Margetts, Bastow, & Tinkler, 2006).

The structure of government in the NPM and e-government models also represents unique differences. In the NPM model, the focus is on departments and public service delivery. Departments rein supreme in the NPM model and they control information flow in the organization. While in the e-government model, there is a centralization of organizational structure and an enterprise

Table 1. Differences between NPM and e-government

	New Public Management	E-Government
Role of Actors	Government responds to citizens with one-way interaction; citizens are viewed as customers	Citizens and government have two-way interaction, with collaboration between partners
Structure	Department focused and decentralized in units	Centralized and enterprise approach to IT development
Rationale	Cost containment and greater efficiency though performance measurement and management	Realignment and reduction of duplication through centralized IT systems
Planning and Management	Reactive with focus on service delivery and promoting customer service	Proactive, but may be conflictual because of change; IT aligned within the strategic planning process
Technology	Websites and other one-way interaction tools	Contact channel alignment through CRM, new social media technologies, and e-participation technologies

approach is practiced. In e-government model there is a consolidation of power and resources through a centralized information system.

The third difference between NPM and e-government is related to the rationale for its adoption. In the NPM model the focus is on cost containment and greater efficiency in service delivery. There is the use of performance measurement and management in the NPM model. Results are used in this model through benchmarks to indicate improvements in performance. In the e-government model the focus is on the realignment and reduction of duplication in information systems through the centralization of IT. In the e-government model, the focus moves away from performance measurement to the realignment of the organization with its mission.

In regards to planning and management, in the NPM model there is a reactive focus on service delivery and promoting customer service. Governments under NPM passively react to customers and change occurs as a result of this reaction. While in the e-government model, planning and management is more proactive and IT is aligned with the mission of the organization, through strategic management and planning.

The final characteristic of the NPM and e-government models is that of technology used. In the NPM model, the technology is one-way and not interactive. In this model, citizens passively look up information on a government website.

While in the e-government model, the technology is more interactive and examples include CRM with contact channels synched together, new social media technologies, and e-participation technologies.

CRM TECHNOLOGY

This section discusses four of the common factors noted in the literature that are predicted to impact CRM adoption in local governments. The enterprise approach is found in the e-government literature as one of the drivers of organizational change. Departmental control is emphasized in the NPM literature, with the focus on functional units in this model and their relative performance. The impact of technology on size of government is found in the IT and public administration and information systems literatures. Each of the four factors is framed in a hypothesis in order to show its influence on CRM adoption.

Enterprise Approach

One of the defining features of CRM technology is its ability to create an enterprise approach to public sector organizations (Pan, Tan, & Lim, 2006; King, 2007). This technology enables citizens to contact a service channel such as the phone and be able to request information or fulfill a service request (Landsbergen & Wolken, 2001). This technology can also track calls and citizens can potentially go online, or through other contact channels, to see the status of their request (Ebbers, Pieterson, & Noordman, 2008). This enterprise approach fits squarely with the e-government model, since there is a centralization of structure to improve information flow to citizens (Hjort-Madsen, 2007). In order to examine the impact of the enterprise approach on CRM adoption the following hypothesis is examined.

H1: The enterprise approach impacts CRM adoption in local governments being consistent with the e-government model.

Department Control

The opposite model to the enterprise approach is the influence of departmental control on public sector agencies. One of the issues with the implementation of CRM technology is the loss of control of information from departments (Bannister, 2001; Fleming, 2008). Under NPM the department is the key player in service delivery as mentioned (Denhardt & Denhardt, 2000). With CRM the department loses control of information since it is done through a centralized customer service system (Fleming, 2008). This study examines the impact of decentralized of control on CRM adoption as having an important impact on organizational change. The reason for decentralization towards departments in the NPM model is to promote an entrepreneurial spirit, because departments are closest in their interactions with citizens and know them best (Dunleavy & Hood, 1994). In order to examine the impact of NPM on CRM adoption the following hypothesis is examined.

H2: Department control impacts CRM adoption in local governments and is consistent with the NPM approach.

Technology

The literature on IT adoption often discusses the impact of advances in IT on greater adoption (Ho & Ni, 2004; Norris and Moon, 2005; Reddick, 2009). The literature discusses that the importance of more advanced information systems being build on previous successes of information systems. This chapter examines whether local governments that have more advanced CRM systems are more likely to have a greater impact on CRM adoption (Reddick, 2009). The IT and public administration literature discusses the importance of creating an internal environment that is supportive of technology, such as CRM, to advance the public sector organizational agenda. In order to examine the impact of the technological sophistication on local government and CRM adoption the following hypothesis examined.

H3: Local governments that have more sophisticated CRM systems are more likely to report a positive impact of these systems on their government.

Size

A final issue identified in the literature that is important to CRM adoption is the size of the local government (Caillier, 2009). The e-government literature has discussed the importance of size to the adoption of IT (Moon & Norris, 2005; Norris & Moon, 2005). This study also examines the impact of size on local CRM adoption, because larger size should indicates that a local government would have more resources to devote towards CRM adoption (Reddick, 2009; Caillier, 2009). This chapter also examines the important issue of size of local government as seen through the following hypothesis.

H4: Larger-sized local governments will indicate a greater impact of CRM on their government.

RESEARCH METHODS

The data examined in this study was taken from a survey of Chief Administrative Officers (CAOs) conducted in April and May 2009. After consulting various sources such as the Websites of local governments that have CRM systems and other published reports there were 113 cities or counties that have confirmed cases (Fleming, 2008). This study focuses on the use in cities and counties of the 311 phone number, which is a dedicated phone number to provide information and services to citizens in a city or county. The Federal Trade Commission (FTC) set up this number in 1997 to divert non emergency calls from the overburdened 911 system (Fleming, 2008). Overall, 311 incorporates CRM as a part of the call center function to answer citizen non emergency calls (Schwester, Carrizales, & Holzer, 2009). In general, 311 systems use CRM software to manage the call intake and management of the data and resources needed to answer citizen inquiries.

A copy of the survey instrument was sent to these 113 cities and counties and 60 of them completed the survey, which is a response rate of 53%. A standardized definition of CRM was provided on the survey as a software application that is used to track interaction with residents in local government on an ongoing basis and allows governments to manage the data. The CAO was sent a copy of the survey to complete because they are the top administrator of the city or county and would know the broad impact of this technology on their government (Moon and Norris, 2005).

TECHNOLOGY USED IN LOCAL GOVERNMENT CRM SYSTEMS

Table 2 provides information on the technologies that are typically used in CRM systems in local governments in the United States. The most common technology used by 96.7% of local governments, that responded to the survey, was assigning tracking numbers to service requests. This was followed by searchable knowledge databases used in 85% of local governments. Geographic Information Systems (GIS) mapping integrated into the CRM system was found in 81.7% of local governments. Some more interactive technologies were not commonly used such as push technology using email blasts (46.7%), wireless technologies to send service requests to workers in the field (53.3%), and Internet kiosks (26.7%). The CRM systems were well integrated, when a citizen contacts government through one channel their contact can be found in subsequent contacts (71.7%). Examining the results in Table 2, local government that have CRM systems do have fairly sophisticated systems, with many of them being well integrated with other contact channels demonstrating some of the importance characteristics of the e-government model (Ebbers, Pieterson, & Noordman, 2008).

TECHNOLOGY, SIZE, DEPARTMENTAL CONTROL, AND ENTERPRISE APPROACH

The following section examines the impact of four dependent variables of size, departmental control, technology, and enterprise approach on the survey questions on CRM adoption. Table 3 provides the descriptive statistics of these four variables. The first variable is technology, which is the number of 311 technologies used in the local governments. This is not an exhaustive list of CRM technologies that can be found in local government, but is representative of some of the most common ones indentified in the literature (Fleming, 2008). If a local government used any of the technologies shown in Table 2 then they would get a point. The descriptive statistics showed that the maximum number of CRM technologies used was 11 and the minimum was zero technologies incorporated in the system. The average number of technologies used for local governments was

Table 2. Technology used in local government CRM systems

	Percent
Assigning tracking numbers to service requests	96.7%
Searchable knowledge database	85.0%
Geographic information Systems (GIS) mapping is integrated into the system	81.7%
When a citizen contacts government through one means such as walk in, this initial contact can be found in subsequent contacts	71.7%
Status of service requests can be checked online	70.0%
Work order management system tied together with GIS	61.7%
Our 311 self service works in conjunction with the phone system	55.0%
Interactive voice response system	53.3%
Using wireless technologies to send requests to service workers in the field	53.3%
Push technology such as email blasts	46.7%
Internet kiosks	26.7%

Note: N=60

seven. Therefore, many of the local governments used the technologies shown in Table 2.

The second dependent variable is the number of full time equivalent (FTE) employees in the local government, which is a measure of government size. The average size of the local government that responded to the survey was 1,000 to 2,499 FTE employees. Therefore, medium-sized local governments were more likely to respond to the survey, which is consistent with evidence found for its adoption in local governments (Reddick, 2009).

The third dependent variable is departmental control. The survey question asked whether CAOs believed that one of the challenges in implementing CRM in their local government was the difficulty of departments not wanting to give up control of their customer management. The Likert scales for this question range from strongly disagree (-2), disagree (-1), neutral (0), agree (1), and strongly agree (2). The mean score showed that agree was the average response for the department control question. Therefore, the issue of department control can be found in the NPM literature and was confirmed with this question as an important issue.

The final dependent variable is whether CRM has enabled a local government to take an enterprise approach, looking at the whole of government, rather than separate departments. This question used the same Likert scales as the

Table 3. Descriptive statistics of technology, size, department control, and enterprise approach dependent variables

	N	Minimum	Maximum	Mean
Number of 311 Technologies used in Local Government *(Technology)*	60	0	11	7.02
Number of full time equivalent employees employed in local government *(Size)*	60	1	7	5.53
Difficulty of departments to give up control of their customer management *(Department Control)*	60	-2	2	0.57
Takes an enterprise approach, looking at the whole of government, rather than separate departments *(Enterprise Approach)*	60	-1	2	1

previous question, and the average response was agree to creating more of an enterprise approach as a result of CRM. This question is used to determine the influence of the e-government model on CRM adoption.

Role of Actors and CRM Technology

Table 4 shows statistics on the role of actors and CRM technology. As previously mentioned, NPM focuses on customer service and e-government focuses on citizens and their interaction with government. This table indicates that CRM in local governments has provided a consistent level of service to citizens, with 90% of CAOs agreeing to this statement. CRM has definitively improved communication with citizens according to 93.3% of CAOs agreeing to this statement. CRM has make customer satisfaction a priority within local government (88.3%). There was the least agreement that CRM enabled local government to redirect resources depending on the needs of citizens (68.4%). There was also the least agreement that CRM has helped local governments anticipate the needs of citizens (68.3%). Overall, the survey results in Table 4 indicated that CRM has impacted the role of actors in and outside of

government. The most striking impact was in its improvement of communication with citizens.

In order to determine which of the four factors explain the role of actors in the process, correlation coefficients were conducted. The Tau-b correlations indicated significant variables that impacted actors in CRM were size, enterprise approach, and the level of technology. However, the greatest number of significant questions was for the enterprise approach. The questions that correlated with the enterprise approach were that CRM helped the local government keep in touch with residents in their community, made customer satisfaction a priority within the local government, provided a consistent level of service to citizens, helped the local government anticipate the needs of citizens, and improved communication with citizens. All of these questions were positive and significant with CAOs indicating that CRM creating a more enterprise approach to their organization.

The size variable showed a negative impact in the correlation coefficient, indicating that the greater the size of the local government, CAOs were less likely to believe the CRM had resolved the needs of customers on the first call with few forwarded calls, made customer satisfaction and

Table 4. Role of actors and CRM technology

CRM in local governments...	Agree	Neutral	Disagree
Has helped to cope with increased service demands of citizens	80.0%	20.0%	0.0%
Has helped us keep in touch with residents in my community with their issues[a]	81.7%	15.0%	3.3%
Has enabled us to redirect resources depending upon needs of citizens[b]	68.4%	26.7%	5.0%
Has resolved the needs of customers on the first call, with few forwarded calls[d]	86.7%	10.0%	3.4%
Has made customer satisfaction a priority within our local government[a,d]	88.3%	11.7%	0.0%
Has provided a consistent level of service to citizens[a,d]	90.0%	10.0%	0.0%
Has helped us anticipate the needs of citizens[a,b]	68.3%	31.7%	0.0%
Has improved communicatio with citizens[a,d]	93.3%	6.7%	0.0%

Notes: a=enterprise approach; b= technology; d=size significant correlations at the 0.05 level.

priority, provided a consistent level of service to citizens, and improved communication. Finally, technology used in the CRM system showed that local governments that had more technological sophisticated systems were more likely to say that this enabled them to redirect resources depending on the needs of citizens and helped local governments anticipate the needs of citizens.

Rationale for CRM Technology

Table 5 shows the rationale for implementing 311 technologies in local governments, another important characteristic outlined in the e-government and NPM models. The most agreement was that CRM enabled the local government to document results of their local government (88.3%) along with helping to indentify high complaint areas for workload and resource allocation (88.3%). Improving local services through results management was important according to 86.7% of CAOs. Overall, the results in Table 5 show strong and consistent impact of CRM as a rationale for changing governments by focusing on results management.

Table 5 also shows significant correlations with the two variables technology and enterprise approach when examining the rationale for CRM technology adoption. There was no evidence that size and departmental control had an impact on the responses to these questions. However, there was a strong impact from the questions on the enterprise approach and technology used impacting CRM adoption. For instance, all of the variables had an impact on CRM creating an enterprise approach for the local government Therefore, local governments that responded that CRM enabled results, created results management, helped to mine data, identified high complaint areas, and enhanced service delivery through data collection also indicated a strong impact of CRM creating an enterprise approach. The rationale for the adoption of CRM was seen by creating a more holistic approach in these local governments that responded to the survey. In addition, the more technology that the local government used, this was positively related to these questions as well. As a result, more technologically enabled governments in their use of CRM systems were more likely to report a strong rationale for it use.

Planning and Management and CRM Technology

Table 6 shows the impact of CRM technology on planning and management for the local government. The results in this table indicated that CRM generally falls within the government's strategic plan (88.3%). There was 68.3% of CAOs who believed that this technology has improved citizens access to municipal services during an emergency. There was only a small number of CAOs that agreed that contact channels such as the web, over the counter, and email lack align-

Table 5. Rationale for CRM technology

CRM in local governments...	Agree	Neutral	Disagree
Documents results of my government[a]	88.3%	8.3%	3.3%
Improves local services through results management[a,b]	86.7%	10.0%	3.3%
Helps us mine the data to look for trends[a,b]	81.7%	16.7%	1.7%
Has indentified high complaint areas for workload and resource allocation[a,b]	88.3%	8.3%	3.3%
We use the data collected to enhance service delivery[a,b]	81.7%	11.7%	6.7%

Notes: a=enterprise approach; b= technology significant correlations at the 0.05 level

Table 6. Planning and management and CRM technology

CRM in local governments...	Agree	Neutral	Disagree
Falls within my government's strategic plan[a,c]	88.3%	10.0%	1.7%
Has allowed upper management to spend more time on long term policy[a,b]	40.0%	46.7%	13.3%
Has the system well integrated with emergency management plans including disaster response and post-disaster information dissemination	53.4%	28.3%	18.3%
Has improved citizen access to municipal services during an emergency[a,b]	68.3%	25.0%	6.7%
Contact channels such as Web, over the counter, and email lack alignment which cause conflict and confusion	23.4%	31.7%	45.0%

Notes: a=enterprise approach; b= technology; c=departmental control significant correlations at the 0.05 level

ment which cause conflict and confusion (23.4%). Only 40% of CAOs believed that CRM had allowed upper management to spend more time on long term policy. Overall, the results in Table 6 showed that the most important planning and management aspect of CRM was that it falls with the local government's strategic plan.

The correlations coefficients showed that size did not register an impact from the planning and management variables. The enterprise approach was significantly correlated with CRM falling with the government's strategic plan. In addition, CRM has allowed upper management to spend more time on long term policy and this was correlated with the enterprise approach. There was the impact of improving citizen access to municipal services during an emergency, which had an impact on the enterprise approach. Finally, local governments that used more CRM technology were more likely to say that it has allowed upper management to spend more time on long-term policy and improved citizen access to municipal services during an emergency.

CONCLUSION

The finding of this chapter indicated that the enterprise approach as seen through the e-government model had the greatest impact on the survey data analyzing. This was seen through CRM and its impact on actors helping to greatly improve communication with citizens under the enterprise model. The results showed that department control, as represented by the NPM model, did not register much of an impact on the survey questions. There is more evidence for the e-government model in the implementation of CRM systems in local governments in the United States, than for the characteristics of the NPM model.

A second factor that registered a consistent impact what the use of more advanced CRM systems. Local governments that have more sophisticated CRM systems were more likely to report an impact on many of the questions asked on the survey; although the technology impact was not as great as the enterprise approach. This implies that local governments that are more technologically enabled are more likely to report positive impacts of CRM on their organization.

Size did not register much of an impact as initially suggested in the e-government literature. In fact, larger local governments were less likely to report an impact from CRM on their organizations. This finding could be the result of smaller local government being more effective at implementing CRM systems because they have fewer stakeholders, which makes it more likely for them to implement change given their relative size. Another reason is that much of the CRM technology used can be easily purchased and modified to fit any organization size, therefore, size may not be an important factor for adoption.

These results of this study imply two important conclusions. First, it is difficult to separate out some of the important principles of NPM and e-government models (Danziger & Andersen, 2002; Kraemer & King, 2006; Bekkers & Homburg, 2007). This is especially the case with the small survey sample used in this study of only 60 cases, which makes it difficult to do more advanced statistical analysis. However, the survey results presented here indicated that the enterprise approach was more consistent with CRM adoption. There was not as much evidence that the NPM approach, of a department focus on service delivery having much of an impact. Second, CRM technology sophistication is a driver of organizational change. Local governments that have more sophisticated systems are more likely to indicate greater impacts from CRM technology on their organization.

FUTURE RESEARCH DIRECTIONS

This study examined CRM and organizational change in local governments in the United States. There are three areas of future research directions that should be noted. First, this study could be replicated in other countries to determine whether there are differences between CRM adoption. In addition, in depth case studies of CRM adoption in perhaps three cities in the United States could be done to examine in more detail some of the issues presented in this chapter. Finally, there could be more research completed on the factors that predict whether a local government is likely to adopt CRM, these factors could be used to aid government's that are thinking of adoption.

REFERENCES

Allen, D., Kern, T., & Havenhand, M. (2002) ERP critical success Factors: An exploration of the contextual factors in public sector institutions. In *Proceedings of the 35th Annual Hawaii International Conference on System Sciences*, Retrieved from http://ieeexplore.ieee.org /xpl/ freeabs_all.jsp? arnumber=994295

Bannister, F. (2001). Dismantling the silos: extracting new value from IT investments in public administration. *Information Systems Journal, 11*(1), 65–84. doi:10.1046/j.1365-2575.2001.00094.x

Bekkers, V., & Homburg, V. (2007). The myths of E-Government: Looking beyond the assumptions of a new and better government. *The Information Society, 23*(5), 373–382. doi:10.1080/01972240701572913

Caillier, J. G. (2009). Centralized customer service: What local government characteristics influence its acceptance and usage of information? *Public Administration and Management, 14*(2), 292–322.

Chadwick, A., & May, C. (2003). Interaction between states and citizens in the age of the Internet: "E-government" in the United States, Britain and the European Union. *Governance, 16*(2), 271–300. doi:10.1111/1468-0491.00216

Crisostomo, D. T. (2008). Management attributes of implementing An ERP system in the public sector. *Journal of International Business Research, 7*(2), 1–15.

Danziger, J. N., & Anderson, K. V. (2002). The impacts of information technology on public administration: An analysis of empirical research from the "Golden Age" of transformation. *International Journal of Public Administration, 25*(5), 591–627. doi:10.1081/PAD-120003292

Denhardt, R. B., & Denhardt, J. V. (2000). The new public service: Serving rather than steering. *Public Administration Review, 60*(6), 549–559. doi:10.1111/0033-3352.00117

Dunleavy, P., & Hood, C. (1994). From old public administration to new public management. *Public Money & Management, 14*(3), 9–16.

Dunleavy, P., Margetts, H., Bastow, S., & Tinkler, J. (2006). New public management is dead- long live digital-era governance. *Journal of Public Administration: Research and Theory, 16*(3), 467–494. doi:10.1093/jopart/mui057

Ebbers, W. E., Pieterson, W. J., & Noordman, H. N. (2008). Electronic government: Rethinking channel management strategies. *Government Information Quarterly, 25*(2), 181–201. doi:10.1016/j.giq.2006.11.003

Ebrahim, Z., & Irani, Z. (2005). E-government and adoption: Architecture and barriers. *Business Process Management Journal, 11*(5), 589–611. doi:10.1108/14637150510619902

Fjermestad, J., & Romano, N. C. (2003). Electronic customer relationship management: Revisiting the general principles of usability and resistance – an integrative implementation framework. *Business Process Management Journal, 9*(5), 572–591. doi:10.1108/14637150310496695

Fleming, C. (2008). *Call 311: Connecting Citizens to Local Government, Final Report*. Retrieved from http://bookstore.icma.org/freedocs/43547.pdf

Fountain, J. E. (2009). Bureaucratic reform and e-government in the United States: An institutional perspective. In Chadwick, A., & Howard, P. N. (Eds.), *Routledge Handbook of Internet Politics*. New York, NY: Routledge.

Frye, D., Gulledge, T., Leary, M., Sommer, R., & Vincent, J. (2007). Public sector enterprise system implementation. *Electronic Government. International Journal (Toronto, Ont.), 4*(1), 76–96.

Grant, G., & Chau, D. (2005). Developing a generic framework for E-government. *Journal of Global Information Management, 13*(1), 1–30. doi:10.4018/jgim.2005010101

Gulledge, T. R., & Sommer, R. A. (2003). Public sector enterprise resource planning. *Industrial Management & Data Systems, 103*(7), 471–483. doi:10.1108/02635570310489179

Hjort-Madsen, K. (2007). Institutional patterns of enterprise architecture adoption in government. *Transforming Government: People. Process and Policy, 1*(4), 333–349.

Ho, A. T. (2002). Reinventing local governments and the E-Government initiative. *Public Administration Review, 62*(4), 434–444. doi:10.1111/0033-3352.00197

Ho, A. T., & Ni, A. Y. (2004). Explaining the adoption of E-Government features: A case study of Iowa county treasurers' offices. *American Review of Public Administration, 34*(2), 164–180. doi:10.1177/0275074004264355

Homburg, V. M. (2008). Red tape and reforms: Trajectories of technological and managerial reforms in public administration. *International Journal of Public Administration, 31*(7), 749–770. doi:10.1080/01900690701690817

Hood, C., & Peters, G. (2004). The middle aging of New Public Management: Into the age of paradox? *Journal of Public Administration: Research and Theory, 14*(3), 267–282. doi:10.1093/jopart/muh019

King, S. F. (2007). Citizens as customers: Exploring the future of CRM in UK local government. *Government Information Quarterly, 24*(1), 47–63. doi:10.1016/j.giq.2006.02.012

Kraemer, K., & King, J. L. (2006). Information technology and administrative reform: Will E-Government be different? *International Journal of Electronic Government Research, 2*(1), 1–20. doi:10.4018/jegr.2006010101

Kumar, V., Maheshwari, B., & Kumar, U. (2002). ERP systems implementation: best practices in Canadian government organizations. *Government Information Quarterly*, *19*(2), 147–172. doi:10.1016/S0740-624X(02)00092-8

Landsbergen, D., & Wolken, G. (2001). Realizing the promise: Government information systems and the fourth generation of information technology. *Public Administration Review*, *61*(2), 206–220. doi:10.1111/0033-3352.00023

Milward, H. B., & Snyder, L. O. (1996). Electronic Government: Linking citizens to public organizations through technology. *Journal of Public Administration: Research and Theory*, *6*(2), 261–275.

Miranda, R. A., & Kavanagh, S. C. (2005). Achieving government transformation through ERP systems. *Government Finance Review*, *21*(3), 36–42.

Moon, M. J., & Norris, D. F. (2005). Does managerial orientation matter? The adoption of reinventing government and e-government at the municipal level. *Information Systems Journal*, *15*(1), 43–60. doi:10.1111/j.1365-2575.2005.00185.x

Norris, D. F., & Moon, M. J. (2005). Advancing e-Government at the grassroots: Tortoise or hare? *Public Administration Review*, *65*(1), 64–75. doi:10.1111/j.1540-6210.2005.00431.x

Pan, S.-L., Tan, C.-W., Eric, T. K., & Lim, E. T. (2006). Customer relationship management (CRM) in e-government: a relational perspective. *Decision Support Systems*, *42*(1), 237–250. doi:10.1016/j.dss.2004.12.001

Raymond, L., Uwizeyemungu, S., & Bergeron, F. (2006). Motivations to implement ERP in e-government: an analysis from success stories. *Electronic Government. International Journal (Toronto, Ont.)*, *3*(3), 225–240.

Reddick, C. G. (2009). The adoption of centralized customer service systems: A survey of local governments. *Government Information Quarterly*, *26*(1), 219–226. doi:10.1016/j.giq.2008.03.005

Reschenthaler, G. B., & Thompson, F. (1996). The information revolution and the New Public Management. *Journal of Public Administration: Research and Theory*, *6*(1), 125–143.

Schellong, A. (2008). *Citizen Relationship Management: A Study of CRM in Government*. Frankfurt am Main: Peter Lang Publishing Group.

Schwester, R. W., Carrizales, T., & Holzer, M. (2009). An examination of municipal 311 system. *International Journal of Organization Theory and Behavior*, *12*(2), 218–236.

Thomas, J. C., & Streib, G. (2003). The new face of government: Citizen-Initiated contacts in the era of E-Government. *Journal of Public Administration: Research and Theory*, *13*(1), 83–102. doi:10.1093/jpart/mug010

Torres, L., Pina, V., & Royo, S. (2005). E-Government and the transformation of public administrations in EU countries: Beyond NPM or just a second wave of reforms? *Online Information Review*, *29*(5), 531–553. doi:10.1108/14684520510628918

Ward, C. J. (2006). ERP integrating and extending the enterprise. *Public Management*, *35*(1), 30–33.

Welch, E. W., Hinnant, C. C., & Moon, M. J. (2004). Linking government satisfaction with E-government and trust in government. *Journal of Public Administration: Research and Theory*, *15*(3), 371–391. doi:10.1093/jopart/mui021

West, D. M. (2004). E-Government and the transformation of service delivery and citizen attitudes. *Public Administration Review*, *64*(1), 15–27. doi:10.1111/j.1540-6210.2004.00343.x

KEY TERMS AND DEFINITIONS

Customer Relationship Management: Customer Relationship Management (CRM) is the use of technology that enables citizens to contact government using different channels such as the phone, email, web, and over the contact with a request for a service or information. The information from the requests can be used to determine areas that might need improvements through data mining and analysis.

Departmental Control: NPM has emphasized the decentralization of decision-making in departments with the view that they are closest to citizens and their needs. This approach advocates for entrepreneurial government, because departments understand their constituents and will more effectively be able to implement change.

E-Government: Electronic Government or E-Government is the use of information and communication technologies for citizens and businesses to interact with government. E-government is different from information technology in that it enables information systems to communicate with each other with the aid of technologies such as the internet.

Enterprise Approach: The enterprise approach to public sector organizations is part of the e-government movement which advocates for the centralization of decisions with the aid of information technology. This approach advocates for the use of strategic planning to influence organization-wide changes from information systems.

New Public Management: New Public Management (NPM) is the use of private sector management principles applied to public sector organizations. The emphasis is on government achieving results for their actions and being rewarded for these results. NPM emphasizes the decentralization of control for decisions in departments.

Chapter 9
E–Governance at the Grass Roots:
Observations at the SAARC Perspective

Hakikur Rahman
SchoolNet Foundation, Bangladesh

ABSTRACT

Ever growing and evolutionary technologies of the Internet have lured nations in utilizing information and communication technologies to upgrade the livelihood of their citizens. Governments of most countries have initiated multi-faceted programs and initiatives to provide enhanced services through means and methods that are being facilitated by the Internet. However, forms and norms of services have taken shapes and domains depending on the ground context, expansion and maturity of ICTs in their countries and communities. This chapter will explore situations of electronic forms of the government, which it argues is a pre-requisite for good governance and thus enable governments to reach the people at large. Particularly, the chapter will review the emancipation of ICTs in eight countries of the South Asian Association for Regional Cooperation (SAARC). It investigates some basic parameters of ICTs retrieving archived data from various institutions and organizations. Later on, the chapter tries to generalize the situation in terms of recommendations.

DOI: 10.4018/978-1-60960-863-7.ch009

INTRODUCTION

Despite the potentiality of the electronic form of the government services (popularly known as e-government), it is somehow unchartered in many countries in terms of implementing the governance system at the local level. In theory it is the local government, in practice it is the lowest tier of the governance system, and for this study it is termed as the grass roots governance. The reality is that the implementation of grass roots governance lack proper incentives, adequate resources, satisfactory management including appropriate leadership, long term management plan and foremost any standardized framework (Zwahr, Rossel & Finger, 2005; Das & Chandrashekhar, 2006; Malhotra, Chariar, Das & Ilavarasan, 2007; Gessi, Ramnarine & Wilkins, 2007).

In recent years, governments throughout the world are in quest of finding novel ways to deliver public services more efficiently and effectively. Incorporation of e-governance in the local governments tier is an option widely discussed, although the expectations often vary. They vary in nature, culture, practice, habits and habitations among communities, states, nations and regions. Various socio-economical motivations, including political commitments may also be reasons for the change as well (Pattakos, 2004; Commonwealth, 2004; Fox & Gurley, 2006; Rahman, 2010).

Moreover, due to non availability of any long term strategy, action plan or vision, and or any accepted or standardized e-governance framework defined to be satisfactory accepted for the grass roots e-governance, some countries and agencies of implementation are still at the stage of simulation or initiation or experimentation or at the state of confusion, even after years of successful operation of e-government system. Countries in the developing and transitional economies are major sufferers of this situation, as most of the time they just try to replicate an established system or try to simply manipulate on their own without

enough researches or try to popularize a political agenda without looking into the innate intricacies surrounding the system.

The consequences are that, not only governments, but also, development actors are revisiting the concept of e-government as many projects on e-governance have failed throughout the globe. Notwithstanding the reasons being indistinct in a short term research finding, some of the international agencies have even shifted their focus area of funding. Perhaps, these could be due to factors related to design, perception, culture, economy, transparency or simple failure due to lack of proper attention (Rahman, 2007). As mentioned, elaborated research work is necessary to make any conclusive recommendation or set a guideline. However, for the sake of this research, the study is following the growth of the very basic parameters of ICTs, which are being accepted by national and international institutions while talking about implementation of electronic form of government around the globe. This chapter likes to see the pattern of progress for some parameters of e-government, such as the governance structure, the ICT policy and strategy, and the e-government ranking; and ICT for development, such the growth of GDP, the number of fixed and mobile telephone, and the number of Internet users (which are very much inter-related for the emancipation of grass roots e-governance) in the SAARC region. From the various patterns of ICT growth as mentioned above, the chapter makes a synthesis and recommendation for future research.

BACKGROUND

Local government can be defined as a city, county, parish, township, municipality, borough, ward, board, district, sub-district, or other general purpose political subdivision of a state or a country[1]. Local governments in different countries are primarily composed of provinces, districts, subdistricts, municipalities, villages and other forms of localities varying by geography, norms, culture, laws, jurisdiction, national integrity, political will and many other parameters. Fox & Gurley (2006:2) supported this by stating, 'Local government size varies dramatically around the world', and so the institutional framework that influences the framework of e-governance. The number and size of municipalities differ widely across countries and governments have to take strategies befitting the ground context to fit into the e-governance framework. Apart from the political vision and will, this research argues that at the administrative context, four major themes may act as the key to run a local government authority; such as leadership, communication and coordination, immediate risk management, and trust, confidence and transparency (CTG, 2003; Chutimaskul & Chongsuphajaisiddhi, 2004; Anttiroiko, 2004).

While applying set of ideas (the intellectual, scientific, and philosophical ideas associated with a particular place, time or group: *Encarta Dictionary – English UK*) with ICTs, one can think of the local e-government system be comprised of an on-line resource designed to assist electronic access to government delivery intermediaries; provide homogeneous linkage to technology, policy and organizational management; promote inter-organizational integration at the local level to information system development, management and institutional partnership; accommodate subsidies, grants and other facilities to empower local communities with greater autonomies; deliver efficient, citizen-centric and cost-effective contents to accelerate participation and partnership-based e-services; integrate communities, societies, and localities to local, national, regional and global e-government initiatives; produce strategic plan to support efficient delivery of government services; identify level of organizational readiness at the local context to prepare for the effectiveness and efficient service delivery; and lead toward the ultimate goal of transformation to offer better citizen services at the grass roots (CTG, 2002;

2003; Austin City Council, 2008; Hoogwout, 2003; Kolsaker, 2005; Perotti & von Thadden, 2006, Government of Jordan, 2006).

Scope of this study will restrict the research limited to see pattern of progress on various elements of basic ICTs, as such nature or role of the GDP; growth of fixed telephone, mobile telephone, Internet penetration (methodology and data are taken from ITU in benchmarking ICT readiness); establishment of national agencies responsible for the development and establishment of ICT policies and Acts (methodology of this research and data taken from literature review); some aspects of ICT strategies; and foremost implementation of any long term action plan (methodology of this research and data taken from literature review) to upgrade the ICT parameters in these SAARC countries, which this research argue, are pre-requisite to implement the grass roots e-governance.

GRASS-ROOTS E-GOVERNANCE

This study is based on observations of some basic parameters of ICT, rather ICT for development and thus effective for implementing and flourishing electronic government in a country. Parameters are taken from ITU, UN and other reputable institutions who are researching in the paradigm of e-governance over the years. This research purview among parameters like, GDP, tele-density, ICT readiness in terms of policy issues and e-government readiness index in terms of applications, and argues that these parameters have direct or consequential effects on the overall development of the governance systems of a country.

Role of GDP and Economic Efficiency

An empirical study (Bavec and Vintar, 2007) finds that the level of economic development has a moderate impact on the e-government development, while national competitiveness and innovation play quite a strong role. Bavec and Vintar (2007) further argue that, there is also a low correlation between overall government efficiency and e-government. There study reveals that economic power (GDP per capita in PPP) has a very moderate impact on the current state of e-governments.

This study after obtaining data from the ITU Statistics observes and illustrates in Figure 1 the ten years of GDP growth pattern of the eight countries under the SAARC. The figure shows four distinct pattern of growth with Maldives being taken the lead; Bhutan and Sri Lanka at the second level; India and Pakistan at the next level; and Afghanistan, Bangladesh and Nepal at the bottom level, which is below USD500.

There is another school of thought that the role of GDP information in the modern economy should not be considered as inevitable (a law of nature) (Van den Bergh, 2007), and also this study finds there is a scarce of research on GDP growth pattern in this region. However, this study states from the finding is that there is a distinct growth of GDP in countries under the SAARC region and it is significant.

Figure 1. 10 years of GDP data from the eight SAARC countries

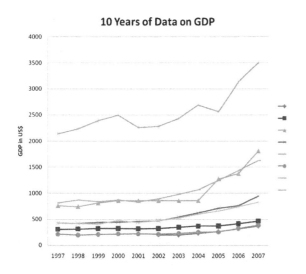

Growth of Internet Users and e-Government

Since the early days of Internet, from various theoretical studies and implementation of small scale pilot projects in many countries have proven the role of Internet in the socio-economic development, especially in the developing countries (Nguyen, 2007). Paul (2007) in her study, which is based on research and personal interviews of selected representatives of the Government of National Capital Territory of Delhi, highlighted the role of Internet, particularly the World Wide Web (WWW), which has made it easier for citizens to locate and download official information and to conduct transactions. Information management agencies or intermediaries such as tele-centres, village kiosks, rural information centers, or knowledge centres play a vital role in supporting transparent and accountable governance in this digital era. However, she emphasized that e-government needs to be integrated into the broader public management framework so as to make a substantial change in the government to citizen (G2C) relationship. Galpaya, Samarajiva and Soysa (2007) also emphasized the role of the Internet in accessing public information from telecenters through their study which has been carried out in India, Pakistan, Philippines, Sri Lanka and Thailand. Many similar researches and reports support this (Reddick, 2004; Lau, 2005; Commission of the European Communities, 2009; EC, 2010). A World Bank / IFC report says for every 10 percentage-point increase in high-speed Internet connections there is an increase in economic growth of 1.3 percentage points (infoDev, 2010).

This study after obtaining the data from ITU observes and shows the ten years of growth pattern of Internet in the SAARC region (see Figure 2). The data (as of 2008) supports that Bhutan, Maldives, Pakistan and Sri Lanka are in better situations in terms of Internet penetration in their countries. This study argues that as a basic parameter of ICT for development, the growth of the Internet users at the local and national level is an essential ingredient of e-government development. However, the point of note is that, there is a general positive trend of development in each country in the region.

Fixed Phone and Cellular Phone vs. e-Governance

From the very beginning of the benchmarking of countries in terms of e-readiness and thereby, e-governance, the role of fixed phone and cellular phone carries significance (Prates, 2001; As-Saber & Hossain, 2008). International agencies like ITU or UN and other research institutions while either making ranking or evaluation or indexing in terms of e-readiness or e-governance, taken consideration on the number of fixed phone users and cellular phone users in their research. Researchers also reveal that both of these instruments have influential role in disseminating and delivering public services and contents for the promotion of e-governance (Galpaya, Samarajiva and Soysa, 2007; CTO, 2008).

Figure 3 and Figure 4 depict the growth of fixed phone and cellular phone in this region as found by this study. The data for Figure 3 shows recent year's emerging growth in Maldives and Sri Lanka, while others still not in a comfortable situation. However, cellular phone growth

shows a general positive trend for all countries, while Maldives has taken the lead. The data has been taken from the ITU statistics, as mentioned in the methodology earlier; however, further investigation may be carried out to find out other parameters that may be involved around these development trends.

GOVERNANCE STRUCTURES

As an entirety, electronic form of governance (e-Governance) cannot be separated from traditional governance, and it cannot be taken as an adjunct of traditional governance, either. It has to be an integral part of the governance structure and pro-

Figure 3. 10 years of fixed phone users' data from the eight SAARC countries

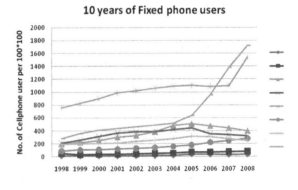

Figure 2. 10 years of Internet users' data from the eight SAARC countries

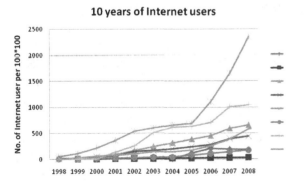

Figure 4. 10 years of cell phone users' data from the eight SAARC countries

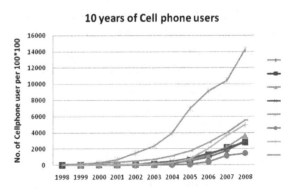

cesses. Thus, every government organization or entity, every government programme or policy and every law and regulation would have to integrate e-Governance modules within itself rather than brought-in as an afterthought or introduced as an adjunct (Govt. of India, 2008). Rahman (2007; 2008; 2010:313) argued that governance structure has an impact in disseminating public information at the grass roots and he suggested a five tier governance structure in an early research. However, for the sake of this research, an exploratory study on governance structure of the SAARC countries is being presented next. Moreover, the research findings and arguments are being provided where applicable, as notes. Efforts were given to find the most dependable source as the authentication.

Governance Structure towards e-Governance

Afghanistan

There are 34 multi-member districts corresponding to the 34 provinces[2], which are further divided into 365 districts (Wentz, Kramer & Starr, 2008). In the House of Elders (*Meshrano Jirga*) 34 members are elected by regional legislatures to serve 4-year terms, 34 members are elected by regional legislatures to serve 3-year terms and 34 members are appointed by the President to serve 5-year terms[3]. In the House of People (*Wolesi Jirga*) 249 members are elected by single non-transferable vote to serve 5-year terms[4]. *Note: The governance pattern shows two forms of administrative measures. There are two tiers of government structure, one bottom-top, and the other one top-bottom. Furthermore, the district council seats are allocated in proportion to provincial population, not geographical boundary.*

Bangladesh

The rural/regional local government, as proposed by the commission on local government in 1997 has four tiers: Gram (Village) Parishads (being reconstituted in 2003 as Sarkers, and later on changed again) (40,392); Union Parishads (4451); Thana/Upazila Parishads (469); and Zila (District) Parishads (64). Urban areas have a separate set of local governments. The Bangladesh Census Commission recognized 522 urban areas in 1991 (with a minimum population of about 5000 or more), but only about 269 of the larger urban areas among these have urban local governments. The six largest cities have a City Corporation status, while the rest are known as Pourashavas or Municipalities, which again are classified according to their financial strength[5]. Note: *There are four tiers of government structure existed in the country.*

Bhutan

Local government in 1991 was organized into four zones, or dzongdey, and eighteen districts, or dzongkhag. Before the zonal administration system was established beginning in 1988 and 1989, the central government interacted directly with district governments. The zonal boundaries were said to be dictated by geophysical and agroclimatic considerations. Eighteen districts comprised local government at the next echelon. Districts were further subdivided into subdistricts (dungkhag) and village blocks or groups (gewog). Ten of the eighteen districts had subdistricts, which were further subdivided into village groups. Bhutan also has two municipal corporations[6]. *Note: There are three tiers of government structure.*

India

There are 28 states and 7 Union territories in the country[7]. The Union Territories are administered by the President through an Administrator. Each state is broken up into several administrative districts. A District is divided into several Community Development Blocks, each of which is headed by a Block Development Officer (BDO). Each Block, in turn, is usually divided into several Tehsils, headed by a Tehsildar. It is probably apparent that the political and administrative set ups are closely interlinked at the district and sub-district levels. For example, the CEO of the Zilla Parishad is a bureaucrat, although the Zilla Parishad itself is made up of elected representatives, including representatives from the Mandal (Praja) Parishads from the different mandals within the district. The Mandal Parishad or Council comprises the heads of the Panchayat Samitis, and some co-opted resource persons. Each Panchayat Samiti, in turn, has representatives from various Gram Panchayats (Village Councils), which is the basic tier of local government[8] (James, 2004). Note: *Note: There are five tiers in the government system; however, there are different administrative channels.*

Maldives

Maldives has 7 provinces each consisting of two to four administrative divisions. The Maldives has twenty-six natural atolls[9] and few island groups on isolated reefs, all of which have been divided into twenty-one administrative divisions (twenty administrative atolls and Malé city). Each atoll is administered by an Atoll Chief (*Atholhu Veriyaa*) appointed by the President. The Ministry of Atoll Administration and its Northern and Southern Regional Offices, Atoll Offices and Island Offices are collectively responsible to the President for Atolls Administration. The administrative head of each island is the Island Chief (Katheeb), appointed by the President. The Island Chief's immediate superior is the Atoll Chief[10]. *Note: There are two tiers in the governance structure, but, there exists three tiers of administrative structure.*

Nepal

Nepal has a *two-tier system of local governance*; with village development committee (VDC) and Municipality as the lower tier, and district development committee (DDC) as the higher tier. In the case of DDCs and VDCs, there is a provision of

classification on the basis of differences in terms of transportation, communication, education and health facilities (including population in the case of VDCs), but such classification has not been completed as yet. Furthermore, the classification does not include the functional bases such as work responsibility, fiscal authority, fiscal attempts and discipline. However, a municipality may be established in any area having access to facilities such as electricity, drinking water supply, roads and transport, education and communication[11]. *Note: Basic human infrastructures are essential elements of the local e-government.*

Pakistan

Local governments in Pakistan exist under the supervision of the various provincial governments, where provincial governments have simply delegated some of their functions and responsibilities to local governments by the promulgation of ordinances. It was a new model of local government pioneered to ensure direct participation of the people in managing their own affairs through representative's bodies set up down to the village level. There were two separate laws for rural (i.e. Basic Democracy Ordinance 1959) and Urban Councils (i.e. Municipal Administration Ordinance 1960). It established a *four tier hierarchical system of local council* throughout the country, namely the Union Councils (for rural areas), Town Committees (for urban areas), Tehsil Councils, and or District Councils and Divisional Councils. The Tehsil Council was the second tier above the Union Council. It was mainly concerned with the development activities in the proclaimed areas[12].

Sri Lanka

The organizational structure of local governance consists of three legal instruments: the Municipal Council Ordinance, the Urban Council Ordinance and the Pradeshiya Sabhas Act. At present there are 18 Municpal Councils, 37 Urban Councils, and 256 Pradeshiya Sabhas (*three tiers*). Local governments used to be divided into wards. Wards have been discontinued under the new proportional system. The composition of a local council is based on the total population of a local authority area and not on a ward basis[13]. *Note: Population is the indicator of local authority area, not geographic boundary.*

ICT POLICY AND STRATEGY

The formulation of appropriate ICT policy and relevant strategy is essential in promoting e-governance within the government and enabling the government in reaching out to the grass roots (Accenture, 2009; Labelle, 2005). This sub-section will discuss relevant ICT policies through a mixed approach, providing a comparative study on various ICT Policies, Acts and establishment of national agencies responsible to carry out any long term vision, or strategy in these countries. First portion of it is an exploratory one and then a table of comparison is being presented.

ICT Policies and Initiatives towards e-Governance

Afghanistan

In October 2002, the Ministry of Communications (MoC) published a national telecommunications development strategy that outlined key ICT infrastructure development initiatives and set the conditions for developing the Afghanistan telecommunications and Internet Policy (ATIP). In October 2003, the ATIP was approved. The Information and Communications Technology Policy was enacted in November 2003 and one of the important objectives among the three was to use ICTs to increase government efficiency and to effectively deliver improved social service. The policy also included a plan to computerize all central government entities by the year 2005, and the

plan to form National ICT Council of Afghanistan (NICTCA). At the same time (November 2003), the Ministry of Communications (MoC) enacted the Telecommunications and Internet Policy containing specific policies related to telecommunications sector (UNDP, 2002; Government of Afghanistan, 2003a; 2003b; 2005; Wentz, Kramer & Starr, 2008).

Bangladesh

Bangladesh Computer Council (BCC), established by Act No IX of 1990 is an autonomous body under the Ministry of Science and Information & Communication Technology, Government of Bangladesh to encourage and provide support for ICT related activities in Bangladesh[14]. In Bangladesh, the focus of capacity-building through ICT is on socio-economic development. Provision of nationwide infrastructure under a national ICT policy, spearheaded by a National ICT task force chaired by the Prime Minister, is designed to facilitate good governance, e-commerce, and as well as e-learning. The human resource development focus of the national ICT policy is to develop ICT professionals and engineers to meet the demand for skilled ICT workers that is growing world-wide, especially for the global software and ICT-enabled services market (Sayo, Chacko & Pradhan, 2004). Ministry of Post and Telecommunications, Ministry of Science and Information and Communications Technology, Bangladesh Telecommunications Regulatory Commission, Bangladesh Telegraph and Telephone Board, Bangladesh Rural Telecom Authority are a few apex bodies which are given the responsibility to formulate policies and national plan and regulate them in the country (Chapagain, 2007).

Bhutan

The first attempt to streamline ICT development in the country was taken in 1994, when the government with assistance from UNDP produced the

Computerization Master Plan of Bhutan for 1997 – 2000. This document outlined necessary steps required to initiate development of ICT in Bhutan. The document also contains some statistics about computer use in Bhutan at that time. In 1999, the Computer Service Center (now Dept of Info and Technology), with assistance from the government of Denmark, conducted a more comprehensive study, resulting in the Bhutan ICT Policy and Strategies (BIPS). This strategy analyzed the ICT situation in the Bhutan in depth, and provided important ICT initiatives to be implemented in the near future, which resulted into the Bhutan ICT Master Plan 2001 and further enhanced its practicality with the introduction of global Internet in June 1999 (Jurmi, 2004; Government of Bhutan, 2003; Government of Bhutan, 2006; Government of Bhutan, 2007).

India

In India, the Department of Electronics (DoE) was established in 1971 for recommending and implementing policies for the country's IT sector. The National Taskforce on Information Technology and Software Development was established by the Prime Minister of India on 28 May 1998 to formulate a long-term National IT Policy for the country and to remove impediments to the growth of the IT industry. The main objective was to assist India emerge as an IT software superpower. In 1999 National Telecoms Policy of India was enacted to provide affordable and effective communication systems for citizens; achieve a balance between the provision of universal service to all uncovered areas and of high-level services capable of meeting the needs of the country's economy; and create a modern and efficient telecommunications infrastructure taking into account the convergence of IT, media, telecom and consumer electronics and thereby propel India into becoming an IT superpower. Later on the IT Act 2000 was adopted

focusing the legal recognition of electronic contracts and digital signatures; created controller for certifying authorities and cyber appellate tribunal (Government of India, 2000; 2006; Pertrazzini & Harindranath, 1997; Lallana, 2004). *Note: To roll out grass roots e-governance a comprehensive and long term vision with requisite action plans are essential.*

Maldives

The Ministry of Communications, Science & Technology (MCST) is responsible for the overall policy development and guidance for the ICT sector in the country. The Telecommunications Authority of Maldives has given the mandate to develop and regulate the telecom sector which covers Internet services as well. The responsibility for establishing a national computer center was given to the Ministry of Communication, Science and technology, which was formed in 1998. The national center for information technology took the key role of guiding the adoption of IT standards within the government. The Maldives telecommunication policy 2001-2005 aimed at the development of the telecommunications sector towards achieving the targets of the Sixth National Development Plan and, ultimately the economic and social development objectives envisaged in *Vision 2020*. The policy also guided the sector in developing ICT services to link the grass roots communities and reduce the impact of geographical isolation and physical separation on the island communities. *Vision 2020* sets a challenging development target to become one of the top-ranking nations among middle-income developing countries by 2020. Vision 2020 also sets a number of goals for social development and quality of life improvement of people at large by addressing issues of equality, security, healthcare delivery, education, gender disparities, environment, work ethics and a caring society.

Nepal

Nepal's Information Technology Policy was developed in 2000 with the aim to put the country on the global IT map by 2005. Its objectives included: making IT accessible to the general public and increasing employment through this means; creating a knowledge-based society; and establishing knowledge-based industries. Nepal's IT plan also identified 16 activities that constitute its IT policy. These include declaring IT a policy priority; providing Internet access to all of the country's Village Development Committees; computerizing the system in all government offices; developing—with private sector participation—IT parks; promoting e-commerce and e-health; and enacting necessary laws. The action plan for implementing the IT policy includes: participation of the private sector in infrastructure development; human resources development; dissemination of IT; promotion of e-commerce, and promotion of e-governance (Lallana, 2003; 2004). *Note: For the promotion of e-governance at the local level, ICT policy should incorporate development activities at the village level, so that people at large could foresee the ultimate economic value and eventually adopt the system as part of their livelihood.*

Pakistan

Pakistan Telecommunications (re-organization) Act was enacted in 1996, and Pakistan IT Commission was established in 2000. Eleven working groups were created under auspices of IT Policy 2000 with emphasis on e-government[15]. The e-Government Program was launched in 2001 with three fold objectives: to encourage ICT's for enabling information and services delivery to the citizens in a cost effective manner; to initiate measures for reengineering of work flow in government departments enabling electronic services delivery to citizens for bringing efficiency in operation; and to bring transparency in government functions and access to information[16]. Promulga-

tion of Electronic Transactions Ordinance in 2002 was another milestone for promoting economic activities at the grass roots strengthening the local government. Furthermore, Telecom Deregulation Policy was approved in 2003 (UNESCAP, 1999; 2003). *Note: Inclusion of economic activities is an essential component of electronic government.*

Sri Lanka

The Government of Sri Lanka first recognized the need for the development of ICT through the National Computer Policy of 1983 (COMPOL), and this was the first attempt from the government that was taken by the Natural Resources, Energy and Science Authority of Sri Lanka (NARESA) on the instructions of the then President. A committee appointed by NARESA produced the National Computer Policy Report. The acceptance of the COMPOL report by the Government gave rise to the establishment of CINTEC by Act No. 10 of 1984 as the "Computer and Information Technology Council of Sri Lanka. Later on, the Science and Technology Development Act No. 11 of 1994 changed the name to "Council for Information Technology" but retained the acronym CINTEC. The "e-Sri Lanka," project launched in November 2002 was tasked to develop an ICT Roadmap for Sri Lanka. The e-Sri Lanka roadmap resulted in the implementation of the ICT Act No. 27 of 2003, which resulted in the establishment of the Information and Communication Technology Agency of Sri Lanka, (ICTA. The mandate of the e-Sri Lanka policy is to build a national information infrastructure, create a framework for the promotion of software and ICT enabled industries, re-engineering the Government and developing ICT-based human resources[17]. *Note: Information infrastructure development, re-engineering of the government, and human resource development are basic ingredients of local e-government development.*

National ICT Strategies towards e-Governance

By taking the opportunities of ubiquitous utilization of ICTs, governments formulated ICT policies and strategies for e-development (rather, e-enhanced development) focusing social and economic development, poverty reduction and foremost the improvement of governance system (Bajwa, 2003; Sarker, 2005; Butt & Sarker, 2009). This research supports this by presenting Table 1 where it has been revealed that initiation of ICT policies and strategies are essential element for overall elevation of ICT platform in a country. It further argues that a long term vision is crucial for sustainable growth of e-governance.

E-GOVERNMENT INDEX (E-GOVERNMENT READINESS INDEX AND RANKING)

Governments are increasingly becoming aware of the importance of employing e-government and e-governance in improving public service delivery to people. The potential of e-government, as a tool for development, hinges upon three pre-requisites-a minimum threshold level of information infrastructure, human capital, and e-connectivity for all. To support the development efforts of UN member states' efforts in e-government the United Na-

tions Department of Economic and Social Affairs (UNDESA) undertook to produce the United Nations Global E-government Surveys (which ranks them through the e-government readiness index) to gauge the comparative state of e-government development in a rapidly globalizing world (UN, 2001). For this parameter, data was taken from the Global E-government Surveys conducted by the United Nations (UN, 2001; 2003; 2004; 2005; 2008). As observed from Table 2, most of the SAARC countries are showing positive trend in their e-government readiness ranking, however, Maldives has taken the lead.

THE SYNTHESIS AND FUTURE RESEARCH

The overall finding of this study has been highlighted with marked texts and notes. However, as the synthesis, this study likes to emphasize on the role of the GDP growth; the growth of Internet and its users; the information infrastructure providing better services through fixed and cellular phones; simplified but transparent and interactive (vertical and longitudinal) governance structure; and effective ICT policies and strategies are essential for strengthening e-governance in a country.

As evident from the governance structure, the top-bottom and bottom-top interactive governance structure with over two tiers to reach the local

Table 1. Years of initiation of ICT policies, acts, and related laws in SAARC countries

	AF	BD	BT	IN	MV	NP	PK	SL
ICT Policy	2003	2002 2008*	2004 2006*	1998	2003	2000	2000	1983[18]
Telecom Act/ Law/ Policy	2005	2001	1999	1999	2001 2006*	1997	1996	1991
National ICT Council	2005	1990	1999[19]	1971[20]	1998	2002[21]	2000	1984 2003*
ICT Act		2006 2009*	2004	2000	2003			2003
ICT Master Plan			2001					

Note: (*) This table is based on exhaustive literature review and may subject to any authentication of years indicated.

Table 2. E-government index/e-government readiness index of SAARC countries

Country	EGI*	EGI		EGRI#		EGRI		EGRI	
	2001	2003		2004		2005		2008	
	Index	Index	Rank	Index	Rank	Index	Rank	Index	Rank
Afghanistan	-	0.118	168	0.1337	171	0.1490	168	0.2048	167
Bangladesh	0.90	0.165	159	0.1788	159	0.1762	162	0.2936	142
Bhutan	-	0.157	161	0.1590	165	0.2941	130	0.3074	134
India	1.29	0.385	87	0.3879	86	0.4001	87	0.3814	113
Maldives	0.93	0.410	79	0.4106	78	0.4321	77	0.4491	95
Nepal	0.94	0.268	130	0.2807	132	0.3021	126	0.2725	150
Pakistan	1.04	0.247	137	0.3042	122	0.2836	136	0.3160	131
Sri Lanka	0.92	0.385	84	0.3748	96	0.3950	94	0.4244	101
Total countries	133		173		178		179		182

*EGI- E-government Index; #EGRI- E-government Readiness Index (Source: UN)

level of the government is significant in this region and similarly population establishes an essential element in distinguishing government management structure. This research finds these as the pre-conditions for the grass roots governance; however, further in-depth studies may be carried out to find out other innate intricacies around the e-governance in this region surrounding other facts, such as economy, culture and politics.

This study has found out the effect of the mentioned parameters (ICT policy and strategy, and adoption of them through effective and transparent infrastructure incorporating the government agencies, intermediaries and institutions) on the e-government readiness index ranking in the SAARC countries. For future research, this study suggests observations on broadband penetration; design, development and management of local content in local languages; increased and effective participation on the Internet through knowledge-based content delivery; and simple quantitative analysis on the parameters discussed earlier and parameters mentioned here. Finally, it recommends a thorough study on long-term vision or master plan on e-governance in this region targeting the overall socio-economic progress.

CONCLUSION

This study finds and argues that GDP growth, Internet penetration and other parameters of basic ICT for development have a definitive and positive impact on the overall e-governance development of a country and thus these pre-conditions effectively improves the e-governance readiness ranking promoting grass roots e-governance. However, it has also observes that long-term vision, action plan or master plan is not prevailing in majority of the countries in SAARC region, not in the form of a sustained pattern, which this study infers, as another extremely important pre-condition for sustained e-governance growth, especially at the local level of the government. Therefore, to achieve an efficient and effective e-governance at the grass roots, countries in the region need to come up with sustainable and long term e-governance master plans.

REFERENCES

Accenture. (2009). *From e-Government to e-Governance: Using new technologies to strengthen relationships with citizens.* Accenture, UK.

Anttiroiko, A. (2004). Towards citizen-centered local e-government: The case of the city of Tampere. In Khosrow-Pour, M. (Ed.), *Annals of cases on information technology* (*Vol. 6*, pp. 371–388). Hershey, PA: Idea Group Publishing.

As-Saber, S. N., & Hossain, K. (2008). Call centres and their role in e-governance: A developing country perspective. *The Journal of Community Informatics*, *4*(3).

Austin City Council. (2008). *Audit report 2008: City of Austin's e-government initiative.* Austin, TX: Office of the City Auditor.

Bajwa, S. B. (2003). ICT policy in India in the era of liberalisation: Its impact and consequences. *Global Built Environment Review*, *3*(2), 49–61.

Baryamureeba, V. (2005). *State of ICT and Local Governance, Needs Analysis and Research Priorities in Uganda.* 3-5 September 2005, Nairobi Kenya.

Bavec, C., & Vintar, M. (2007). What matters in the development of the e-government in the EU? In Wimmer, M. A., Jochen Scholl, H., & Anke, G. (Eds.), *Electronic government* (pp. 424–435). Berlin, Germany: Springer. doi:10.1007/978-3-540-74444-3_36

Butt, D., & Sarker, P. P. (2009). ICT for development in Asia Pacific: Emerging themes in a diverse region. In *Digital Review of Asia Pacific 2009-2010* (pp. 3–13). Orbicom and the International Development Research Centre.

Chapagain, D. P. (12-14 December 2007). *Regional overview of policy and legislations on provision of ICT access for disadvantaged communities through public-private partnership.* Expert Group Meeting on the Provision of ICT Access for Disadvantaged Communities through Public-Private Partnership, Bangkok

Chutimaskul, W., & Chongsuphajaisiddhi, V. (2004). A framework for developing local e-government. In M. A. Wimmer (Ed.), *Proceedings of Knowledge Management in Electronic Government: 5th IFIP International Working Conference*, KMGov 2004, Krems, Austria, May 17-19, 2004 (pp. 319-324).

Commission of the European Communities. (2009). *Europe's Digital Competitiveness Report, Vol. 1: i2010 — Annual Information Society Report 2009 and Benchmarking i2010: Trends and main achievements.* Commission of the European Communities, Brussels.

Commonwealth. (2004). *Commonwealth local government handbook: Modernisation, Council structures, finance, e-government, local democracy, partnerships, representation.* Commonwealth Local Government Forum, Commonwealth Secretariat, 2004.

CTG. (2002). *New foundations: Annual report 2002.* Center for Technology in Government, University at Albany, State University of New York.

CTG. (2003). *Annual report 2003.* Center for Technology in Government, University at Albany, State University of New York.

CTO. (2008). *Towards effective e-governance: The delivery of public services through local e-content.* Global Summary Report, Commonwealth Telecommunications Organization.

Das, S. R., & Chandrashekhar, R. (2006). *List of Asia Pacific e-government case studies. UNDP-APDIP, Digital Review of Asia Pacific 2005/2006.* UNDP-APDIP.

Duggal, P. (2005). Harmonization of e-commerce laws and regulatory systems in South Asia. In TID (Ed.), *Harmonized development of legal and regulatory systems for e-commerce in Asia and the Pacific: Current challenges and capacity-building needs* (pp. 23-36). New York, NY: UN Publications.

Ebrahim, Z., & Irani, Z. (2005). E-government adoption: Architecture and barriers. *Business Process Management Journal, 11*(5), 589–611. doi:10.1108/14637150510619902

EC. (2010). *Europe's digital competitiveness report: Main achievements of the i2010 strategy 2005-2009.* Luxembourg: European Commission.

Fox, W. F., & Gurley, T. (2006, May). *Will consolidation improve sub-national governments?* (World Bank Policy Research Working Paper WPS3913). Washington, DC: World Bank.

Galpaya, H., Samarajiva, R., & Soysa, S. (2007). Taking e-government to the bottom of the pyramid: Dial-a-gov? *Proceedings of the 1st International Conference on Theory and Practice of Electronic Governance,* Vol. 232 (pp. 233-241). Macao, China: ACM.

Gessi, T., Ramnarine, D., & Wilkins, J. (2007). Introducing a new e-governance framework in the commonwealth: From theory to practice. *The Asia Pacific Journal of Public Administration, 29*(2), 131–151.

Government of Afghanistan. (2003a). *Afghanistan telecommunications and Internet policy.*

Government of Afghanistan. (2003b). *Information and communications technology policy.*

Government of Afghanistan. (2005, April). *Afghanistan country report: Telecommunications, Ministry of Communications.*

Government of Bhutan. (2003). *Information and communications technology (ICT) policy for Bhutan: A White Paper.* Ministry of Information and Communications, Royal Government of Bhutan, Thimphu; Bhutan.

Government of Bhutan. (2006). *Technical guidelines on information and communications technology (ICT) for preparation of the tenth five year plan (2008-2013). August 2006.* Thimphu, Bhutan: Ministry of Information and Communications, Royal Government of Bhutan.

Government of Bhutan. (2007). *Information, communications and transport sectors in Bhutan: A Special Report. July 2007.* Thimphu, Bhutan: Ministry of Information and Communications, Royal Government of Bhutan.

Government of India. (2000). *The Information Technology Act 2000.* Ministry of Communications and Information Technology/Dept of IT.

Government of India. (2006). *Information Technology: Annual report 2006-2007.* Ministry of Communications and Information Technology/ Dept of IT.

Government of Jordan. (2006). *Jordan e-government-2006: E-government strategy. Jordan e-Government Program, Ministry of Information and Communications technology (MoICT).* Government of Jordan.

Government of Maldives. (2001). *Maldives telecommunication policy 2001-2005.* Ministry of Communication, Science and Technology, Maldives, 1 August 2001.

Government of Maldives. (2002). *Maldives government information technology initiative – The progress.* A paper at the 2nd APT Meeting on Asia-Pacific Initiatives for the Information Society (AIIS), 5-9 August 2002, Negara, Burunai Darussalam, Post & Telecom, Ministry of Communication, Science & Technology, Government of Maldives.

Government of Maldives. (2003). *E-Maldives: The Republic of Maldives national information and communications technology policy.* Ministry of Communication, Science and Technology. Draft. 2003.

Government of Maldives. (2006) *Maldives telecommunication policy 2006-2010: Towards one island nation through effective telecommunications.* Minister of Transport & Communication, 1 August 2006.

Hanna, N. K. (2003). *Why national strategies are needed for ICT-enabled development.* ISG Staff Working Papers No. 3

Heeks, R. (2006). *Implementing and managing e-government.* Vistaar Publications.

Hoogwout, M. (2003). super pilots, subsidizing or self-organization: Stimulating e-government initiatives in Dutch local governments. In R. Traunmüller (Ed.), *Proceedings of Electronic Government: Second International Conference,* (pp. 85-90). EGOV 2003, Prague, Czech Republic, September 1-5, 2003, Springer. i4D. (2005) E-government: Evolution or revolution? *Information for Development (i4D), 3*(6). infoDev. (2010). *High-speed Internet drives economic growth.* Retrieved November 18, 2010, from http://www.infodev.org /en/Article.522.html

Ilyas, A. (2004). *Statistics and indicators on ICTs in Maldives.* Global Indicators Workshop on Community Access to ICTs, Mexico City, 16-19 November 2004.

Jurmi, K. (2004). *A paper on Bhutan's information and communication technology.* 1st International Conference by the Italian Chamber of Deputies, 6 & 7 Oct. 2004, Rome, Italy.

Kolsaker, A. (2005). Third way e-government: The case for local devolution. In M. H. Böhlen, J. Gamper, W. Polasek, & M. A. Wimmer (Eds.), *Proceedings of E-Government: Towards Electronic Democracy: International Conference,* TCGOV 2005 Bolzano, Italy, March 2-4, 2005, (pp. 70-80). Springer.

Labelle, R. (2005). *ICT policy formulation and e-strategy development: A comprehensive guidebook. United Nations Development Programme-Asia Pacific Development Information Programme.* UNDP-APDIP.

Lallana, E. C. (2003). *Comparative analysis of ICT polices and e-strategies in Asia.* A presentation at the Asian Forum on ICT Policies and e-Strategies, 20-22 October, Kuala Lumpur: UNDP-APDIP.

Lallana, E. C. (2004). *An overview of ICT policies and e-strategies of select Asian economies. United Nations Development Programme-Asia Pacific Development Information Programme (UNDP-APDIP) – 2004.* Reed Elsevier India Private Limited.

Lau, E. (2005). *E-government and the drive for growth and equity. Belfer Center for Science and International Affairs (BCSIA).* Harvard University.

Malhotra, C., Chariar, V. M., Das, L. K., & Ilavarasan, P. V. (2007). ICT for rural development: An inclusive framework for e-Governance. In Sahu, G. P. (Ed.), *Adopting e-governance* (pp. 216–226). New Delhi, India: GIFT Publishing.

Mendel, T. D. (2009). *Assessment of media development in the Maldives: Based on UNESCO's media development indicators* (p. 24). UNESCO.

Nguyen, A. (2007). *Public information network as computing and e-government infrastructure in developing countries.* Invited talk at the 7th Global Forum on Reinventing Government: Building Trust in Government, Vienna, Austria, June 2007.

Pattakos, A. N. (2004). The search for meaning in government service. *Public Administration Review, 64*(1), 106–112. doi:10.1111/j.1540-6210.2004.00350.x

Paul, S. (2007). A case study of e-governance initiatives in India. *The International Information & Library Review, 39*(3-4), 176–184. doi:10.1016/j.iilr.2007.06.003

Perotti, E. C., & von Thadden, E.-L. (2006). Corporate governance and the distribution of wealth: A political-economy perspective. [JITE]. *Journal of Institutional and Theoretical Economics, 162*(1), 204–217. doi:10.1628/093245606776166660

Pertrazzini, B. A., & Harindranath, G. (1997). Information infrastructure initiative in emerging economies: The case of India. In Kahin, B., & Wilson, E. (Eds.), *National information infrastructure initiatives: Vision and policy design* (p. 220). Cambridge, MA: MIT Press.

Prates, C. A. (2001). *E-government – Realising the benefits of Information Technologies and improving public services delivering. A paper presented on the seminars preceding the III Global Forum – Fostering Democracy and Development through e-government*. Naples.

Rahman, H. (2007). Role of ICTs in socioeconomic development and poverty reduction. In Rahman, H. (Ed.), *Information and communication technologies for economic and regional developments* (pp. 188–219). Hershey, PA: Idea Group Inc. doi:10.4018/9781599041865.ch010

Rahman, H. (2008). An overview on strategic ICT implementations toward developing knowledge societies. In Rahman, H. (Ed.), *Developing successful ICT strategies: Competitive advantages in a global knowledge-driven society* (pp. 1–39). New York, NY: Information Science Reference.

Rahman, H. (2010). Local e-government management: A wider window of e-governance. In Rahman, H. (Ed.), *Handbook of research on e-government readiness for information and service exchange: Utilizing progressive information communication technologies* (pp. 295–323). Hershey, PA: IGI Global.

Reddi, U. V., & Sinha, V. (2003). ICT use in education. In Farrell, G., & Wachholz, C. (Eds.), *Metasurvey on the use of technologies in education in Asia and the Pacific 2003-2004* (pp. 253–265). Maldives: UNESCO.

Reddick, C. G. (2004). Empirical models of e-government growth in local governments. *e-Service Journal, 3*(2), 59-84

Sarker, S. (2005). ICT policy: Perspectives and challenges. *Information for Development, 3*(6), 6–7.

Sayo, P., Chacko, J. G., & Pradhan, G. (Eds.). (2004). *ICT policies and e-strategies in the Asia-Pacific: A critical assessment of the way forward. United Nations Development Programme-Asia Pacific Development Information Programme (UNDP-APDIP) – 2004*. Reed Elsevier India Private Limited.

UN. (2001). *Benchmarking e-government: A global perspective-Assessing the UN Member States*. New York, NY: United Nations.

UN. (2003). *Global e-government survey 2003: E-government at the crossroads*. New York, NY: United Nations.

UN. (2004). *Global e-government readiness report: Towards access for opportunity*. New York, NY: United Nations.

UN. (2005). *Global e-government readiness report: From e-government to e-inclusion*. New York, NY: United Nations.

UN. (2008). *United Nations e-government survey 2008: From e-government to connected governance*. New York, NY: United Nations.

UNDP. (2002). *Information and communications technology policy for Afghanistan*. Final Report, Asia-Pacific Development Information Programme, UN Development Programme, October 2002.

UNESCAP (Ed.). (1999). *Local government in Asia and the Pacific: A comparative study of fifteen countries*. Bangkok, Thailand: UN Economic and Social Commission for Asia and the Pacific (UNESCAP).

UNESCAP. (2003). *Country reports on local government systems*. Pakistan: United Nations Economic and Social Commission for Asia and Pacific.

Van Den, B. L., Van Der, M. L., Van, W. W., & Woets, P. (2006). *E-governance in European and South African cities: The cases of Barcelona, Cape Town, Eindhoven, Johannesburg, Manchester, Tampere, The Hague, and Venice*. Ashgate Publishing, Ltd.

van den Bergh, J. C. J. M. (2007). *Abolishing GDP Tinbergen Institute discussion paper. TI 2007-019/3*. Vrije Universiteit Amsterdam, and Tinbergen Institute.

Wentz, L., Kramer, F., & Starr, S. (2008). *Information and communication technologies for reconstruction and development: Afghanistan challenges and opportunities*. Washington, DC: Center for technology and National Security Policy, National Defense University.

Zwahr, T., Rossel, P., & Finger, M. (2005). Towards electronic governance – A case study of ICT in local government governance. *Proceedings of 2005 International Conference on Digital Government Research*, Atlanta, May 15-18, 2005.

KEY TERMS AND DEFINITIONS

E-Governance: A network of organizations or institutions to include government, nonprofit, and private-sector entities for establishing electronic form of governance.

E-Governance Framework: A form of standardized pattern incorporating policy, governance and infrastructure of the government to facilitate the e-government system.

E-Government: A form of delivery of the government services and information through electronic means such as the internet, digital television and other digital technologies to create a comfortable, transparent, and cheap interaction between government and citizens (G2C – government to citizens), government and business.

E-Readiness: The capability of a nation or an entity to use information and communication technologies (ICTs) to widen one's economy and to foster one's welfare.

E-Readiness Ranking: A form of accepted bench marking across the countries of the world utilizing different parameters as the index rank.

Local Government: The lowest infrastructural tier of a government system, which incorporate a county, city, city and county, special district, joint powers agency or other political subdivision of a country or state.

ENDNOTES

1. Google definition
2. https://www.cia.gov/library/publications/the-world-factbook/geos/af.html
3. Each Provincial Council elects one of its members to the House of Elders under a two-round system (4-year term). Each District Council elects one of its members to the House of Elders under a two-round system (3-year term).
4. http://www.electionguide.org/country.php?ID=2
5. http://www.unescap.org/huset/lgstudy/newcountrypaper/Bangladesh/Bangladesh.pdf
6. http://www.mongabay.com/reference/country_studies/bhutan/GOVERNMENT.html
7. http://www.india.gov.in/knowindia/state_uts.php
8. http://en.wikipedia.org/wiki/ Administrative_divisions_of_India; http://www.oifc.in/ViewFolder.aspx?FolderName=Understanding_the_States&FolderID=65
9. http://www.statoids.com/umv.html
10. http://en.wikipedia.org/wiki/Maldives
11. http://www.unescap.org/huset/lgstudy/newcountrypaper/Nepal/Nepal.pdf
12. http://www.unescap.org/huset/lgstudy/newcountrypaper/Pakistan/Pakistan.pdf
13. http://www.unescap.org/huset/lgstudy/newcountrypaper/SriLanka/SriLanka.pdf
14. http://www.bcc.net.bd/

15   http://www.apdip.net/projects/dig-rev/info/pk/

16   http://www.apdip.net/projects/dig-rev/info/pk/

17   http://www.ifip.or.at/minutes/GA2005/Rep_SriLanka1.pdf

18   National Computer Policy Report

19   Division of Information Technology (DIT)

20   Department of Electronics (DoE)

21   National Information Technology Center (NITC)

Chapter 10

Evaluating Web Sites of Municipal Corporations:
A Case Study of Leading Cities in India

Muneesh Kumar
University of Delhi South Campus, India

Mamta Sareen
University of Delhi, India

ABSTRACT

While evaluation of government websites has been a matter of interest for researchers, the perspectives and parameters of such evaluation used in these have been diverse. It is primarily because the evaluated web sites had different objectives and only a general matrix could be used for their assessment. Fortunately, web sites of Municipal Corporations have a unique advantage in this respect. The kind of information needs and citizen services required in different cities do not differ significantly in most cases. In this chapter, an attempt has been made to evaluate municipal websites of twenty major cities in India. It also examines the relationship between the income levels of the city and the quality of municipal website. While the glaring differences were observed among municipal web sites of different cities, no significant relationship could be established between the quality of municipal websites and income levels in the city.

INTRODUCTION

One of the major tasks of any e-government initiatives is to improve citizen's access to public information and services. The increasing use of

DOI: 10.4018/978-1-60960-863-7.ch010

Enterprise Resource Planning (ERP) Systems in e-government is shifting the focus of such initiative to internal integration of processes. However, any e-government initiative with focus on optimization of internal processes will serve only a limited purpose. Rather, use of ERP systems should enable governments to provide a more effective platform for delivery of information and service to citizen more conveniently and in a transparent manner. The channel used for providing access to information and services is generally a web site/ portal. Despite the increased use of ERP systems by governments for this purpose, the gap between the information needs and available information in digital form remains significant. The information gap is compounded by the inefficiencies in the content and design of the web interfaces of e-governance initiatives. Though most of the e-government initiatives in different countries have made extensive use of Internet technologies and infrastructure in developing their web interface, the success in its effective use is far from satisfactory (Welch, Hinnant and Moon, 2005; Jones et al. 2006). Thus, the need for evaluating e-government web sites and constant improvement in them cannot be over-emphasized.

While evaluation of government websites has been a matter of interest for researchers, the perspectives and parameters of such evaluation used in these have been diverse. It is primarily because, the evaluated web sites had different objectives and only a general matrix could be used for their assessment. Fortunately, web sites of Municipal Corporations (local governments) have a unique advantage in this respect. The kind of information needs and citizen services required in different cities do not differ significantly in most cases. In this chapter, an attempt has been made to evaluate municipal websites of twenty major cities in India. It also examines relationship between the income levels of the city and the quality of municipal website.

BACKGROUND

The day-to-day interactions of citizens with the government relate to the mundane governance activities that are primarily in the domain of municipal corporations that are responsible for development and maintenance of common services and facilities. As citizens use these common services extensively and on regular basis, their perceptions about and relationship with local government are influenced by the way the information and services are delivered. It is, therefore, imperative for any government to provide for delivery of services promptly and without any major inconvenience. These web sites have the potential to improve relations with citizens and reverse the trend of declining trust in governments (Nye, 1997). While the craze, among governments at various levels, for use of e-government initiatives as a tool for improving service quality is on, the issue is whether and to what extent this objective is actually achieved.

The evaluation of web sites of Municipal Corporations and comparisons overtime can help in assessing not only the change in the quality of these web sites but also helps in gauging the level of commitment of the local government in improving its citizens services and access to information. This chapter focuses on the evaluation municipal websites of 20 major cities in India

Related Work

A number of studies have attempted to assess the websites in general (Nielsen, 2000; Alexander and Tate, 1999; Bauer and Scharl, 2000). These studies quality of website can be assessed on the basis of a number of characteristic features relating to information content, navigation, design and general appearance, accessibility, security and relevance of information. Methods and tools have also been proposed to facilitate the process of web site assessment. Wang et al. (2005) suggest the dimensions that may be used for evaluation of web sites and also identifies the factors responsible for observed success or failure of a web site. A few recent studies also attempted to evaluation of web sites for different segments such as e-commerce web sites (Oppenheim and Ward, 2006; Basu, 2002; Huang et al., 2006, Kumar and Sareen, 2010), academic and e-learning web sites (Olsina et al., 1999; Buenadicha et al. 2001, Bu ¨yu ¨ko ¨zkan et al., 2007) and healthcare services web sites (Bilsel et al., 2006 Welch and Pandey, 2007;). There have been a few studies that focused on framework for evaluation of e-Government web site as well (Middleton, 2007, Miranda et. al., 2009)

A few studies have also focused specifically on evaluating web sites of local bodies, (popularly called Municipal Corporations in India and in many other countries). Some of these studies were country specific (Aramouni, Pando & Calamari, 2006; Sandoval-Almazan & Gil-Garcia, 2010), while others attempted international comparisons (Melitski, et al. 2005, Rodríguez, 2008). Though each of these studies used a diverse set of criteria for assessment of these web sites, common set of concepts in this regard can easily be observed in these studies. Some of the leading studies are discussed in the following paragraphs.

Based on the experiences of e-commerce web sites and the factors commonly used for their evaluation, Wood et al. (2003), suggested use of a multidimensional web evaluation strategy focusing on usability testing, user feedback, usage data, and web and Internet performance, etc.

Wang et al. (2005) emphasized on citizen centric approach in design and evaluation of e-government web sites and proposed and tested a model for evaluation of e-government services. Though, the model was designed for performance evaluation of an e-government system, it also serves as a tool for understanding why e-government websites succeed or fail in achieving their objectives.

Parajuli (2007) used factors like transparency, interactivity, accessibility, and usability to evaluate ministerial websites of Nepal. A number of weaknesses in most of the ministerial web sites and suggested establishment of standards for web site design in order to ensure that exploit and also continuously evolve citizens' information needs and expectations are met.

Alshawi et al (2007) identified various issues in evaluation of e-government websites under three broad categories namely the technical issues, the economical issues, and the social issues. While the technical issues relate to performance and accessibility; the economical issues primarily consisted of cost saving. The social issue related to trust. The study used 'openness' and 'perceived ease of use' and 'usefulness' for evaluation of e-government websites.

Perhaps one of the most comprehensive studies in this regard is the one by West (2008). It analyzed 1,667 government websites in 98 nations using 18 measures. These measures related to volume of available information, degree of interaction with users, and updation of information. The findings indicated that much needs to be done to reach the desired levels in this regard. The study ranked North America and Africa ranked at the top and the bottom respectively, of the list.

Holzer et. al (2008) examined the municipal websites of a sample of 98 world cities, and classified them, using cluster analysis, into four types:

1. digitally mature cities,
2. digitally moderate cities,
3. digitally minimal cities, and
4. digitally marginal cities.

The evaluation factors included security and privacy; usability; content; services; and citizen participation. The gap between OECD and non-OECD member countries in average scores was found to be significant and widening.

The framework for evaluation of web sites of public authorities proposed by Panopaulou et al. (2008) consisted of four axes. The first two related to assessment of general characteristics and content of the web sites while the other two focused on assessment of specific functionalities. The general characteristics axis focused on information availability, ease of use, feedback process and privacy concerns. The e-content axis referred to the web site's general content, specific content and news and updating aspect of the websites. The e-services axis focused on availability of public services online. The e-participation primarily related to opportunity for public participation in decision-making processes of the public authority. Their model measured only a predetermined set of services.

Miranda et al. (2009) evaluated 84 European municipal web sites using a model that focused on four categories of factors: accessibility, speed, navigability and content to access the quality of web pages. Their findings highlighted the variation in the value of the index that exists within Europe as some of the web sites of European cities were only in the beginning in terms of functionality. For example, it was observed that only 44.7 percent of the web sites offered feedback tools for users and 38.82 percent offered contact information.

MAIN FOCUS OF THE CHAPTER

There are an increasing number of governments investing in Enterprise Resource Planning (ERP) systems as their basic technological infrastructure for e-government. The major objectives include integrating various information systems, achieve process efficiencies and enable online services and citizen relationship management (Raymond et al., 2005). The success in effective delivery of public services and information online depends, to a great extent, upon the quality of the web interface of such projects.

Issues and Problems

Though, there is growing body of literature on evaluation of quality of e-government sites in general and municipal web sites in particular, there are no standard measure for evaluation of such web sites (Wei et al., 2009). In fact, quite diverse dimensions/categories of factors have been considered while evaluating such web sites. Another issue relates to the weighting system used

in the process of evaluation. This chapter focuses on the framework for evaluation of municipal web sites and the also uses the proposed framework in evaluation of the websites of 20 top cities in India.

Solutions and Recommendations

A number of dimensions/categories of factors have been considered in the assessment of websites in general and e-government websites in particular. However, there seems to be convergence of thoughts on few of these dimensions in so far as assessment of e-government web sites is concerned. These dimensions include content, navigation, transparency, interactivity, accessibility, and usability. Table 1 presents a brief description of these dimensions and the studies that used them in the assessment of the websites of public authorities.

A combination of these dimensions could be used to build a framework for evaluation of e-government websites. It may be noticed that the above dimensions are from the prospective of the citizen user and are related to the effectiveness of websites in meeting the information and service needs of the user. In that sense, they define the quality of the web site. A number of factors could be considered under each of these dimensions for the purposes of assessing the quality of the websites. A brief description of the factors considered under each of the dimensions has been presented in the following paragraphs.

Content: One of the primary motives of any citizen visiting any municipal website is to obtain relevant information regarding the services and the facilities available. The factors that determine the quality of website content include completeness (Miranda et al, 2009; West, 2007; Henriksson et al., 2006), relevance, accuracy, reliability (Garcia et al., 2005; Smith, 2001), and consistency (Garcia et al., 2005; Smith, 2001). The content should also be well structured in order to effectively convey the information (Radha and Murphy, 1992; Gay et al., 1991: Utting and Yankelovich, 1989; Mo-

Table 1. *Dimensions used in assessment of municipal websites*

Dimension	Description	Researchers Contribution
Content	Relevance and Structure of information	West (2007); Henriksson et al. (2006), Garcia et al. (2005); Holzer and Kim (2005); Smith (2001); Radha and Murphy (1992);
Navigation	Ability to effectively navigate around the site in search of required information	Olsina et al. (2008), Henriksson et al. (2006), Garcia et al. (2005); Merwe and Bekker (2003); Basu (2002); Smith (2001); Bauer and Scharl (2000);
Transparency	Availability of decisions/ guidelines /rulings/ reports etc.	Blakemore et al (2007) ; Parajuli (2007) ; Akkermann et al (2004) ; Phillips (2001); Zhu K.(2002);
Interactivity	Coexistence and convergence of various means to interact with users	UN (2005); Phillips (2001); Norris (2001); Misic and Johnson (1999);
Accessibility	Being easy to meet or deal with the web site	West (2007); Henriksson et al. (2006), Holzer and Kim (2005); Garcia et al. (2005); Henry (2002); Smith (2001);
Usability	Determines the structure of navigational ease and search engine effectiveness.	Middleton (2007); Melitski et al (2005); Tolbert and Mossberger (2003) Nielson (2000); Newman and Landay (2000); Shubin and Meehan (1997);

hageg, 1992). Suitable graphics or photographs without much self-congratulatory phrases help in improving the comprehension of information.

Navigation: As the website consists of large number of web pages, its quality to a large extent depends upon the way one can navigate through these pages. No amount of "sparkle" in the website can overcome the weakness of poor navigation features (Lohse, 1999). According to Nielsen J. (1999), a good navigation system should answer three questions: 'where am I? Where have I been? Where can I go?' The site's navigation system should answer all three questions very clearly. The navigation should be such that when visitors navigate through the site, they end up where the site hoped they would (Prigent, 1996), finding what they were looking for, or are they hitting a "dead end" in the chosen navigation route. Consistency in terms of layout, coloring and terminology (Miranda et al, 2009; Henriksson et al., 2006; Garcia et al., 2005; Smith, 2001;) makes navigation more effective. Moreover, features like navigation menus (Smith, 2001) and site maps (Panopaulou et al, 2008; Holzer and Kim, 2005; Smith, 2001; Henriksson et al., 2006) also play an important role in determining the quality of navigation. Another factor in this regard is the availability of

web site's internal search engine. These internal search engines serve as a useful navigational aid for those sites that contain large volumes of information (Alexander and Tate, 1999; Gehrke and Turban, 1999), as they provide an easy and quick way for locating the information sought for.

Transparency: Transparency is defined as the degree of visibility and accessibility of information (Zhu K., 2004). In the website of public authority, information transparency is essential and would primarily relate to the availability of the information regarding laws/rulings/policies/notifications/ guideline/previous decisions/reports/ press releases etc. A regularly updated and fresh site shows the seriousness of the public authority in disseminating and sharing timely information with the citizens and adds to the transparency and openness in the decision-making (Akkermann et al, 2004). According to Kim, et al., (1999), the "currency of information" as measured by the frequency of update, freshness, and maintenance of the site also add to the transparency dimension. Display of site statistics is another important factor in determining the transparency of any website.

Interactivity: An effective municipal website must provide opportunities/possibilities of interaction of the user/citizen with the concerned public authority. A number of factors determine the interactivity of a municipal website. These would include availability of online contact details (Misic and Johnson, 1999), possibility of citizens to communicate through Chats/Blogs/eForums (Phillips, 2001; UN, 2005), participation in discussion forums/opinion polls/bulletin boards (Moon, 2002), availability of other contact details of the different departments, facility for citizens requesting additional information regarding the public services, etc.

Accessibility: Accessibility means that users are able to find information quickly and easily. It makes it easy for users to extract needed information; provide clues that reduce the efforts by users to find the required information. Accessibility dimension reflects the inclusive approach of the public authority and is a feature of the web site that extends its use to various categories of users in more situations (Terry Ma, and Zaphiris, 2003). Specifically, it can be accessed by people of different physical abilities (West, 2007; Garcia et al., 2005; Holzer and Kim, 2005; Henriksson et al., 2006; Smith, 2001;), having different technical compatibilities in terms of both hardware and software (Henriksson et al., 2006; Smith, 2001). Citizens/users with different linguistic backgrounds should be able to access the information from various municipal websites (West, 2007; Henriksson et al., 2006; Holzer and Kim, 2005). In order words, municipal websites should be accessible to all regardless of expertise, personality, literacy, ethnicity, and disability (Shneiderman, 2000; Zahedi, Pelt, and Song, 2001). Another important factor that enhances accessibility of a website is its high ranking in popular search engines (Miranda et al., 2009). Features such as Frequently Asked Questions (FAQs) and text-only option also help in improving the accessibility of the website. The site that insists on use of any particular software of accessing information reduces accessibility unless it also provides a link for downloading that software.

Usability: Usability is the measure of the ease of use and convenience in interaction with the web interface. Primarily, usability of a web site is enhanced by features that improve the quality of user experience. Usability has also been defined as the characteristic of a web site that makes the visit of the user effective, whatever their interests and needs, by removing barriers (Sweden Canada Link, 2001). "A good user experience is one where a user achieves his/her goals and is highly satisfied with the process; it encourages reuse and recommendation of the site. If a website does not have usability quality, the user would generally, leave the site and may not come back again to visit the web site. Melitski et al. (2005) found usability as one of the major factors in the evaluation of e-government websites. A number of factors determine the usability of the website. In the context of municipal web sites, factors like good contrast that enhances the readability, legibility of site with respect to font size and type aspect, uniformity of terminology throughout the site (Middleton, 2007), grammatical correctness, due emphasis on more relevant information with a combination of header tags, bold type, color, or lists, clean and tidy look with text and images aligned, determine the usability of a municipal website. Moreover, consistency in colors, style, fonts, typography, or layout that makes the visitor understand that they are moving through separate pages with different information of the same website. Facility of filling online forms wherever possible also improves usability of a website.

EVALUATION OF MUNICIPAL WEBSITES: A CASE STUDY OF SELECT INDIAN CITIES

In this chapter, an attempt has been made to make an assessment of municipal web sites of select Indian cities using the framework for evaluation as described above. The evaluation is based on the data collected during a survey of the municipal web sites of twenty top Indian cities. These twenty cities had the highest annual household income in the country according to a study by National Council of Applied Economic Research (NCEAR)[1]. These cities collectively account for almost one-third of India's disposable income and generate around 60% of India's surplus income and also accounted for almost $100 billion of consumption expenditure in 2007-08.

The Instrument

A spreadsheet describing the above six dimensions and the relevant factor under each of these dimensions was developed as an instrument of data collection during the survey of the select municipal websites. In total forty items each representing a factor that determines the quality of the municipal web site, were included in the instrument. With regard to the item scoring, each dimension was awarded 10 points which were equally distributed among the factors describing that dimension. In order to avoid the evaluator's subjectivity, the items were designed in a manner that permitted only standardized/quantitative assessment.

In order to test the independence of the six dimensions of an effective municipal web site, Spearman's rho was calculated. The correlation matrix of the six dimensions is presented in the Table 2.

As may be observed from Table 2, high degree of correlation exists between the scores for each of the dimension with other dimension. The Spearman's correlation co-efficient was found to be greater than 0.5 and statistically significant in all cases with only one exception. This would indicate that the website that scores high on one dimension generally also scores high on other dimensions and vice-versa.

Evaluation

Each sample website was evaluated independently by ten different evaluators for each of the 40 items included in the instrument. The evaluation was carried out during November-December, 2010. The participants were IT savvy in the age range of 30-45 years and came from a variety of background like employees from public sector, employees from private sector, employees from banking sector, employees from education sector and business men. In this manner, each participant gave 40 ratings for each website. Hence, a total of 800 ratings were received from each of the 10 participants (Table 3).

For the purposes of analysis, the average score for each factor has been used.

Table 2. Correlations among various dimensions of municipal website quality

Spearman's rho	Accessibility	Content	Interactivity	Navigation	Transparency	Usability
Accessibility	1.0					
Content	0.559*	1.0				
Interactivity	0.532*	0.769**	1.0			
Navigation	0.663**	0.868**	0.837**	1.0		
Transparency	0.446	0.695**	0.609**	0.814**	1.0	
Usability	0.524*	0.688**	0.747**	0.837**	0.744**	1.0

* Correlation is significant at 0.05 level (2 tailed)

** Correlation is significant at 0.01 level (2 tailed)

Table 3. Basic information about the survey

Attributes	Responses
Number of Websites	20
No. of Participants	10
No. of items to be assessed for each Website	40
Completed Questionnaires	200
Total ratings from each participant	800

Results and Discussions

The descriptive statistics in respect of the mean evaluation scores given by the participants of the survey of municipal websites of leading twenty Indian cities are presented in Table 4.

As may be observed from Table 4, the standard error of mean was found to be fairly low (< 0.6 in all cases) and thus, the means for each of the dimension can be considered to be statistically significant. The mean scores were found to be comparatively lower in case of dimension like accessibility and transparency.

The mean evaluation scores for each of the twenty leading Indian city in each of the dimension are presented in Table 5.

As may be observed from Table 5, cities differ from each other significantly in terms of the total mean score and they range between 10.50 and 49.50. This is inspite of the fact that there is fair amount of uniformity in the information and the services needs of the citizens of the cities. Further,

the significant differences can be observed within each dimension as well.

In order to examine the relationship between the quality of the municipal website and income levels in the city, correlation coefficient was estimated between the total mean scores of the websites and the average annual household income of the city. The Pearson's Coefficient of correlation was found to be 0.403 indicating low degree of correlation. Similar observations can be made from the Table 6, which presents the ranking of the cities on the basis of average annual household income and mean total evaluation scores of their municipal websites. Interesting, significant differences were observed between the rankings on the basis of income and rankings on the basis of average total evaluation scores of their municipal websites.

Thus, it may be concluded that the there is no significant relationship between the quality of municipal website and the income levels of the city. It is perhaps the level of commitment of the local authority for meeting the information and service needs that determine what quality standards maintained in respect of the websites of these authorities.

FUTURE RESEARCH DIRECTIONS

Like any other study of this kind, the analysis presented above suffers from a number of limitations. Limited size of the sample is one of the major

Table 4. Evaluation score for dimensions of websites: select descriptive statistics

Dimension	N	Mean		Standard Deviation
		Statistic	Std Error	Statistic
Accessibility	20	3.6750	0.4635	2.0728
Content	20	6.3250	0.4132	1.8480
Interactivity	20	4.6000	0.4049	1.8108
Navigation	20	6.4500	0.5521	2.4691
Transparency	20	3.5750	0.3601	1.6102
Usability	20	6.6625	0.5670	2.5356

Table 5. Mean evaluation scores for sample cities

CITY	ACCESSIBILITY	CONTENT	INTERACTIVITY	NAVIGATION	TRANSPARENCY	USABILITY	TOTAL
Ahmedabad	2.50	8.00	5.75	8.25	4.25	9.25	38.00
Amritsar	2.00	6.00	3.75	2.25	1.75	2.75	18.50
Bangalore	5.50	6.50	6.00	9.50	5.00	8.75	41.25
Bhopal	7.00	6.00	6.25	6.25	2.50	6.00	34.00
Chandigarh	1.50	6.50	6.50	7.50	4.75	6.25	33.00
Chennai	2.50	5.25	5.25	6.25	3.50	9.50	32.25
Coimbatore	3.00	7.75	5.50	7.50	2.00	4.50	30.25
Delhi	2.50	3.25	3.00	5.25	4.25	7.75	26.00
Faridabad	1.50	2.50	1.00	2.25	0.50	2.75	10.50
Hyderabad	6.50	5.00	5.25	6.75	3.25	8.50	35.25
Jaipur	6.00	7.50	4.00	8.50	6.00	7.00	39.00
Jalandhar	3.00	5.75	2.50	5.00	1.50	4.00	21.75
Kanpur	1.00	5.00	3.00	3.25	1.00	3.25	16.50
Kolkata	6.00	8.75	6.25	9.25	6.00	8.75	45.00
Lucknow	2.50	4.25	4.00	3.75	3.00	3.75	21.25
Ludhiana	2.50	6.25	2.00	4.00	4.00	5.50	24.25
Mumbai	4.50	9.25	6.50	9.00	5.25	9.75	44.25
Nagpur	3.00	6.50	2.25	5.50	4.00	5.75	27.00
Pune	2.50	7.00	6.25	9.00	4.00	9.50	38.25
Surat	8.00	9.50	7.00	10.00	5.00	10.00	49.50
Maximum	**8.00**	**9.50**	**7.00**	**10.00**	**6.00**	**10.00**	**49.50**
Minimum	**1.00**	**2.50**	**1.00**	**2.25**	**0.50**	**2.75**	**10.50**
RANGE	**7.00**	**7.00**	**6.00**	**7.75**	**5.50**	**7.25**	**39.00**

limitations of the above analysis. Another limitation of the study is its India focus. Being a single country study, the opportunities for generalization of its findings would be limited. Similar studies in different parts of the world and at different times may offer different results. The arbitrary weights assigned to different factors, thought determined with consistency, also affect the reliability of results. Similar study with different weighting may not offer similar results. The possibility of subjectivity in evaluation by participants, though expected to be averaged-out, cannot be ruled out and thus may adversely affect the results.

There is increasing research interest in the area of identification of the factors that determine the effectiveness of websites of e-government projects in general and municipal web sites in particular. Unfortunately, most of it has been in form of bit and pieces. No comprehensive study seems to have been made that puts in a complete framework for development and evaluation of municipal web sites. Like this study, a few other studies have also pointed out significant differences in the quality of municipal web site of different cities in the same country and quite similar in income levels. Future research that identifies what factors explain such differences could be very useful in

Table 6. Ranking of sample cities: on basis of income and website quality

S. No.	Cities	Rank based on Avg. Household Income	Rank based on Mean Total Score
1	Ahmedabad	15	14
2	Amritsar	6	3
3	Bangalore	13	17
4	Bhopal	2	12
5	Chandigarh	20	11
6	Chennai	16	10
7	Coimbatore	4	9
8	Delhi	17	7
9	Faridabad	5	1
10	Hyderabad	8	13
11	Jaipur	12	16
12	Jalandhar	11	5
13	Kanpur	1	2
14	Kolkata	10	19
15	Lucknow	9	4
16	Ludhiana	7	6
17	Mumbai	19	18
18	Nagpur	14	8
19	Pune	3	15
20	Surat	18	20

understanding what drives a local government to maintain high quality standards of its web site. Future research may also attempt to provide insight into broad issues of information architecture and the directions of information integration in the public service organizations. The issue of security and privacy continue to haunt the users of web sites in general and public services web sites in particular. As most municipal web sites permit online payment of taxes and other dues from the user, it is essential not only to ensure security and privacy of information, but also to demonstrate it though the web sites using alternative mode. A study devoted to improving understanding of these issues particularly with perspective on trust in the web site may be useful.

CONCLUSION

The findings of this case study suggests that there are significant differences in the quality of municipal web sites of different cities of the same country though the web sites of some of the leading Indian cities score high in respect of content, usability, and navigation. Other cities are falling behind and in general making very little progress in meeting the information and service needs of their citizens and are at the initial stages on the maturity curve, in so far as the effectiveness of their web sites is concerned. These findings are in line with the findings of Miranda et.al. (2009) regarding the municipal websites of cities in Europe.

Like any other study of this kind, the analysis presented above suffers from a number of limitations. Limited size of the sample is one of the major limitations of the above analysis. Another limitation of the study is its India focus. Being a single country study, the opportunities for generalization of its findings would be limited. Similar studies in different parts of the world and at different times may offer different results. The arbitrary weights assigned to different factors, thought determined with consistency, also affect the reliability of results. Similar study with different weighting may not offer similar results. The possibility of subjectivity in evaluation by participants, though expected to be averaged-out, cannot be ruled out and thus may adversely affect the results.

However, the strength of this study lies in identification of a comprehensive list of dimensions/ categories of factors that determine the quality of municipal websites. The examination of relationship between the income in the city and quality of websites is also a unique feature of this analysis and may provoke examination of relationship of quality of websites with other feature of local governments. This chapter is perhaps one of the very few studies that have South Asia context.

REFERENCES

Akkermans, H., Bogerd, P., & van Doremalen, J. (2004). Travail, transparency and trust: a case study of computer-supported collaborative supply chain planning in high-tech electronics. *European Journal of Operational Research*, *153*, 445–456. doi:10.1016/S0377-2217(03)00164-4

Al-awadhi, S., & Morris, A. (2008). The Use of the UTAUT Model in the Adoption of e-Government Services in Kuwait. In *Proceedings of the 41st Hawaii International Conference on System Sciences*. 1-11.

Al-Kibsi, G., de Boer, K., Mourshed, M., & Rea, N. P. (2001). Putting citizens on-line, not in line'. *The McKinsey Quarterly*, *2*, 65–73.

Alexander, J. E., & Tate, M. A. (1999). *Web Wisdom: How to Evaluate and Create Information Quality on the Web*. Mahwah, NJ: Lawrence Erlbaum Associates.

Alshawi, S., Alahmary, A., & Alalwany, H. (2007). E-Government Evaluation Factors: Citizen's Perspective. In *Proceedings of European and Mediterranean Conference on Information Systems* June 2007, Polytechnic University of Valencia, Spain www.emcis.org

Aramouni, G., Pando, D., & Calamari, M. (2006). *Midiendo el Gobierno Electrónico Análisis de Páginas Web Municipales en Argentina*, San Andrés University, Argentina, available at: http://www.udesa.edu.ar/files/cee/e-gov/webs_municip.pdf.

Basu, C. (2002). Context-driven assessment of commercial web sites. In *Proceedings of the 36th Hawaii International Conference on System Sciences*, 6-9 January 2003, Island of Hawaii, (Big Island), available at: www.hicss.hawaii.edu/ HICSS36/HICSSpapers/ INMIW01.pdf.

Bauer, C., & Scharl, A. (2000). Quantitative evaluation of web site content and structure. *Internet Research: Electronic Networking Applications and Policy*, *10*(1), 31–43. doi:10.1108/10662240010312138

Bilsel, R.U., Bu ̈yu ̈ko ̈zkan, G., & Ruan, D. (2006). A fuzzy preference-ranking model for a quality evaluation of hospital web sites. *International Journal of Intelligent Systems*, *21*(11), 1181–1197. doi:10.1002/int.20177

Bu ̈yu ̈ko ̈zkan, G., Ruan, D., & Feyzioglu, O. (2007). Evaluating e-learning web site quality in a fuzzy environment. *International Journal of Intelligent Systems*, *22*, 5, 567-86.

Buenadicha, M., Chamorro, A., & Miranda, F.J., & Gonza ́lez, O.R. (2001). A new web assessment index: Spanish universities analysis. *Internet Research: Electronic Networking Applications and Policy*, *11*(3), 226–234. doi:10.1108/10662240110396469

Garcia, A. C. B., Maciel, C., & Pinto, F. B. (2005). A quality inspection method to evaluate e-government sites. in Wimmer, M.A., Traunmu¨ller, R., Gro¨nlund,A. and Andersen, K.V. (Eds), Electronic Government: 4th International Conference, EGOV 2005, In *Proceedings:Lecture Notes in Computer Science, Vol. 3591,* Copenhagen, Denmark, pp. 198-209, available at: www.informatik.uni-trier.de/, ley/db/conf/egov/egov2005.html.

Henriksson,A., Yi, Y., Frost, B., & Middleton, M. (2007). Evaluation instrument for e-government websites. Electronic Government. *International Journal (Toronto, Ont.), 4*(2), 204–226.

Holzer, M., & Kim, S.-T. (2005). *Digital Governance in Municipalities Worldwide (2005), A Longitudinal Assessment of Municipal Web sites throughout the World.* The e-Governance Institute, available at: http://andromeda.rutgers.edu

Howard, M. (2001). E-Government Across the Globe: How Will 'e' Change Government. *Government Finance Review, 17*(4), 6–9.

Huang, W., Le, T., Li, X., & Gandha, S. (2006). Categorizing web features and functions to evaluate commercial web sites. *Industrial Management & Data Systems, 106*(4), 523–539. doi:10.1108/02635570610661606

Jones, S., Irani, Z., Sharif, A., & Themistocleous, M. (2006). E-government Evaluation: Reflections on Two Organizational Studies. In *Proceedings of the 39th Hawaii International Conference on System Sciences.*

Kim, P., Eng, T. R., Deering, M. J., & Maxfield, A. (1999). Published criteria for evaluating health related Web sites [Review]. *British Medical Journal, 318,* 647–649.

Kumar, M., & Sareen, M. (2009). Building Trust in E-Commerce through Web Interface. *International Journal of ICT and Human Development, 1*(1), 64–74. doi:10.4018/jicthd.2009092205

Lohse, G. L., & Spiller, P. (1998). Electronic Shopping: Quantifying the Effect of Customer Interfaces on Traffic & Sales. *Communications of the ACM,* 417.

Melitski, J. (2005). Digital government worldwide: an e-government assessment of municipal Web sites. *International Journal of Electronic Government Research, 1*(1), 1–19. doi:10.4018/jegr.2005010101

Middleton, M. (2007). Approaches to evaluation of websites for public sector services. In P. Kommers (Ed.), In *Proceedings of the IADIS International Conference,* e-Society 2007, Lisbon, Portugal (pp. 279-284). Lisbon: IADIS.

Miranda, F. J., Sanguino, R., & Bañegil, T. M. (2009). Quantitative assessment of European municipal web sites: Development and use of an evaluation tool. *Internet Research, 19*(4), 425–441. doi:10.1108/10662240910981380

Moon, J.-W., & Kim, Y.-G. (2001). Extending the TAM for a World-Wide-Web Context. *Information & Management, 38,* 217–230. doi:10.1016/S0378-7206(00)00061-6

Nielsen, J. (2000). *Designing Web Usability: The Practice of Simplicity.* Indianapolis, IN: New Riders Publishing.

Nye, J. Jr. (1997). Introduction: The decline of confidence in government. In Nye, J. Jr, Zelikow, P., & King, D. (Eds.), *Why people don't trust government* (pp. 1–18). Cambridge, MA: Harvard University Press.

Olsina, L., Godoy, D., Lafuente, G., & Rossi, G. (1999). Assessing the quality of academic websites. *New Review Hypermedia Multimedia Journal, 5,* 81–103. doi:10.1080/13614569908914709

Oppenheim, C., & Ward, L. (2006). Evaluation of web sites for B2C e-commerce. *Aslib Proceedings, 58*(3), 237–260. doi:10.1108/00012530610701022

Palmer, J. W. (2002). Website usability, design, and performance metrics. *Information Systems Research, 13*(2), 151–167. doi:10.1287/isre.13.2.151.88

Panopoulou, E., Tambouris, E., & Tarabanis, K. (2008). A framework for evaluating web sites of public authorities. *Aslib Proceedings, 60*(5), 517–546. doi:10.1108/00012530810908229

Parajuli, J. (2007). A content analysis of Selected Government Websites: A case Study of Nepal. *The Electronic. Journal of E-Government, 5*(1), 87–94.

Pascual, P. J. (2003). E-government. New York: Asia-Pacific Development Information Programme, United Nations Development Programme, eprim ers.apdip.net/series.

Phillips, D. (2001). *Online public relations*. London, UK: Kogan Page Limited.

Poskitt (2002) recommended from Sarmad Alshawi, Ali Alahmary, Hamid Alalwany (2007) E-government Evaluation factors: Citizen's Perspective. *Proceedings of European and Mediterranean Conference on Information Systems* 2007.

Radha, R., & Murphy, C. (1992). Searching Versus Browsing in Hypertext. *Hypermedia, 4*(1), 1–31.

Raymond, L., Uwizeyemungu, S., & Bergeron F. (2006). ERP Adoption for E-Government: *Electronic Government, an International Journal, 3*(3).

Rodríguez, R. A., Welicki, L., Giulianelli, D. A., & Vera, P. M. (2008). Measurement framework for evaluating e-governance on municipalities websites. In *Proceedings of the 2nd International Conference on Theory and Practice of Electronic Governance* (pp. 381--387). Cairo, Egypt: ACM.

Sandoval-Almazan, R., & Gil-Garcia, R. A. (2010). Assessing local e-government: an initial exploration of the case of Mexico. *In Proceedings of the 4th International Conference on Theory and Practice of Electronic Governance* (ICE-GOV '10). ACM, New York, NY, USA, 61-65. DOI=10.1145/1930321.1930335

Selz, D., & Schubert, P. (1997). Web assessment: a model for the evaluation and the assessment of successful electronic commerce applications. *Electronic Markets, 7*(3), 46–48. doi:10.1080/10196789700000038

Serafeimidis, V., & Smithson, S. (2009). Information Systems Evaluation in Practice: a Case Study of Organizational Change. *Journal of Information Technology, 15*(2), 93–105. doi:10.1080/026839600344294

Shneiderman, B. (2000a). Universal usability. *Communications of the ACM, 43*(5), 85–91. doi:10.1145/332833.332843

Shneiderman, B. (2000b). Designing information-abundant Web sites: Issues and recommendations. *International Journal of Human-Computer Studies, 47*, 5–29. doi:10.1006/ijhc.1997.0127

Shubin, H., & Meehan, M. M. (1997). Navigation in Web application. *Interactions (New York, N.Y.), 4*(6), 13–17. doi:10.1145/267505.267508

Simeon, R. (1999). Evaluating domestic and international web site strategies. Internet Research. *Electronic Networking Applications and Policy, 9*(4), 297–308. doi:10.1108/10662249910286842

Skietrys, E., Raipa, A., & Bartkus, E. V. (2008). Dimensions of the Efficiency of Public - Private Partnership. *Inzinerine Ekonomika-Engineering Economics, 3*, 45–50.

Smith, A. G. (2001). Applying evaluation criteria to New Zealand government web sites. *International Journal of Information Management, 21*(2), 137–149. doi:10.1016/S0268-4012(01)00006-8

Sterne, J. (2002). *Web metrics: Proven methods for measuring Web site success*. New York, NY: John Wiley and Sons, Inc.

Symonds, M. (2000). Government and the Internet: The next revolution. *The Economist, August.*

Utting, K., & Yankelovich, N. (1989). Context and Orientation in Hypermedia Networks. *ACM Transactions on Information Systems, 7*(1), 58–84. doi:10.1145/64789.64992

van der Merwe, R., & Bekker, J. (2003). A framework and methodology for evaluating e-commerce web sites'. *Internet Research: Electronic Networking Applications and Policy, 13*(5), 330–341. doi:10.1108/10662240310501612

von Dran, G. M., et al. (1999). Quality Websites: An application of the Kano Model to Website Design. *Proceedings of the 5th Americas Conference in Information Systems* (AMCIS'99).

Wang, L., Bretschneider, S., & Gant, J. (2005). Evaluating web-based e-government services with a citizen-centric approach. Proceedings of the 38th Hawaii International Conference on System Sciences, 3-6 January 2005, Island of Hawaii (Big Island), 5, 1292.

Wauters P., & Lörincz B. (2008). User satisfaction and administrative simplification within the perspective of eGovernment impact: Two faces of the same coin? *European Journal of ePractice, 4*, 1-10.

Welch, E. W., Hinnat, C. C., & Moon, M. J. (2005)... *Journal of Public Administration: Research and Theory, 15*(3).

Welch, E. W., & Pandey, S. (2007). Multiple measures of web site effectiveness and their association with service quality in health and human service agencies. In *Proceedings of the 40th Hawaii International Conference on System Science*, 3-6 January, 107.

Welling, R., & White, L. (2006). Web site performance measurement: promise and reality. *Managing Service Quality, 16*(6), 664–670. doi:10.1108/09604520610711954

West, D. M. (2007). *Global E-government*, available at: http://www.insidepolitics.org /egovt07int.pdf.

Wilson, T. D., et al, (1999).Uncertainty in information seeking. Final report to the Birtish Library Research and Innovation Centre/Library and Information Commission on a research project carried out at the Department of Information Studies, University of Sheffield, December.

Wood, F.B. et al 2003. *A practical approach to E-government Web evaluation. IT Professional*, May|June 2003, 22-28.

World Bank. (n.d.). *World Bank* Retrieved Sept. 2009, from http://go.worldbank.org / M1JHE0Z280

Wrightsman, L. S. (1991). Interpersonal Trust and Attitudes Toward Human Nature. In Robinson, J. P. (Eds.), *Measures of Personality and Social Psychological Attitudes* (pp. 373–412). San Diego, CA: Academic Press.

Young, D., & Benamati, J. (2000). Difference in public web sites: the current state of large US firms. *Journal of Electronic Commerce Research, 1*, 3.

Yücel, G., & Özok, A. F. (2008). A Methodology for Developing and Evaluating of Ergonomic Quality of Governmental Websites base on Fuzzy Approach. *Proceedings of the 2nd International Conference on Applied Human Factors and Ergonomics*.

Zahedi, M. F., van Pelt, W. V., & Song, J. (2001). A conceptual framework for international Web design. *IEEE Transactions on Professional Communication, 44*(2), 83–103. doi:10.1109/47.925509

Zhu, K. (2002). *Information Transparency in electronic marketplaces: Why data transparency may hinder the adoption of B2B Exchanges*. Electronic Market.

KEY TERMS AND DEFINITIONS

Accessibility: Accessibility means that users are able to find information quickly and easily thereby reducing their searching/surfing efforts.

Content: It determines the completeness, relevance, accuracy, reliability, and consistency of the information displayed on the website.

Evaluation: It refers to the assessment of municipal web sites of select cities using a prescribed framework.

Interactivity: It relates to the presence of on-line contact details, possibility of communication through Chats/Blogs/ eForums, participation in discussion forums/opinion polls/bulletin boards and availability of other contact details of the different departments.

Transparency: Transparency is defined as the degree of visibility and accessibility of information.

Usability: Usability is the measure of the ease of use and convenience in interaction with the web interface so as to improve the quality of user experience.

ENDNOTE

[1] www.ncear.org/downloads/mediaClips/ Press/Ecotimes-top20citieshold.pdf

Chapter 11
Information Security Threats in ERP Enabled E-Governance:
Challenges and Solutions

Geetanjali Sahi
Lal Bahadur Shastri Institute of Management, India

Sushila Madan
University of Delhi, India

ABSTRACT

E-governance offers different e-Services to its citizens so that they can interact with the government in a more effective way. Enterprise Resource Planning (ERP), when implemented in the e-governance domain, combines all the government functions together into one single integrated system with a central database. This system serves the information needs of all the departments across geographies, while allowing them to communicate with each other. For this it is necessary to understand that government has become more dependent on modern technologies that have the potential to create seamless, responsive, and citizen-centric government for the benefit of all. At the same time, it has become increasingly vulnerable to a range of risks, from interruption of operations that are based on computers to loss of confidential data. Government agencies at all levels (national, provincial, and local) must protect the computer systems that they own and operate. Information security requires a combination of business, management, and technical measures in an on-going process. Security is costly, but like privacy, it should be addressed in the design phase and periodically reviewed. This chapter contributes to the ERP enabled e-governance literature for understanding threats and risks, clarification and investigation of the techniques in mitigating these challenges and issues involved in improving e-governance security. The interest generated by the ERP phenomenon in the public sector, and the peculiarities of this sector make specific studies of ERP in government organizations necessary. This is an issue which has not yet been widely addressed in the open literature.

DOI: 10.4018/978-1-60960-863-7.ch011

INTRODUCTION

E-Governance

E-Governance refers to the use of information technology by government agencies that have the ability to transform relations with citizens, businesses, and its other arms. ERP system can be defined as an IT solution that helps organizations to achieve enterprise wide integration which results in faster access to accurate information required for decision making. These two different concepts when combined, can serve a variety of different ends viz. better delivery of government services to citizens, improved interactions with business and industry, citizen empowerment through access to information, or more efficient government management. The resulting benefits can be less corruption, increased transparency, greater convenience, revenue growth, and/or cost reductions" (World Bank, 2004)

Technology developments are changing all aspects of societies. E-governance is a key instrument for modernisation and reforms as the government faces the continuous pressure of increasing their performance and adapting to the pressure of new information society (Wang and Hang, 2009). Good, reliable and trustworthy public services built around the needs of the citizen are essential to a modern, fair and dynamic society. As many public sector organizations are either planning for or implementing major e-governance projects, there is a growing need to understand how these projects can be successfully managed for maximum realization of their potential benefits (Lee, 2005). Moreover, we know public and private organizations are facing a wide range of information threats hence Information security is a crucial component in their information systems. With the increasing reliance on technologies connected over open data networks, effective management of information security has become one of the most crucial success factors for public and private organizations alike. Requirements and guidelines

for effective information security management practices are a prerequisite of e-governance in order to promote the necessary steps to ensure successful outcomes.

E-Governance was born out of the Internet boom. However, it is not limited to Internet use or publicly accessible systems for direct use by customers or citizens (Garcia and Moyano, 2007). In some ways, the use of the Internet (and all of its underlying technologies) has become the primary means by which the organization interacts with its environment, while this brings tremendous opportunities, it also exposes the organization to new risks that must be identified, mitigated, and managed so as not to impede the organization's quest to meet its mission (Caralli et al).Along with the rapid growth of the Internet there has been a substantial rise in online transactions. The government sector has been no exception to these facts and it has embraced IT in general and Internet-based technologies in particular, in order to extend the benefits of governance to all citizens—urban and rural through a series of e-governance projects. In fact, e-governance has received more and more importance and it can provide non-stop government information services to citizens, enterprises, public officers, government administrations and agencies over a network (Hwang et al, 2004).

The term e-governance emerged in the late 1990s, but the history of computing in government organizations can be traced back to the beginnings of computer history. A literature on "IT in government," goes back at least to the 1970s. (Kraemer, et al, 1979, Danziger and Andersen,2002).E-governance is the application of IT to the processes of governments functioning to bring about Simple Moral Accountable Responsive and Transparent (SMART) governance that works for improving the service delivered to the citizen on dimensions such as speed, quality, reliability, convenience and cost. E-governance as defined by (Turban et al., 2002) is: "The use of information technology in general and e-commerce in particular, to provide citizens and organizations with more convenient access to government information and services, and to provide delivery of public services to citizens, business partners and suppliers, and those working in the public sector." (Sprecher, 2000) considers e-governance as anyway technology is used to help simplify and automate transactions between government and constituents, businesses, or other governments. According to (McClure, 2000) Electronic government refers to government's use of technology, particularly web-based Internet applications to enhance the access to and delivery of government information and services to citizens, business partners, employees, other agencies and entities. E-governance can be defined as government use of information technologies in order to communicate externally in the public sector (with citizens and businesses [i.e. G2C and G2B]) and internally (with other government departments G2G) (Ebrahim and Irani, 2005; Gilbert et al., 2004; Heeks, 2003; World Bank).

The Basic Structure of E-Governance

The purpose of an e-governance system is to provide access to government services anywhere at any time over open networks. This leads to issues of security and privacy in the management of the information systems. In developing e-governance services, the readiness of citizen groups to use self-service channels must be taken into account, as must the complexity and requirements of the service. (Layne and Lee, 2001) described a four-stage growth model to develop a fully functional e-governance. Based on technical, organizational and managerial feasibilities, the four stages of a growth model developed for e-governance are:

- Cataloguing (Information)
- Transaction
- Vertical integration (Interactive)
- Horizontal integration (Strategic, interactive) or transformation

The stages are arranged in terms of complexity and different levels of integration. The first stage is *"cataloguing"* because efforts are focused on cataloguing government information and presenting it on the web. The second stage *"Transaction,"* where e-governance initiatives are focused on connecting the nternal government system to on-line interfaces. However, the critical benefits of implementing e-governance are actually derived from the integration of underlying processes across different level of government. This integration may happen in two ways: vertical and horizontal. *Vertical integration* refers to local and central administration connected for any functions or services of government, while *horizontal integration* refers integration across different functions and services.

Enterprise Resource Planning

Enterprise Resource Planning (ERP) when implemented in the e-governance domain combines all the government functions together into one single integrated system with a single central database. This system serves the information needs of all the departments across geographies, while allowing them to communicate with each other.

The Key strength of ERP is integration. It integrates all the functions of an organization. The success of ERP also depends upon the synergy between technology and management. ERP software not only uses cutting edge technology but also embeds the best of the breed management practices from the leading edge companies such as Intel, Compaq, Microsoft, GM, Philips, to name a few(Jhaand Saini, 2009). It serves the information needs of all the departments across geographies, while allowing them to communicate with each other. Before ERP came into existence, different departments had their own software system to meet their requirements. This resulted in information being fragmented and redundantly stored on different systems, factories etc. sometimes spread across the world. This made it impossible to get accurate information on time. In 1990s, globalization led to immense competition and companies, especially in the manufacturing sector, realized the need for more customer focus and shortened product life cycles which resulted in corporations moving towards agile manufacturing, continuous improvement of business processes and business process reengineering (Kale et. al, 2007). This required an integration of manufacturing with other functional areas like accounting, marketing, HR, etc. This led to the evolution of MRPII to ERP systems (Sadagopan, 1999).

Objectives of ERP Based E-Governance Design

The objective of the integration is to provide efficient services to citizens, administrators and comparators by implementing ERP Based Solutions to enable organizational processes and workflows. Key objectives of such a project are as follows:

- Improve the quality of Citizen Service Delivery System and offer these services with optimal effectiveness and transparency.
- Allow data sharing across different departments, thus bringing about the efficiency in administration functioning.
- Facilitate the decision making process of top management by furnishing the right information at right time.
- Help different departments to improve their revenue collection efficiency.
- Harness the use of technology to create sense of achievement amongst employees and citizens

Challenges to Effective ERP Enabled E-Governance

E-governance presents challenges and opportunities to transform both the operational process of

government and the nature of governance itself. It impacts on most functions in government and agencies, the private sector and civil society. In the long term, it has the potential to positively change the government operations and the interaction of citizens and businesses with government. An e-governance project, like any other IT-enabled project, also runs on a network. A government department deals with a considerable amount of information that may be critical to several other government departments concerned as well as external parties and citizens.

ERP vendors' advice government departments' to mould their functions to ERP's way of working, considering that ERP systems bring with them best business practices, this is the plain vanilla approach which would bring down the cost of implementation (Kale et al., 2007). But most government departments have processes that have evolved over time and hold very dear to their hearts. As a result, these departments are having the entire ERP system customized to meet their requirements which increases the overall cost of implementation which could be a major hindrance in government wide implementation of ERP (Kale et al., 2007). A good approach would be to keep the customization to a minimum.

One third of ERP implementations worldwide fail owing to various factors (Sirigindi, 2000). One of the other major reasons why ERP implementations nationwide have been known to fail is due to the implementation being considered as an automation project instead of one that involves change management which results in the system being put in place but not being used effectively as people are not ready to accept the change (Kale et al., 2007). Hence, a thorough analysis of the reasons for which an organization, be it public or private, undertakes an ERP project is deemed essential, as many studies have found such projects to be very costly and risky (e.g., Besson, 1999; Umble and Umble, 2002).

The real difficulty in implementing an ERP isn't because it's a new system or because it means making changes. The challenge is that it instils discipline into an undisciplined organization and while it helps the organization as a whole, employees don't necessarily see this cultural change as an improvement(Mashari, 2002).

ERP ENABLED E-GOVERNANCE INFORMATION SECURITY LITERATURE REVIEW

While e-governance is subject to the same threats as e-business, e-governance operates within different constraints. Most businesses deal only with a subset of the population, and they can choose the how and the when they do it. But the government must deal with everyone (Stibbe, 2005). Therefore, in order to service the huge number of users and transactions, and sensitivity of this field, like citizen's private information or government's secret information, and other issues, securing governmental networks is more important than businesses (Conklin and White, 2006). A barrier frequently cited is the need to ensure adequate security and privacy in an e-governance strategy (Daniels, 2002; James, 2000; Joshi et al., 2001; Lambrinoudakis et al., 2003; Layne and Lee, 2001; Sanchez et al., 2003;). (Bonham et al. 2001 and Gefen et al. 2002) agree that one of the most significant barriers for implementing e-governance applications is computer security, privacy and confidentiality of the personal data. For instance, one of the sophisticated applications of e-governance is e-voting, which uses electronic ballots that allow voters to transmit their vote to election officials over the internet. This application requires extensive security approaches to secure the voting process and protect the voter personal data.

(Henriksson et al., 2006) divided the factors that influence the quality of government websites into 6 major categories: (1) Security and Privacy; (2) Usability; (3) Content; (4) Services; (5) Citizen

Participation; and (6) Features. (Wimmer and Bredow, 2001) proposed a holistic concept that integrates security aspects from the strategic level down to the data and information level in order to address different security aspects of e-governance in a comprehensive way. Their holistic approach consists of 4 layers: strategic, process level, interaction and information. (Hof and Reichstädter, 2004) surveyed security, peculiarities and implementations of security requirements within governmental structures, based on three interaction points (citizen to government C2G, government to government G2G and government to citizen G2C).

According to (Allen, Kern & Havenhand, 2002) Enterprise Resources Planning (ERP) systems need to develop a body of knowledge specific to public organizations in order to increase its relevancy and acceptance. In the same context, (Blick, Gulledge and Sommer, 2000) show that ERP implementation approaches used in the private sector must be adapted to the culture and regulations peculiar to the public sector. Recognizing the importance of ERP in e-governance (Sprecher, 1999; Miranda, 1998) state that the interest generated by the ERP phenomenon in the public sector and the particularities of this sector thus generate e-government issues for the information systems field (Grönlund and Horan) and make specific studies of ERP in government and public organizations necessary.

(Chang *et al.*, 2000) state that public agencies, are increasingly adopting ERP systems to replace their operational and control systems, as ERP enabled organizations are more efficient. In the same context, while studying public sector institutions of higher learning in the United Kingdom, Allen *et al.* (2002) found four basic reasons for which these organizations had adopted an ERP system: a) to simplify the complex environment of these institutions, through a common system-interface, (b) to avoid fragmentation and duplication of resources and services, c) to reduce confusion and waste, and d) to allow these institutions to adapt more effectively and more quickly to changes in their environment.

Studies have also been conducted to investigate specific ERP functions such as Customer Relationship Management (CRM). In the government sector, CRM is particularly important since it aims at building an interface between the government and its citizens in order to better meet the citizen's needs (Louis et al., 2005).

SECURITY IN ERP BASED E-GOVERNANCE

The availability of multiple channels like Internet, digital television, mobiles, smartcards, biometrics and other new technologies, present their own challenges and demand support for trusted services, authentication, integrity and confidentiality. With multiple agencies frequently involved in the development of e-governance integrated with other functional projects, the information security infrastructure is invariably the element most open to compromise and the one that frequently presents the greatest risk to e-governance projects (Omari, 2006). Security issues in ERP based e-governance can be understood by firstly having a basic idea of the dynamicity of its environment.

ERP Based E-Governance Environment

ERP enabled e-governance environment is a very complex one may comprise of MIS, GIS, In order to support the proposed MIS and GIS applications, various other IT Management solutions are required. The list of such requirements is given below:

a. RDBMS
b. Application Server for MIS/GIS
c. Web Server

Along with IT Management Applications specified in above section, it requires Server Side Infrastructure components such as:

a. Database Server
b. Application Servers
c. Web Servers
d. Domain Server

It allows multiple access channels for citizens including PCs, laptops, PDA's, data centre servers, mobile phones etc., multiple service access portals, multiple back ends, networks spread across multiple locations, diversity in the user environment etc. Due to its complexity the e-governance environment poses many information threats thus; information security has become a crucial component of the information systems of both public and private organizations. Increasing reliance on technologies connected over open data networks dictates effective management of information security to ensure successful outcomes. (Alfawazand Mohanak, 2008). ERP based e-governance implementation can be observed in Figure 1.

Information Security Threats

E-governance security requirements can be understood after examining the overall process, beginning with the consumer and ending with the e-governance server (Mazumdar, 2009). Hence, we divide the threats according to the stage and location of data (i.e. data may be at client end, destination end, or in transit).

Threats at client end: Some common threats at client end could be encryption cracking, system failure or unavailability of information system, corruption / loss or damage of back up media, denial of service attacks and theft of credentials

Threats for data in transit: Common threats for data in transit could be loss of decryption keys, system failure, corruption / loss or damage of back up media, cross-site scripting, query

Figure 1. Nine stepped approach for implementing ERP enabled e-governance

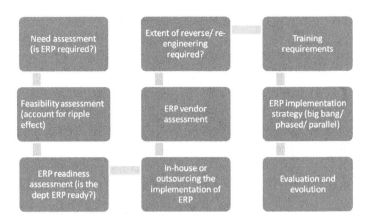

string manipulation, network eavesdropping, impersonation, cookie manipulation, HTTP header manipulation, inability to identify actual user

Threats at destination end: at the side of end user the threats may be any of the following (i.e. inability to identify actual user, denial of service attacks, loss of decryption keys, encryption cracking).

Information Security Challenges

Data cannot be confined to one place; the importance of data lies in sharing it. When data is shared, it is spread across several devices including PCs, laptops etc. and that is where threats like defacing of websites, virus attacks, malware, bots, hacking into servers, Denial-of-service attacks, key-loggers, phishing and spoofing originate. In e-governance scenario we need to secure all tangible and intangible assets comprising of data, information, knowledge assets, hardware, software, communication networks etc. Although emerging IT solutions provide intriguing opportunities for supporting the design and implementation of an e-governance infrastructure, use of these technologies, the highly sensitive nature of information it maintains, critical transactions it processes, and the national security issues the government processes bring forth, create significant infrastructure

security challenge (Joshi, et al., 2001). The US Government Accountability Office (GAO), 2004 report indicates that while interconnectivity of heterogeneous domains is a basic need for an efficient e-governance system, it significantly raises the potential for unauthorized access to personal and confidential data and exposes the critical infrastructures to new vulnerabilities.

Also due to the fact that e-governance projects are very complex in nature, have multiple legacy environments, command high performance and low response time, it is difficult to design a security framework for them. A significant challenge is thus, to provide an integrated e-governance infrastructure that ensures secure integration of services and information sources, fosters security assured partnerships among public and private sectors, and securely manage government resources. Hence, challenges with respect to information security in the e-governance scenario arise due to the following factors:

- Excessive dependency on information systems
- Difficulty in controlling enormous information
- Threats from increased use of remote access facility
- High degree of information sharing

- Dealing with highly sensitive citizen's and business data
- Concerns National security
- Consequences of security breach can be detrimental

TECHNIQUES FOR OVERCOMING INFORMATION SECURITY CHALLENGES

The Internet is an open environment, protecting the data flowing on the Internet from attacks is therefore a pressing e-governance issue. Therefore, there is a need to define some security standards. These standards among other things can help in following:

- Provide a realistic and unified security framework
- Target all components of IT infrastructure
- Safeguard against internal users who could be possible threats
- Improving Network Performance
- Addressing the multi-level complexities in network threats
- Provide Secure Converged Communication
- Seamlessly integrating new applications with the legacy applications

The basic concepts and principles of information security services and mechanisms remain the same no matter where, geographically, ICT is applied. Information security systems are often defined as systems that protect information assets from harm or misuse. Traditionally the main information security services are the preservation of confidentiality, integrity and availability of information. Other properties such as authenticity, accountability, non-repudiation and reliability are also involved (ISO/IEC 17799:2005). Security mechanisms and practices are the technologies that provide the security services, such as Firewalls and Digital Signatures. Technical infrastructure

that is capable of handling the required volume and type of transactions in a secure manner is a necessity in achieving the information assurance objectives. Three such techniques are discussed below briefly.

- Adhering to the guidelines of Information Security Management System (ISMS)/ ISO 27001
- Implementing Public Key Infrastructure (PKI)
- Steganology

Information security infrastructure, in general lacks the necessary security technology structures (Aljifri et al, 2003), such as Public Key Infrastructures (PKI) and adequate encryption systems, to enable a high quality of electronic information. These types of technologies can ensure confidentiality and provide access control, integrity, authentication and non-repudiation services for organizations moving into the information age.

ISO 27001

Information security standards are the essential starting point for any organization that is commencing an information security project. ISO 27001 is a generic standard; it has to be adapted to the associated e-governance environment. It provides good practice guidance on designing, implementing and auditing Information Security Management Systems (ISMS) to protect the confidentiality, integrity and availability of the information on which we all depend. ISO 27001 requires that management:

- Systematically examine the organization's information security risks, taking account of the threats, vulnerabilities and impacts;
- Design and implement a coherent and comprehensive suite of information security controls and/or other forms of risk treatment (such as risk avoidance or risk trans-

fer) to address those risks that are deemed unacceptable; and

- Adopt an overarching management process to ensure that the information security controls continue to meet the organization's information security needs on an ongoing basis.

Public Key Infrastructure (PKI)

Creating trust in electronic environment involves assuring the transacting parties about the integrity and confidentiality of the content of documents along with authentication of the sending and receiving parties in a manner that ensures that both the parties cannot repudiate the transaction. PKI is a set of hardware, software, people, policies, and procedures needed to create, manage, distribute, use, store, and revoke digital certificates (JoelWeise). A PKI enables users of an unsecure public network such as the Internet to securely and privately exchange data and money through the use of a public and a private cryptographic key pair that is obtained and shared through a trusted authority. The implementation of a PKI is intended to provide mechanisms to ensure trusted relationships are established and maintained. The specific security functions in which a PKI can provide foundation are confidentiality, integrity, non-repudiation and authentication.

The paper based concepts of identification; declaration and proof are carried out through the use of digital signatures in an electronic environment. Digital signatures, a form of electronic signatures, are created and verified using Public Key Cryptography, is based on the concept of a pair of keys (public and private), generated by a mathematical algorithm. The private key, used to digitally sign a document, is securely held by the owner, while the public key is made known to everyone for verifying the digital signature. Knowing the public key, one cannot compute the private key belonging to its owner. Thus by providing digital signatures to the people in government,

authenticity of communication can be established, especially in electronic transactions that happen in E-governance and other service delivery.

A public key infrastructure consists of:

- A certificate authority (CA) that issues and verifies digital certificate. A certificate includes the public key or information about the public key
- A registration authority(RA) that acts as the verifier for the certificate authority before a digital certificate is issued to a requestor
- One or more directories where the certificates (with their public keys) are held
- A certificate management system

Challenges of PKI

- One of the functions of Controller of Certifying Authorities (CCA) is to ensure the standards which are prescribed are fully adopted. The compliance of these standards, practice and procedures are to be audited at regular intervals.
- The private key, which is used to create digital signature should be in the safe custody of subscriber else anyone holding the private key can misuse it.
- Several large applications, especially in banking and insurance sector are still to adapt to Digital Signature Certificate (DSC) based secure transaction in their citizen services.
- Further there are issues relating to the interoperability. The certificates issued by different licensed CAs are not acceptable to some applications due to lack of uniform certificate norms.
- Some of the application providers feel that DSCs are inconvenient.

Prior to considering how a PKI can support an e-governance application, an in-depth study into the specific threats that exist in the environment must be and the requirements for different security mechanisms that a PKI can enable must be identified.

Steganology

As computing power keeps increasing and the techniques of cryptanalysis keep advancing, contemporary cryptosystems cannot and will not work forever. Cryptography is not adequate in some applications. At the 24th Annual International Cryptology Conference (CRYPTO'04), MD5 and a series of related cryptosystems, which are currently in widespread use, were proved unreliable (Wang *et al.*, 2004).

From the last decade, *steganology*, the technique for digitally hiding and detecting information is attracting more attention. It is already regarded as a powerful complement to cryptology and a promising technique for ensuring e-governance security. Unlike cryptology, which renders the encrypted information completely meaningless, steganology keeps the host media perceptually unchanged after hiding the secret information.(Kahn, 1995) defined steganography as "the art and science of communicating in a way which hides the existence of the communication. In contrast to cryptography, where the enemy is allowed to detect, intercept and modify messages without being able to violate certain security premises guaranteed by a cryptosystem, the goal of steganography is to hide messages inside other innocent messages in a way that does not allow any enemy to even detect that there is a second message present."

CONCLUSION

India's experience in ERP based e-governance / ICT initiatives has demonstrated significant success in improving accessibility, cutting down costs, reducing corruption, extending help and increased access to un-served groups. In this phase of *experimentation*, e-governance initiatives have reached millions of people belonging to these sections of society. Improved access to information and services has provided economic and social development opportunities, facilitated participation and communication in policy and decision-making processes and empowerment of the weakest groups. This has led to fostering a sense of ownership and building of social capital, which in turn, constitute a basis for local re-vitalization.

Potential key factors are security mechanisms and practices, security and privacy legislation, management commitment, management style, senior management and user awareness, skills and training, management change and information security infrastructure.

REFERENCES

Alfawaz, S., May, L., & Mohanak, K. (2008). *E-governance security in developing countries: A managerial conceptual framework*. International Research Society for Public Management Conference, Queensland University of Technology, Brisbane, Australia.

Ali, A. K., Mehdi, A. K., & Mohammad, A. (2009). A Foresight based Framework For E-governance Strategic Planning. *Journal of Software*, *4*(6).

Aljifri, H. A., Pons, A., & Collins, D. (2003). Global e-commerce: a framework for understanding & overcoming the trust barrier. *Information Management & Computer Security*, *11*(3), 130–138. doi:10.1108/09685220310480417

Allen, D., Kern, T., & Havenhand, M. 2002. ERP critical success factors: An exploration of the contextual factors in public sector institutions. In *Proceedings of the 35th Hawaii International Conference on System Sciences.*http://www.computer.org/proceedings /hicss/1435/volume8 /14350227abs.htm

Besson, P. (1999). Les ERP à l'épreuve de l'organisation. *Systèmes d'Information et Management, 4*(4), 21–51.

Blick, G., Gulledge, T., & Sommer, R. 2000. Defining business process requirements for large-scale public sector ERP implementations: A case study. *Proceedings of the European Conference on Information Systems,* WirtschaftsUniversität, Wien.

Bonham, G., Seifert, J., & Thorson, S. (2001). The transformational potential of e-government: the role of political leadership. Paper presented at 4th Pan European International Relations Conference, University of Kent.

Caralli, A. R., & William, R. W. (n.d.). *The challenges of security management.* White paper of Survivable Enterprise Management Team, Networked Systems Survivability Program, Software Engineering Institute.

Chang, S. I., Gable, G., Smythe, E., & Timbrell, G. 2000. A Delphi examination of public sector ERP implementation issues. *Proceedings of the Twenty First International Conference on Information Systems*, Brisbane, Queensland, Australia, 494-500.

Conklin, A., & White, G. B. (2006). E-government & Cyber Security: The Role of Cyber Security exercises. In *Proceedings of the 39th Annual Hawaii International Conference on System Sciences*.

Daniels, M. (2002). *E-Government Strategy: Simplified Delivery of Services to Citizens.* Washington, DC: Office of Management & Budget.

Danziger, J. N., & Anderson, K. V. (2002). The impacts of information technology on public administration: an analysis of empirical research from the "golden age" of transformation. *International Journal of Public Administration, 1*(22).

Ebrahim, Z., & Irani, Z. (2005). E-government adoption: architecture & barriers. *Business Process Management Journal, 11*(5), 589–611. doi:10.1108/14637150510619902

Garcia, J. R., & Moyano, I. J. M. (2007). Understanding the evolution of e-government: The influence of systems of rules on public sector dynamics. *Government Information Quarterly,* (2): 266–290. doi:10.1016/j.giq.2006.04.005

Gefen, D., & Pavlou, P. (2002). E-government adoption. Paper presented at Americas Conference on Information Systems, Tampa, FL.

Gilbert, D., Balestrini, P., & Littleboy, D. (2004). Barriers & benefits in the adoption of e-government. *International Journal of Public Sector Management, 17*(5), 286. doi:10.1108/09513550410539794

Grönlund, Å., & Horan, T. A. (2004). Introducing e-Gov: History, definitions, and issues. *Communications of the AIS, 15,* 713–729.

Hae, D., & Lee, D. (2005). Contextual IT Business Value & Barriers: An E-Government & E-Business Perspective. In *Proceedings of the 38th Annual Hawaii International Conference on System Sciences* (HICSS'05) - Track 5, Hawaii.

Heeks, R. (2003). Most E-government Development Projects Fail: How Can Risks be Reduced? *iGovernemnt Working Paper Series,* Paper no. 14.

Henriksson, A. Yi, Frost, Y.B., & Middleton, M. (2006). Evaluation instrument for e-government websites. In *Proceedings Internet Research 7.0: Internet Convergences*, Brisbane, Queensland, Australia.

Hof, S., & Reichstädter, P. (2004). *Securing e-Government.* EGOV 2004, Springer-Verlag, 336-341.

Hwang, M. S., Ta, L. C., Ji, S. J., & Chu, Y. P. (2004). Challenges in E-governance & Security of Information. *International Journal of Information Security, 15*(1).

James, G. (2000). Empowering bureaucrats. *MC Technology Marketing Intelligence, 20*(12), 62–80.

Joshi, J., & Ghafoor, A. (2001). Digital government security infrastructure design challenges. *IEEE Computer*, *34*(1), 66–72.

Joshi, J. B. D., Anttiroiko, A. V., & Malkia, M. (2007). *Information Security Issues & Challenges*. Encyclopaedia of Digital Government.

Kale, P. T., Banwait, S. S., & Laroiya, S. C. (2007). Enterprise Resource Planning Implementation in Indian SMEs: Issues and Challenges. *National Institute of Technical Teachers' Training and Research*, Retrieved from www.csi-sigegov.org/critical_pdf/27_242-248.pdf

Kraemer, K. L., & Perry, J. L. (1979). The Federal Push to Bring Computer Applications to Local Governments. *Public Administration Review*, *39*(3), 260–270. doi:10.2307/975951

Lambrinoudakis, C., & Gritzalis, S. (2003). Security requirements for e-government services: a methodological approach for developing a common PKI-based security policy. *Computer Communications*, *26*(16), 1873–1883. doi:10.1016/S0140-3664(03)00082-3

Layne, K., & Lee, J. (2001). Developing Fully Functional e- Government: A Four Stage Model. *Government Information Quarterly*, *18*(2), 122–136. doi:10.1016/S0740-624X(01)00066-1

Louis, R., Sylvestre, U., & François, B. (2005). "Erp Adoption For E-Government: An Analysis Of Motivations." *e*Government Workshop, Brunel University, West London. UK.

Mashari, M. A. (2002). ERP Systems: A Research Agenda. *Industrial Management & Data Systems*, *102*(3).

Mazumdar, C., Kumar, A., & Banerjee, P. (2009). *On Information Security Issues in E-governance: Developing Country Views*. CSDMS Journal.

McClure, D. L. (statement of David L. McClure) (2000). *U.S. General Accounting Office, before the subcommittee on Government Management*, Information & technology, committee on Government reform, Retrieved from http://www.gao.gov.

Miranda, R. (1998). The rise of ERP technology in the public sector. *Government Finance Review*, *15*(4), 9–17.

Omari, H. A., & Omari, A. A. (2006). Building an E-governance e-Trust Infrastructure. *American Journal of Applied Sciences*, *3*(11), 2122–2130. doi:10.3844/ajassp.2006.2122.2130

Rashmi, J., & Saini, A. K. (2009). How to Tap ERP's Hidden Potential in India? Proceedings of the 3rd National Conference; INDIACom- 2009, Computing For Nation Development.

Sadagopan, S. (1999). *ERP: A Managerial Perspective*. New Delhi, India: Tata McGraw Hill.

Sanchez, A., & Koh, C. (2003). The relationship between IT for communication & e-government barriers. Paper presented at Americas Conference on Information Systems, Tampa, FL.

Signore O., Chesi, F. & Pallotti, M. (2005). E-governance: challenges & opportunities. CMG Italy - XIX annual conference.

Siriginidi, S. R. (2000). Enterprise Resource Planning in re-engineering business. *Business Process Management Journal*, *6*(5), 376–391. doi:10.1108/14637150010352390

Sprecher, M. H. (2000). Racing to E-governance: using the Internet for citizen service delivery. *Government Finance Review*, *16*(5), 21–22.

Stibbe, M. (2005). E-government security. *Infosecurity Today*, *2*(3), 8–10. doi:10.1016/S1742-6847(05)70272-X

Turban, E. (2002). *Electronic commerce- A managerial perspective* (2nd ed.). Prentice Hall.

Umble, E. J., & Umble, M. M. (2002). Avoiding ERP implementation failure. *Industrial Management (Des Plaines)*, *44*(1), 25–33.

Wang, J. F., & Duo, H. (2009). Customer-centered e-government service quality evaluation: framework & case study. ISECS International Colloquium on Computing, Communication, *Control, &. Management*, *8*(3), 198–202.

Wang, X., & Feng, D. Lai, X., & Yu, H. (2004). Collisions for Hash Functions MD4, MD5, HAVAL-128 & RIPEMD. *Cryptology ePrint Archive*, Report 2004/199. Retrieved from http://eprint.iacr.org/2004/199.pdf.

Weise, J. (2001). *Public Key Infrastructure Overview*. SunPSSM Global Security Practice, SunBluePrintsOnLine.

Wimmer, M., & Bredow, B. (2001). E-Government: Aspects of Security on Different Layers. In *Proceedings of the 12th International Workshop on Database & Expert Systems Applications* (DEXA'01. WorldBank (n.d.). *Definition of E-Government*. Retrieved from: http://go.worldbank.org

KEY TERMS AND DEFINITIONS

Cryptography: means sending the message not as plain text but in some coded language that can only be deciphered by the authorized users and to all others the message appears as a set of junk characters.

E-Governance: When government agencies use information technology and web technologies in particular to provide services to citizens, businesses and other governmental departments, it is called E-governance.

Information Security: can be defined as the protection information and information systems against unauthorized access, use or modification.

Public Key Infrastructure: is a mechanism that helps the users of open and insecure networks such as internet to securely exchange information with help of public and private keys.

Steganology: is the method in which we hide the message to be sent behind some other message so that it cannot be misused.

Compilation of References

Accenture. (2009). *From e-Government to e-Governance: Using new technologies to strengthen relationships with citizens.* Accenture, UK.

Adenso-Di'Az, B., & Canteli, A. (2001). Business Process Reengineering and University Organisation: a normative approach from the Spanish case. *Journal of Higher Education Policy and Management, 23*(1), 63–73. doi:10.1080/13600800020047243

Akkermans, H., & van Helden, K. (2002). Vicious and Virtuous Cycles in ERP Implementation: A Case Study of Interrelations between Critical Success Factors. *European Journal of Information Systems, 11*, 35–46. doi:10.1057/palgrave/ejis/3000418

Akkermans, H., Bogerd, P., & van Doremalen, J. (2004). Travail, transparency and trust: a case study of computer-supported collaborative supply chain planning in high-tech electronics. *European Journal of Operational Research, 153*, 445–456. doi:10.1016/S0377-2217(03)00164-4

Al-awadhi, S., & Morris, A. (2008). The Use of the UTAUT Model in the Adoption of e-Government Services in Kuwait. In *Proceedings of the 41st Hawaii International Conference on System Sciences.* 1-11.

Aldowaisan, T., & Gaafar, L. (1999). BPR: An approach for process mapping. *Omega, 27*, 515–524. doi:10.1016/S0305-0483(99)00015-8

Alexander, J. E., & Tate, M. A. (1999). *Web Wisdom: How to Evaluate and Create Information Quality on the Web.* Mahwah, NJ: Lawrence Erlbaum Associates.

Alfawaz, S., May, L., & Mohanak, K. (2008). *E-governance security in developing countries: A managerial conceptual framework.* International Research Society for Public Management Conference, Queensland University of Technology, Brisbane, Australia.

Ali, A. K., Mehdi, A. K., & Mohammad, A. (2009). A Foresight based Framework For E-governance Strategic Planning. *Journal of Software, 4*(6).

Aljifri, H. A., Pons, A., & Collins, D. (2003). Global e-commerce: a framework for understanding & overcoming the trust barrier. *Information Management & Computer Security, 11*(3), 130–138. doi:10.1108/09685220310480417

Al-Kibsi, G., de Boer, K., Mourshed, M., & Rea, N. P. (2001). Putting citizens on-line, not in line'. *The McKinsey Quarterly, 2*, 65–73.

Allen, D., Kern, T., & Havenhand, M. (2002). ERP critical success factors: An exploration of the contextual factors in public sector institutions. Paper presented at the *Proceedings of the 35th Hawaii International Conference on System Sciences*, Hawaii.

Al-Mashari, M., Irani, Z., & Zairi, M. (2001). Business process reengineering: a survey of international experience. *Business Process Management Journal, 7*(5), 437–455. doi:10.1108/14637150110406812

Al-Mashari, M., Al-Mudimigh, A., & Zairi, M. (2003). ERP: A Taxonomy of Critical Factors. *European Journal of Operational Research, 146*, 352–364. doi:10.1016/S0377-2217(02)00554-4

Alpar, P., & Olbrich, S. (2005). Legal Requirements and Modelling of Processes in e-Government. *The Electronic. Journal of E-Government, 3*(3), 107–116.

Alshawi, S., Alahmary, A., & Alalwany, H. (2007). E-Government Evaluation Factors: Citizen's Perspective. In *Proceedings of European and Mediterranean Conference on Information Systems* June 2007, Polytechnic University of Valencia, Spain www.emcis.org

Altova, F. (2009), 'Database mapping. Altova (http://www.altova.com/ products/mapforce/xml_to_db_ database _mapping.html accessed March 2009. Bouret, R., (2005), XML and Databases, XML Guild, September, file://C:\TEMP\3EERCYBR.html accessed March 2009.

Andersen, K. (1999). Reengineering public sector organisations using information technology. *Reinventing government in the information age*: 312-330.

Anttiroiko, A. (2004). Towards citizen-centered local e-government: The case of the city of Tampere. In Khosrow-Pour, M. (Ed.), *Annals of cases on information technology* (*Vol. 6*, pp. 371–388). Hershey, PA: Idea Group Publishing.

Anttiroiko, A.-V. (2008). Social responsibility: Structure, content and process. In Sharma, S. (Ed.), *Transformative Pathways: Attainable Utopia* (pp. 52–81). Jaipur: Pratiksha Publications.

Aramouni, G., Pando, D., & Calamari, M. (2006). *Midiendo el Gobierno Electrónico Análisis de Páginas Web Municipales en Argentina*, San Andrés University, Argentina, available at: http://www.udesa.edu.ar /files/ cee/e- gov/ webs_municip.pdf.

Arnold, V. (2006). Behavorial research opportunities: Understanding the impact of enterprise systems. *International Journal of Accounting Information Systems*, 7, 7–17. doi:10.1016/j.accinf.2006.02.001

As-Saber, S. N., & Hossain, K. (2008). Call centres and their role in e-governance: A developing country perspective. *The Journal of Community Informatics*, *4*(3).

Austin City Council. (2008). *Audit report 2008: City of Austin's e-government initiative*. Austin, TX: Office of the City Auditor.

Aversano, L., Canfora, G., De Lucia, A., & Gallucci, P. (2002). Business process reengineering and workflow automation: a technology transfer. *Journal of Systems and Software*, *63*(1), 29–44. doi:10.1016/S0164-1212(01)00128-5

Bagchi, S., Kanungo, S., & Dasgupta, S. (2003). Modeling use of enterprise resource planning systems: A path analytic study. *European Journal of Information Systems*, *12*(2), 142. doi:10.1057/palgrave.ejis.3000453

Bajjaly, S. T. (1999). Managing emerging information systems in the public sector. *Public Productivity and Management Review*, *23*, 40–47. doi:10.2307/3380791

Bajwa, S. B. (2003). ICT policy in India in the era of liberalisation: Its impact and consequences. *Global Built Environment Review*, *3*(2), 49–61.

Banker, R., Davis, G. B., & Slaughter, S. A. (1988). Software Development Practices, Software Complexity, and Software Maintenance Performance: A Field Study. *Management Science*, *44*(4), 433–451. doi:10.1287/mnsc.44.4.433

Bannister, F. (2001). Dismantling the silos: extracting new value from IT investments in public administration. *Information Systems Journal*, *11*(1), 65–84. doi:10.1046/j.1365-2575.2001.00094.x

Barker, T., & Frolick, M. (2003). ERP Implementation Failure: A Case Study. *Information Systems Management*, *20*(4), 43–49. doi:10.1201/1078/43647.20.4.20030901/77292.7

Baryamureeba, V. (2005). *State of ICT and Local Governance, Needs Analysis and Research Priorities in Uganda*. 3-5 September 2005, Nairobi Kenya.

Basu, C. (2002). Context-driven assessment of commercial web sites. In *Proceedings of the 36th Hawaii International Conference on System Sciences, 6-9 January 2003, Island of Hawaii, (Big Island),* available at: www.hicss.hawaii.edu/ HICSS36/HICSSpapers/ INMIW01.pdf.

Bauer, C., & Scharl, A. (2000). Quantitative evaluation of web site content and structure. *Internet Research: Electronic Networking Applications and Policy*, *10*(1), 31–43. doi:10.1108/10662240010312138

Bavec, C., & Vintar, M. (2007). What matters in the development of the e-government in the EU? In Wimmer, M. A., Jochen Scholl, H., & Anke, G. (Eds.), *Electronic government* (pp. 424–435). Berlin, Germany: Springer. doi:10.1007/978-3-540-74444-3_36

Bekkers, V., & Homburg, V. (2007). The myths of E-Government: Looking beyond the assumptions of a new and better government. *The Information Society*, *23*(5), 373–382. doi:10.1080/01972240701572913

Berenson, H., Bernstein, P., Gray, J., Melton, J., O'Neil, E., & O'Neil, P. (1995). A Critique of ANSI SQL Isolation Levels. In *Proc ACM SIGMOD Conf.*, pp. 1-10.

Besson, P. (1999). Les ERP à l'épreuve de l'organisation. *Systèmesd'Information et Management, 4*(4), 21–51.

Bhatnagar, S. (2003). Administrative Corruption: How Does E-Government Help? In *Proceedings of Global Corruption Report 2003*, Transparency International. Retrieved June 30, 2007 from http://www.gipi.az/ssi_eng /egov/20030324.pdf.

BIH. (n.d.). *Business in Haryana.* Retrieved June 23, 2006 from http://www.haryana-online.com/business.htm.

Bilsel, R.U., Buʻyuʻkoʻzkan, G., & Ruan, D. (2006). A fuzzy preference-ranking model for a quality evaluation of hospital web sites. *International Journal of Intelligent Systems, 21*(11), 1181–1197. doi:10.1002/int.20177

Blick, G., Gulledge, T., & Sommer, R. 2000. Defining business process requirements for large-scale public sector ERP implementations: A case study. *Proceedings of the European Conference on Information Systems,* WirtschaftsUniversität, Wien.

Bliemel, M., & Hassanein, K. (2004). E-health:applying business process reengineering principles to healthcare in Canada. *International Journal of Electronic Business, 2*(6), 625–643. doi:10.1504/IJEB.2004.006129

Bonaiuti G. (2006). *E-Learning 2.0 futuro dell'appren dimento in rele tra formale e- informale.* Trento: Erickson.

Bonham, G., Seifert, J., & Thorson, S. (2001). The transformational potential of e-government: the role of political leadership.Paper presented at 4th Pan European International Relations Conference, University of Kent.

Booth, P., Matolcsy, Z., & Wieder, B. (2000). The impacts of enterprise resource planning systems on accounting practice.*The Australian experience. Australian Accounting Review, 16,* 4–18. doi:10.1111/j.1835-2561.2000. tb00066.x

Boudreau, M., & Robey, D. (2005). Enacting Integrated Information Technology: A Human Agency Perspective. *Organization Science, 16*(1), 3–18. doi:10.1287/ orsc.1040.0103

Breibart, Y., Garcia-Molina, H., & Silberschatz, A. (1992). Overview of Multidatabase Transaction Management. *The VLDB Journal, 2,* 181–239. doi:10.1007/BF01231700

Bresnahan, T. F., & Brynjolfsson, E. (2000). Information technology, workplace organization, and the demand for skilled labor: Firm-level evidence. *The Quarterly Journal of Economics, 117*(1), 339–376. doi:10.1162/003355302753399526

Brown, C., and I. Vessey, (2003) Managing the Next Wave of Enterprise Systems: Leveraging Lessons from ERP, MIS Quarterly Executive, 2(1).

Buʻyuʻkoʻzkan, G., Ruan, D., & Feyzioglu, O. (2007). Evaluating e-learning web site quality in a fuzzy environment. *International Journal of Intelligent Systems, 22,* 5, 567-86.

Buchanan, D. (1997). The limitations and opportunities of business process re-engineering in a politicized organizational climate. *Human Relations, 50*(1), 51. doi:10.1177/001872679705000103

Buenadicha, M., Chamorro, A., & Miranda, F.J., & Gonza ́lez, O.R. (2001). A new web assessment index: Spanish universities analysis. *Internet Research: Electronic Networking Applications and Policy, 11*(3), 226–234. doi:10.1108/10662240110396469

Burns, J., & Vaivio, J. (2001). Management accounting change. *Management Accounting Research, 12,* 389–402. doi:10.1006/mare.2001.0178

Business Software, (2008), Top 10 ERP Vendors – 2008 Profiles of the Leading Vendors, Business Software.com.

Butt, D., & Sarker, P. P. (2009). ICT for development in Asia Pacific: Emerging themes in a diverse region. In *Digital Review of Asia Pacific 2009-2010* (pp. 3–13). Orbicom and the International Development Research Centre.

Byrge, C. & Hansen. (2009). The Creative platform: A didactic approach for unlimited application of knowledge in interdisciplinary and intercultural groups. *European Journal of Engineering Education, 34*(3), 235–250. doi:10.1080/03043790902902914

Cacciaguidi-Fahy, S., Currie, J., & Fahy, M. (2002). Financial Shared Services Centres: Opportunities and Challenges for the Accounting Profession. *ACCA Research Report, 79*.

Caglio, A. (2003). Enterprise Resource Planning systems and accountants: towards hybridization? *European Accounting Review, 12*, 123–153. doi:10.1080/0963818031000087853

Caillier, J. G. (2009). Centralized customer service: What local government characteristics influence its acceptance and usage of information? *Public Administration and Management, 14*(2), 292–322.

Caniel, M. C. J. (2004). Teaching competencies efficiently through Internet: A practical example. *European Journal of Vocational Training, 34*, 40–48.

Caralli, A. R., & William, R. W. (n.d.). *The challenges of security management*. White paper of Survivable Enterprise Management Team, Networked Systems Survivability Program, Software Engineering Institute.

Carman, J. H. (1990). Consumer perceptions of service quality: an assessment of the SERVQUAL dimensions. *Journal of Retailing, 66*(1), 33–55.

Carroll, A. B. (1991). The pyramid of corporate social responsibility: Toward the moral management of organizational stakeholders," *Business Horizon*, July-August 1991. RetrievedonJune26,2010,fromhttp://www.rohan.edsu.edu/faculty /dunnweb/rprnts.pyramidofcsr.pdf.

Chadwick, A., & May, C. (2003). Interaction between states and citizens in the age of the Internet: "E-government" in the United States, Britain and the European Union. *Governance, 16*(2), 271–300. doi:10.1111/1468-0491.00216

Chang, S.-I., Gable, G., Smythe, E., & Timbrell, G. (2000). A Delphi examination of public sector ERP implementation issues. Paper presented at the *Proceedings of the 21st International Conference on Information Systems*, Brisbane, Queensland, Australia.

Chapagain, D. P. (12-14 December 2007). *Regional overview of policy and legislations on provision of ICT access for disadvantaged communities through public-private partnership.* Expert Group Meeting on the Provision of ICT Access for Disadvantaged Communities through Public-Private Partnership, Bangkok

Chutimaskul, W., & Chongsuphajaisiddhi, V. (2004). A framework for developing local e-government. In M. A. Wimmer (Ed.), *Proceedings of Knowledge Management in Electronic Government: 5th IFIP International Working Conference*, KMGov 2004, Krems, Austria, May 17-19, 2004 (pp. 319-324).

Clayton, G. E. (2005). *A Case Study and Comparison of Enterprise Resource Planning Systems: Implementation and Performance*, Master's Thesis, Penn State Harrisburg, Harrisburg, PA

Commission of the European Communities. (2009). *Europe's Digital Competitiveness Report, Vol. 1: i2010—Annual Information Society Report 2009 and Benchmarking i2010: Trends and main achievements*. Commission of the European Communities, Brussels.

Commonwealth. (2004). *Commonwealth local government handbook: Modernisation, Council structures, finance, e-government, local democracy, partnerships, representation*. Commonwealth Local Government Forum, Commonwealth Secretariat, 2004.

Conklin, A., & White, G. B. (2006). E-government & Cyber Security: The Role of Cyber Security exercises. In *Proceedings of the 39th Annual Hawaii International Conference on System Sciences*.

Cooper, R., & Zmud, R. (1990). Information technology implementation research: a technological diffusion approach. *Management Science, 36*(2), 123–142. doi:10.1287/mnsc.36.2.123

Cordella, A. (2006). Transaction costs and information systems: does IT add up? *Journal of Information Technology, 21*, 195–202. doi:10.1057/palgrave.jit.2000066

Cordella, A. (2001), *Does Information Technology Always Lead to Lower Transaction Costs?* The 9th European Conference on Information Systems, Bled, Slovenia, June 27-29.

Cordella, A., & Simon, K. A. (1997), *The Impact of Information Technology on Transaction and Coordination Cost*, Conference on Information Systems Research in Scandinavia (IRIS 20), Oslo, Norway, August 9-12.

Cornell, J., Ferres, N., & Traveglione, T. (2003). Engendering trust in manager-subordinate relationships: Predictors and outcomes. *Personnel Review, 32*(5), 569–587. doi:10.1108/00483480310488342

Corner, M. L. (2007). *Informal learning*. Retrieved on May 13, 2010 from http//: agelesslearner.com/ intros/ informal.html.

Coulson-Thomas, C. (1998). Managing innovation in public services: European and international experience. *Total quality management & Business Excellence, 9*(2), 213-222.

Crisostomo, D. T. (2008). Management attributes of implementing An ERP system in the public sector. *Journal of International Business Research, 7*(2), 1–15.

Cronin, J. J., & Taylor, S. A. (1992). Measuring service quality: a re-examination and extension. *Journal of Marketing, 56*(July), 55–68. doi:10.2307/1252296

CTG. (2002). *New foundations: Annual report 2002*. Center for Technology in Government, University at Albany, State University of New York.

CTG. (2003). *Annual report 2003*. Center for Technology in Government, University at Albany, State University of New York.

CTO. (2008). *Towards effective e-governance: The delivery of public services through local e-content*. Global Summary Report, Commonwealth Telecommunications Organization.

Daniels, M. (2002). *E-Government Strategy: Simplified Delivery of Services to Citizens*. Washington, DC: Office of Management & Budget.

Danziger, J. N., & Anderson, K. V. (2002). The impacts of information technology on public administration: An analysis of empirical research from the "Golden Age" of transformation. *International Journal of Public Administration, 25*(5), 591–627. doi:10.1081/PAD-120003292

Danziger, J. N., & Anderson, K. V. (2002). The impacts of information technology on public administration: an analysis of empirical research from the "golden age" of transformation. *International Journal of Public Administration, 1*(22).

Das, S. R., & Chandrashekhar, R. (2006). *List of Asia Pacific e-government case studies. UNDP-APDIP, Digital Review of Asia Pacific 2005/2006*. UNDP-APDIP.

Davenport, T. (1998). Putting the enterprise into the enterprise system. *Harvard Business Review, 76*(4), 121–131.

Davenport, T. H. (1998). Putting the enterprise into the enterprise system. *Harvard Business Review, 76*(July-August), 123–131.

Davidson, G. (1997). Managing by process in private and public organizations: Scientific Management in the Information Revolution. *Journal of Post Keynesian Economics, 20*(1), 25–45.

Davis, F. D. (1989). Perceived usefulness, perceived ease of use, and user acceptance of information technology. *Management Information Systems Quarterly, 13*(3), 319–340. doi:10.2307/249008

Davis, F. D., Bagozzi, R. P., & Warshaw, P. R. (1989). User acceptance of computer technology: A comparison of two theoretical models. *Management Science, 35*, 982–1003. doi:10.1287/mnsc.35.8.982

Deloitte (2008). *In fighting shape?*. 2008 survey of cost-improvement trends in the Fortune 500', Deloitte.

Deloitte Research Study. (2002). *The keys to smart enterprise transformation for the public sector*. Retrieved from http://www.deloitte.com/assets/DcomGlobal/Local%20 Assets/Documents/ DTT_DR_keyspublicsector.pdf

Denhardt, R. B., & Denhardt, J. V. (2000). The new public service: Serving rather than steering. *Public Administration Review, 60*(6), 549–559. doi:10.1111/0033-3352.00117

Department of Defense. (2009). *Defense Materiel Organization*. Australian Government.

Downes, S. (2005). E-learning 2.0. *Elearn magazine*, October 17, 2005. Retrieved on June 20, 2010 from http:// www.elearnmag.or /subpage.cfm.

Duggal, P. (2005). Harmonization of e-commerce laws and regulatory systems in South Asia. In TID (Ed.), *Harmonized development of legal and regulatory systems for e-commerce in Asia and the Pacific: Current challenges and capacity-building needs* (pp. 23-36). New York, NY: UN Publications.

Dunleavy, P., & Hood, C. (1994). From old public administration to new public management. *Public Money & Management, 14*(3), 9–16.

Dunleavy, P., Margetts, H., Bastow, S., & Tinkler, J. (2006). New public management is dead- long live digital-era governance. *Journal of Public Administration: Research and Theory, 16*(3), 467–494. doi:10.1093/jopart/mui057

Dwivedi, Y. K., Weerakkody, V., & Williams, M. D. (2007). Interorganzational Information Integration: A key enabler for digital government. *Government Information Quarterly, 24*, 691. doi:10.1016/j.giq.2007.08.004

Dzhumalieva, S., & Helfert, M. (2008). A Conceptual Framework for Handling Complex Administrative Processes in E-Government. *Information Systems and E-Business Technologies, 417-428.*

Ebbers, W. E., Pieterson, W. J., & Noordman, H. N. (2008). Electronic government: Rethinking channel management strategies. *Government Information Quarterly, 25*(2), 181–201. doi:10.1016/j.giq.2006.11.003

Ebrahim, Z., & Irani, Z. (2005). E-government and adoption: Architecture and barriers. *Business Process Management Journal, 11*(5), 589–611. doi:10.1108/14637150510619902

Ebrahim, Z., & Irani, Z. (2005). E-government adoption: Architecture and barriers. *Business Process Management Journal, 11*(5), 589–611. doi:10.1108/14637150510619902

EC. (2010). *Europe's digital competitiveness report: Main achievements of the i2010 strategy 2005-2009.* Luxembourg: European Commission.

Financial Times Higher Education Supplement. (2008). *University Rankings, Financial Times Higher Education Supplement.* New York, NY: Financial Times.

Fjermestad, J., & Romano, N. C. (2003). Electronic customer relationship management: Revisiting the general principles of usability and resistance – an integrative implementation framework. *Business Process Management Journal, 9*(5), 572–591. doi:10.1108/14637150310496695

Fleming, C. (2008). *Call 311: Connecting Citizens to Local Government, Final Report.* Retrieved from http://bookstore.icma.org/freedocs/43547.pdf

Fountain, J. E. (2009). Bureaucratic reform and e-government in the United States: An institutional perspective. In Chadwick, A., & Howard, P. N. (Eds.), *Routledge Handbook of Internet Politics.* New York, NY: Routledge.

Fox, W. F., & Gurley, T. (2006, May). *Will consolidation improve sub-national governments?* (World Bank Policy Research Working Paper WPS3913). Washington, DC: World Bank.

Frank, L., & Zahle, T. (1998). Semantic ACID Properties in Multidatabases Using Remote Procedure Calls and Update Propagations. *Software, Practice & Experience, 28*, 77–98. doi:10.1002/(SICI)1097-024X(199801)28:1<77::AID-SPE148>3.0.CO;2-R

Frank, L. (2008). Smooth and Flexible ERP Migration between both Homogeneous and Heterogeneous ERP Systems/ERP Modules. In *Proc of the 2ⁿᵈ Workshop on 3ʳᵈ Generation Enterprise Resource Planning Systems,* Copenhagen business School.

Frank, L. (2010). *Design of Distributed Integrated Heterogeneous or Mobile Databases.* Saarbrücken, Germany: LAP LAMBERT Academic Publishing AG & Co. KG, Germany, 1-157.

Frank, L., & Andersen, S. K. (2010). Evaluation of Different Database Designs for Integration of Heterogeneous Distributed Electronic Health Records. In *Proc. of the International Conference on Complex Medical Engineering* (CME2010), IEEE Computer Society.

Frank, L., & Susanne Munck. (2008). An Overview of Architectures for Integrating Distributed Electronic Health Records. In *Proceeding of the 7th International Conference on Applications and Principles of Information Science* (APIS2008), 297-300.

Frye, D., & Gulledge, T. (2007). End-to-end business process scenarios. *Industrial Management & Data Systems, 107*(6), 749–761. doi:10.1108/02635570710758707

Frye, D., Gulledge, T., Leary, M., Sommer, R., & Vincent, J. (2007). Public sector enterprise system implementation. *Electronic Government. International Journal (Toronto, Ont.), 4*(1), 76–96.

Gallivan, M. J., Spitler, V. K., & Koufaris, M. (2005). Does Information Technology Training Really Matter? A Social Information Processing Analysis of Coworkers' Influence on IT Usage in the Workplace. *Journal of Management Information Systems, 22*(1), 153–192.

Galpaya, H., Samarajiva, R., & Soysa, S. (2007). Taking e-government to the bottom of the pyramid: Dial-a-gov? *Proceedings of the 1st International Conference on Theory and Practice of Electronic Governance*, Vol. 232 (pp. 233-241). Macao, China: ACM.

Garcia, J. R., & Moyano, I. J. M. (2007). Understanding the evolution of e-government: The influence of systems of rules on public sector dynamics. *Government Information Quarterly*, (2): 266–290. doi:10.1016/j.giq.2006.04.005

Garcia, A. C. B., Maciel, C., & Pinto, F. B. (2005). A quality inspection method to evaluate e-government sites. in Wimmer, M.A., Traunmu¨ller, R., Gro¨nlund,A. and Andersen, K.V. (Eds), Electronic Government: 4th International Conference, EGOV 2005, In *Proceedings: Lecture Notes in Computer Science, Vol. 3591,* Copenhagen, Denmark, pp. 198-209, available at: www.informatik. uni-trier.de/, ley/db/conf/egov/egov2005.html.

Garcia-Molina, H., & Polyzois, C. (1990). *Issues in disaster recovery. IEEE Compcon*. New York, NY: IEEE.

Garcia-Molina, H., & Salem, K. (1987). *Sagas*. In *Proceeding of the ACM SIGMOD Conf*, pp 249-259.

Gattiker, T., & Goodhue, D. (2005). What happens after ERP Implementation: Understanding the Impact of Inter-Dependence and Differentiation on Plant-Level Outcomes. *Management Information Systems Quarterly*, *29*(3), 559–584.

Gefen, D., & Pavlou, P. (2002). E-government adoption. Paper presented at Americas Conference on Information Systems, Tampa, FL.

Gessi, T., Ramnarine, D., & Wilkins, J. (2007). Introducing a new e-governance framework in the commonwealth: From theory to practice. *The Asia Pacific Journal of Public Administration*, *29*(2), 131–151.

Gilbert, D., Balestrini, P., & Littleboy, D. (2004). Barriers & benefits in the adoption of e-government. *International Journal of Public Sector Management*, *17*(5), 286. doi:10.1108/09513550410539794

Gonella, L., & Panto, E. (2005). *Didactic architecture and organization models; A process of mutual adaptation*. Retrieved on June 20, 2010 from www.elearningeuropa. info /files/media.

Government of Afghanistan. (2003a). *Afghanistan telecommunications and Internet policy.*

Government of Afghanistan. (2003b). *Information and communications technology policy.*

Government of Afghanistan. (2005, April). A*fghanistan country report: Telecommunications, Ministry of Communications.*

Government of Bhutan. (2006). *Technical guidelines on information and communications technology (ICT) for preparation of the tenth five year plan (2008-2013). August 2006.* Thimphu, Bhutan: Ministry of Information and Communications, Royal Government of Bhutan.

Government of Bhutan. (2007). *Information, communications and transport sectors in Bhutan: A Special Report. July 2007.* Thimphu, Bhutan: Ministry of Information and Communications, Royal Government of Bhutan.

Government of Bhutan. (2003). *Information and communications technology (ICT) policy for Bhutan: A White Paper*. Ministry of Information and Communications, Royal Government of Bhutan, Thimphu; Bhutan.

Government of India. (2000). *The Information Technology Act 2000*. Ministry of Communications and Information Technology/Dept of IT.

Government of India. (2006). *Information Technology: Annual report 2006-2007*. Ministry of Communications and Information Technology/Dept of IT.

Government of Jordan. (2006). *Jordan e-government-2006: E-government strategy. Jordan e-Government Program, Ministry of Information and Communications technology (MoICT)*. Government of Jordan.

Government of Maldives. (2001). *Maldives telecommunication policy 2001-2005*. Ministry of Communication, Science and Technology, Maldives, 1 August 2001.

Government of Maldives. (2002). *Maldives government information technology initiative – The progress*. A paper at the 2nd APT Meeting on Asia-Pacific Initiatives for the Information Society (AIIS), 5-9 August 2002, Negara, Burunai Darussalam, Post & Telecom, Ministry of Communication, Science & Technology, Government of Maldives.

Government of Maldives. (2003). *E-Maldives: The Republic of Maldives national information and communications technology policy*. Ministry of Communication, Science and Technology. Draft. 2003.

Government of Maldives. (2006) *Maldives telecommunication policy 2006-2010: Towards one island nation through effective telecommunications*. Minister of Transport & Communication, 1 August 2006.

Granlund, M., & Malmi, T. (2002). Moderate impact of ERPs on management accounting: a lag or permanent outcome? *Management Accounting Research, 13*, 299–321. doi:10.1006/mare.2002.0189

Grant, G., & Chau, D. (2005). Developing a generic framework for E-government. *Journal of Global Information Management, 13*(1), 1–30. doi:10.4018/jgim.2005010101

Gray, J., & Reuter, A. (1993). *Transaction Processing*. San Francisco, CA: Morgan Kaufman.

Gray, P. (2003). *In depth: RMIT's PeopleSoft disaster*. Australia: ZDNet.

Greasley, A. (2006). Using process mapping and business process simulation to support a process-based approach to change in a public sector organization. *Technovation, 26*(1), 95–103. doi:10.1016/j.technovation.2004.07.008

Grönlund, Å., & Horan, T. A. (2004). Introducing e-Gov: History, definitions, and issues. *Communications of the AIS, 15*, 713–729.

Groznik, A., Kovacic, A., & Trkman, P. (2008). The role of business renovation and information in eGovernment. *Journal of Computer Information Systems, 49*(1), 81–89.

Gulledge, T., & Sommer, R. (2002). Business process management: public sector implications. *Business Process Management Journal, 8*(4), 364–376. doi:10.1108/14637150210435017

Gulledge, T. R., & Sommer, R. A. (2003). Public sector enterprise resource planning. *Industrial Management & Data Systems, 103*(7), 471–483. doi:10.1108/02635570310489179

Gupta, A. (2000). Enterprise Resource Planning: The Emerging Organizational Value Systems. *Industrial Management + Data Systems. 100*, (3), 114-.

Gyorgy, M., & Szeged, Z. D. M. (2003). Didactic approach for teaching non-determinism in automata theory. *Analysis, 35*(2), 48–61.

Hae, D., & Lee, D. (2005). Contextual IT Business Value & Barriers: And E-Government & E-Business Perspective. In *Proceedings of the 38th Annual Hawaii International Conference on System Sciences* (HICSS'05) - Track 5, Hawaii.

Halachmi, A., & Bovaird, T. (1997). Process reengineering in the public sector: Learning some private sector lessons. *Technovation, 17*(5), 227–235. doi:10.1016/S0166-4972(96)00123-X

Hanna, N. K. (2003). *Why national strategies are needed for ICT-enabled development*. ISG Staff Working Papers No. 3

Harrington, B., McLoughlin, K., & Riddell, D. (1997). Business Process Re-engineering in the Public Sector: a Case Study of the Contributions Agency. *New Technology, Work and Employment, 13*(1), 43–50. doi:10.1111/1468-005X.00037

Heeks, R. (2006). *Implementing and managing e-government*. Vistaar Publications.

Heeks, R. (2003). Most E-government Development Projects Fail: How Can Risks be Reduced? *iGovernemnt Working Paper Series,* Paper no. 14.

Henriksson, A. Yi, Frost, Y.B., & Middleton, M. (2006). Evaluation instrument for e-government websites. In *Proceedings Internet Research 7.0: Internet Convergences*, Brisbane, Queensland, Australia.

Hesson, M. (2007). Business process reengineering in UAE public sector A naturalization and residency case study. *Business Process Management Journal, 13*(5), 707–727. doi:10.1108/14637150710823174

Hesson, M., Al-Ameed, H., & Samaka, M. (2007). BPR in UAE Public Sector: a town planning study. *Business Process Management Journal, 13*(3), 348–378. doi:10.1108/14637150710752281

Hjort-Madsen, K. (2007). Institutional patterns of enterprise architecture adoption in government. *Transforming Government: People. Process and Policy, 1*(4), 333–349.

Ho, A. T. (2002). Reinventing local governments and the E-Government initiative. *Public Administration Review*, *62*(4), 434–444. doi:10.1111/0033-3352.00197

Ho, A. T., & Ni, A. Y. (2004). Explaining the adoption of E-Government features: A case study of Iowa county treasurers' offices. *American Review of Public Administration*, *34*(2), 164–180. doi:10.1177/0275074004264355

Hof, S., & Reichstädter, P. (2004). *Securing e-Government*. EGOV 2004, Springer-Verlag, 336-341.

Holzer, M., & Kim, S.-T. (2005). *Digital Governance in Municipalities Worldwide (2005), A Longitudinal Assessment of Municipal Web sites throughout the World*. The e-Governance Institute, available at: http://andromeda.rutgers.edu

Homburg, V. M. (2008). Red tape and reforms: Trajectories of technological and managerial reforms in public administration. *International Journal of Public Administration*, *31*(7), 749–770. doi:10.1080/01900690701690817

Hong, K, K. and Kim, Y. G. (2002). The Critical Success Factors for ERP Implementation: An Organizational Fit Perspective. *Information & Management*, *40*(1), 25–40. doi:10.1016/S0378-7206(01)00134-3

Hood, C., & Peters, G. (2004). The middle aging of New Public Management: Into the age of paradox? *Journal of Public Administration: Research and Theory*, *14*(3), 267–282. doi:10.1093/jopart/muh019

Hoogwout, M. (2003). super pilots, subsidizing or self-organization: Stimulating e-government initiatives in Dutch local governments. In R. Traunmüller (Ed.), *Proceedings of Electronic Government: Second International Conference*, (pp. 85-90). EGOV 2003, Prague, Czech Republic, September 1-5, 2003, Springer.

Howard, M. (2001). E-Government Across the Globe: How Will 'e' Change Government. *Government Finance Review*, *17*(4), 6–9.

Huang, W., Le, T., Li, X., & Gandha, S. (2006). Categorizing web features and functions to evaluate commercial web sites. *Industrial Management & Data Systems*, *106*(4), 523–539. doi:10.1108/02635570610661606

Hughes, M., Scott, M., & Golden, W. (2006). The role of business process redesign in creating e-Government in Ireland. *Business Process Management Journal*, *12*(1), 76–87. doi:10.1108/14637150610643779

Hwang, M. S., Ta, L. C., Ji, S. J., & Chu, Y. P. (2004). Challenges in E-governance & Security of Information. *International Journal of Information Security*, *15*(1).

i4D. (2005) E-government: Evolution or revolution? *Information for Development (i4D)*, *3*(6). infoDev. (2010). *High-speed Internet drives economic growth*. Retrieved November 18, 2010, from http://www.infodev.org /en/ Article.522.html

Ilyas, A. (2004). *Statistics and indicators on ICTs in Maldives*. Global Indicators Workshop on Community Access to ICTs, Mexico City, 16-19 November 2004.

Indihar Stemberger, M., & Jaklic, J. (2007). Towards E-government by business process change-A methodology for public sector. *International Journal of Information Management*, *27*(4), 221–232. doi:10.1016/j.ijinfomgt.2007.02.006

James, G. (2000). Empowering bureaucrats. *MC Technology Marketing Intelligence*, *20*(12), 62–80.

Jones, S., Irani, Z., Sharif, A., & Themistocleous, M. (2006). E-government Evaluation: Reflections on Two Organizational Studies. In *Proceedings of the 39th Hawaii International Conference on System Sciences*.

Joshi, J., & Ghafoor, A. (2001). Digital government security infrastructure design challenges. *IEEE Computer*, *34*(1), 66–72.

Joshi, J. B. D., Anttiroiko, A. V., & Malkia, M. (2007). *Information Security Issues & Challenges*. Encyclopaedia of Digital Government.

Jurmi, K. (2004). *A paper on Bhutan's information and communication technology*. 1st International Conference by the Italian Chamber of Deputies, 6 & 7 Oct. 2004, Rome, Italy.

Jutras, C. (2007, July). *The Total Cost of ERP Ownership in Mid Sized Companies*. Boston, MA: Aberdeen Group.

Kale, P. T., Banwait, S. S., & Laroiya, S. C. (2007). Enterprise Resource Planning Implementation in Indian SMEs: Issues and Challenges. *National Institute of Technical Teachers' Training and Research*, Retrieved from www.csi-sigegov.org/ critical_pdf/27_242-248.pdf

Khosrow-Pour, M. (2006). Emerging Trends and Challenges in Information Technology Management, *Information Management Association*, International Conference, Idea Group Inc.

Kim, P., Eng, T. R., Deering, M. J., & Maxfield, A. (1999). Published criteria for evaluating health related Web sites [Review]. *British Medical Journal, 318*, 647–649.

King, W. (2005). *Ensuring ERP implementation success. Information Systems Management*. Hershey, PA: IGI Global.

King, S. F. (2007). Citizens as customers: Exploring the future of CRM in UK local government. *Government Information Quarterly, 24*(1), 47–63. doi:10.1016/j.giq.2006.02.012

Knox, C. (2008). Kazakhstan: modernizing government in the context of political inertia. *International Review of Administrative Sciences, 74*(3), 477. doi:10.1177/0020852308095314

Koch, C., & Wailgum, T. (2008). *ERP Definitions and Solutions*. CIO.

Kohn, A. (1999). Getting back to basics: Unlearn how to learn. *Washington Post*, October 10,1999. Retrieved on June 26, 2010 from www.alfiekohn.org/teaching / alagbtb.htm

Kolsaker, A. (2005). Third way e-government: The case for local devolution. In M. H. Böhlen, J. Gamper, W. Polasek, & M. A. Wimmer (Eds.), *Proceedings of E-Government: Towards Electronic Democracy: International Conference,* TCGOV 2005 Bolzano, Italy, March 2-4, 2005, (pp. 70-80). Springer.

Kraemer, K., & King, J. L. (2006). Information technology and administrative reform: Will E-Government be different? *International Journal of Electronic Government Research, 2*(1), 1–20. doi:10.4018/jegr.2006010101

Kraemer, K. L., & Perry, J. L. (1979). The Federal Push to Bring Computer Applications to Local Governments. *Public Administration Review, 39*(3), 260–270. doi:10.2307/975951

Kumar, V., Maheshwari, B., & Kumar, U. (2002). ERP systems implementation: Best practices in Canadian government organizations. *Government Information Quarterly, 19*, 147–172. doi:10.1016/S0740-624X(02)00092-8

Kumar, M., & Sareen, M. (2009). Building Trust in E-Commerce through Web Interface. *International Journal of ICT and Human Development, 1*(1), 64–74. doi:10.4018/jicthd.2009092205

Kwak, N., & Lee, C. (2002). Business process reengineering for health-care system using muticriteria mathematical programming. *European Journal of Operational Research, 140*(2), 447–458. doi:10.1016/S0377-2217(02)00082-6

Kwon, T., & Zmud, R. (1987). *Unifying the fragmented models of information systems implementation: Critical issues in Information Systems Research*. New York, NY: John Wiley.

Labelle, R. (2005). *ICT policy formulation and e-strategy development: A comprehensive guidebook. United Nations Development Programme-Asia Pacific Development Information Programme*. UNDP-APDIP.

Lallana, E. C. (2004). *An overview of ICT policies and e-strategies of select Asian economies. United Nations Development Programme-Asia Pacific Development Information Programme (UNDP-APDIP) – 2004*. Reed Elsevier India Private Limited.

Lallana, E. C. (2003). *Comparative analysis of ICT polices and e-strategies in Asia*. A presentation at the Asian Forum on ICT Policies and e-Strategies, 20-22 October, Kuala Lumpur: UNDP-APDIP.

Lambrinoudakis, C., & Gritzalis, S. (2003). Security requirements for e-government services: a methodological approach for developing a common PKI-based security policy. *Computer Communications, 26*(16), 1873–1883. doi:10.1016/S0140-3664(03)00082-3

Landsbergen, D., & Wolken, G. (2001). Realizing the promise: Government information systems and the fourth generation of information technology. *Public Administration Review, 61*(2), 206–220. doi:10.1111/0033-3352.00023

LaTour, S. A., & Peat, N. C. (1979). Conceptual and methodological issues in consumer satisfaction research. Wilkie, W.F. (Ed.), *Advances in Consumer Research, 6*, Association for Consumer Research, Ann Arbor, Ml, 431-437.

Lau, E. (2005). *E-government and the drive for growth and equity. Belfer Center for Science and International Affairs (BCSIA)*. Harvard University.

Layne, K., & Lee, J. (2001). Developing fully functional E-government: A four stage model. *Government Information Quarterly, 18*(2), 122–136. doi:10.1016/S0740-624X(01)00066-1

Levy, Y., & Ellis, T. (2006). A systems approach to conduct an effective literature review in support of information systems research. *Informing Science: International Journal of an Emerging Transdiscipline, 9*, 181–212.

Limam Mansar, S., Reijers, H. A., & Ounnar, F. (2009). Development of a decision-making stategy to improve the efficiency of BPR. *Expert Systems with Applications, 36*(2), 3248–3262. doi:10.1016/j.eswa.2008.01.008

Linden, R. (1994). *Seamless Government: A Practical Guide to Re-engineering in the Public Sector*. Jossey-Bass Publishers.

Lohse, G. L., & Spiller, P. (1998). Electronic Shopping: Quantifying the Effect of Customer Interfaces on Traffic & Sales. *Communications of the ACM, 417*.

Louis, R., Sylvestre, U., & François, B. (2005). "Erp Adoption For E-Government: An Analysis Of Motivations."*e*Government Workshop, Brunel University, West London, UK.

Ludwigshafen University Of Applied Sciences. (2004). *Enhanced Project Success Through SAP Best Practices*. Germany: International Benchmarking Study, Ludwigshafen University.

MacIntosh, R. (2003). BPR: alive and well in the public sector. *International Journal of Operations & Production Management, 23*(3/4), 327–345. doi:10.1108/01443570310462794

Malhotra, C., Chariar, V. M., Das, L. K., & Ilavarasan, P. V. (2007). ICT for rural development: An inclusive framework for e-Governance. In Sahu, G. P. (Ed.), *Adopting e-governance* (pp. 216–226). New Delhi, India: GIFT Publishing.

Markoff, J. (2009a). *Worm Infects Millions of Computers Worldwide*. New York, NY: The New York Times.

Martin, R., & Montagna, J. (2006). Business process reengineering role in electronic government. *The past and Future of Information Systems: 1976-2006 and Beyond: 77-88*

Martinez-Moyano, I., & Gil-Garcia, J. (2004). Rules, Norms, and Individual preferences for action: An Institutional Framework to Understand the dynamics of eGovernment Evolution. *Electronic. Journal of E-Government*, 194–199. doi:10.1007/978-3-540-30078-6_32

Mashari, M. A. (2002). ERP Systems: A Research Agenda. *Industrial Management & Data Systems, 102*(3).

Mazumdar, C., Kumar, A., & Banerjee, P. (2009). *On Information Security Issues in E-governance: Developing Country Views*. CSDMS Journal.

McAdam, R., & Corrigan, M. (2001). Re-engineering in public sector health care: a telecommunication case study. *International Journal of Health Care Quality Assurance, 14*(5), 218–227. doi:10.1108/09526860110401340

McAdam, R., & Micheli, P. (1998). Development of Business process reengineering Model applicable to the public sector. *Total Quality Management, 9*(4), 160–163. doi:10.1080/0954412988802

McClure, D. L. (statement of David L. McClure) (2000). *U.S. General Accounting Office, before the subcommittee on Government Management*, Information & technology, committee on Government reform, Retrieved from http://www.gao.gov.

McNulty, T., & Ferlie, E. (2004). Process transformation: Limitations to radical organizational change within public service organizations. *Organization Studies, 25*(8), 1389. doi:10.1177/0170840604046349

Mehrotra, S., Rastogi, R., Korth, H., & Silberschatz, A. (1992). A transaction model for multi-database systems. In *Proc International Conference on Distributed Computing Systems*, pp. 56-63.

Melitski, J. (2005). Digital government worldwide: an e-government assessment of municipal Web sites. *International Journal of Electronic Government Research*, *1*(1), 1–19. doi:10.4018/jegr.2005010101

Mendel, T. D. (2009). *Assessment of media development in the Maldives: Based on UNESCO's media development indicators* (p. 24). UNESCO.

Meneklis, V., & Douligeris, C. (2007). Enhancing the design of e-government: identifying structures and modelling concepts in contemporary platforms. *Proceedings of the 1st international conference on Theory and practice of electronic governance:* ACM, 108-116.

Mengesha, G., & Common, R. (2007). Public sector capacity reform in Ethiopia: a tale of success in two ministries? *Public Administration and Development*, *27*(5), 367–380. doi:10.1002/pad.456

Meta Group. (2010). Longhaus. Retrieved from http://www.longhaus.com/ research/naked-chief-blog-link/tags /META-Group/

Michnowski, L. (2008). Ecohumanism as a developing crossing. In Sharma, S. (Ed.), *Transformative Pathways: Attainable Utopia* (pp. 107–136). Jaipur, India: Pratiksha Publications.

Middleton, M. (2007). Approaches to evaluation of websites for public sector services. In P. Kommers (Ed.), In *Proceedings of the IADIS International Conference*, e-Society 2007, Lisbon, Portugal (pp. 279-284). Lisbon: IADIS.

Milward, H. B., & Snyder, L. O. (1996). Electronic Government: Linking citizens to public organizations through technology. *Journal of Public Administration: Research and Theory*, *6*(2), 261–275.

Miranda, R. A., & Kavanagh, S. C. (2005). Achieving government transformation through ERP systems. *Government Finance Review*, *21*(3), 36–42.

Miranda, F. J., Sanguino, R., & Bañegil, T. M. (2009). Quantitative assessment of European municipal web sites: Development and use of an evaluation tool. *Internet Research*, *19*(4), 425–441. doi:10.1108/10662240910981380

Miranda, R. (1998). The rise of ERP technology in the public sector. *Government Finance Review*, *15*(4), 9–17.

Mittal, V., Kumar, P., & Tsiros, M. (1999). Attribute-level performance, satisfaction and behavioral intentions over time: a consumption-system approach. *Journal of Marketing*, *63*(April), 88–101. doi:10.2307/1251947

Mookerjee, R. (2005, November). Maintaining Enterprise Software Applications. *Communications of the ACM*, *48*(11), 75–79. doi:10.1145/1096000.1096008

Moon, M. J., & Norris, D. F. (2005). Does managerial orientation matter? The adoption of reinventing government and e-government at the municipal level. *Information Systems Journal*, *15*(1), 43–60. doi:10.1111/j.1365-2575.2005.00185.x

Moon, J.-W., & Kim, Y.-G. (2001). Extending the TAM for a World-Wide-Web Context. *Information & Management*, *38*, 217–230. doi:10.1016/S0378-7206(00)00061-6

Moore, J. (2000). One Road to Turnover: An Examination of Work Exhaustion in Technology Professionals. *Management Information Systems Quarterly*, *24*(1), 141–168. doi:10.2307/3250982

Motwani, J., Kumar, A., Jiang, J., & Youssef, M. (1998). Business process reengineering: a theoretical framework and an integrated model. *International Journal of Operations & Production Management*, *18*(9/10), 964–977. doi:10.1108/EUM0000000004536

Nadler, L. (1984). *The handbook of HRD*. New York, NY: John Wiley and Sons.

Nah, F., Zuckweiler, K., & Lau, J. (2003). ERP Implementation: Chief Information Officers' Perceptions of Critical Success Factors. *International Journal of Human-Computer Interaction*, *16*(1), 5–22. doi:10.1207/S15327590IJHC1601_2

Narsimhan, R., & Jayaram, J. (1998). Reengineering Service Operation: a longitudinal casse study. *Journal of Operations Management*, *17*(1), 7–22. doi:10.1016/S0272-6963(98)00029-1

Nguyen, A. (2007). *Public information network as computing and e-government infrastructure in developing countries.* Invited talk at the 7th Global Forum on Reinventing Government: Building Trust in Government, Vienna, Austria, June 2007.

Nielsen, J. (2000). *Designing Web Usability: The Practice of Simplicity.* Indianapolis, IN: New Riders Publishing.

Nonaka, I., & Takeuchi, H. (1995). *The knowledge creating company: How Japanese company create the dynamics of innovations.* Oxford, UK: Oxford University Press.

Norris, D. F., & Moon, M. J. (2005). Advancing e-Government at the grassroots: Tortoise or hare? *Public Administration Review, 65*(1), 64–75. doi:10.1111/j.1540-6210.2005.00431.x

Nunnally, J. C. (1978). *Psychometric Theory* (2nd ed.). New York: McGraw-Hill.

Nye, J. Jr. (1997). Introduction: The decline of confidence in government. In Nye, J. Jr, Zelikow, P., & King, D. (Eds.), *Why people don't trust government* (pp. 1–18). Cambridge, MA: Harvard University Press.

Olsina, L., Godoy, D., Lafuente, G., & Rossi, G. (1999). Assessing the quality of academic websites. *New Review Hypermedia Multimedia Journal, 5,* 81–103. doi:10.1080/13614569908914709

Omari, H. A., & Omari, A. A. (2006). Building an E-governance e-Trust Infrastructure. *American Journal of Applied Sciences, 3*(11), 2122–2130. doi:10.3844/ajassp.2006.2122.2130

O'Neill, P., & Sohal, A. (1999). Business Process Reengineering A review of recent literature. *Technovation, 19*(9), 571–581. doi:10.1016/S0166-4972(99)00059-0

Ongaro, E. (2004). Process management in the public sector: the experience of one-stop shops in Italy. *International Journal of Public Sector Management, 17*(1), 81–107. doi:10.1108/09513550410515592

Oppenheim, C., & Ward, L. (2006). Evaluation of web sites for B2C e-commerce. *Aslib Proceedings, 58*(3), 237–260. doi:10.1108/00012530610701022

Palmer, J. W. (2002). Website usability, design, and performance metrics. *Information Systems Research, 13*(2), 151–167. doi:10.1287/isre.13.2.151.88

Pan, S.-L., Tan, C.-W., Eric, T. K., & Lim, E. T. (2006). Customer relationship management (CRM) in e-government: a relational perspective. *Decision Support Systems, 42*(1), 237–250. doi:10.1016/j.dss.2004.12.001

Panopoulou, E., Tambouris, E., & Tarabanis, K. (2008). A framework for evaluating web sites of public authorities. *Aslib Proceedings, 60*(5), 517–546. doi:10.1108/00012530810908229

Parajuli, J. (2007). A content analysis of Selected Government Websites: A case Study of Nepal. *The Electronic. Journal of E-Government, 5*(1), 87–94.

Parasuraman, A., Zeithaml, V. A., & Berry, L. L. (1988). SERVQUAL: a multiple-item scale for measuring customer perceptions of service quality. *Journal of Retailing, 64*(Spring), 12–40.

Parr, A., & Shanks, G. (2000). A model of ERP project implementation. *Journal of Information Technology, 15,* 289–303. doi:10.1080/02683960010009051

Pascual, P. J. (2003). E-government. New York: Asia-Pacific Development Information Programme, United Nations Development Programme, eprim ers.apdip.net/series.

Pattakos, A. N. (2004). The search for meaning in government service. *Public Administration Review, 64*(1), 106–112. doi:10.1111/j.1540-6210.2004.00350.x

Patton, M. Q. (2002). *Qualitative Evaluation & Research Methods* (3rd ed.). Thousand Oaks, CA: Sage Publications.

Paul, S. (2007). A case study of e-governance initiatives in India. *The International Information & Library Review, 39*(3-4), 176–184. doi:10.1016/j.iilr.2007.06.003

Perotti, E. C., & von Thadden, E.-L. (2006). Corporate governance and the distribution of wealth: A political-economy perspective. [JITE]. *Journal of Institutional and Theoretical Economics, 162*(1), 204–217. doi:10.1628/093245606776166660

Pertrazzini, B. A., & Harindranath, G. (1997). Information infrastructure initiative in emerging economies: The case of India. In Kahin, B., & Wilson, E. (Eds.), *National information infrastructure initiatives: Vision and policy design* (p. 220). Cambridge, MA: MIT Press.

Peslak, A., Subramanian, G., & Clayton, G. (2008). The Phases of ERP Software Implementation and Maintenance: A Model for Predicting Preferred ERP Use. *Journal of Computer Information Systems*, 48(2), 25–33.

Phillips, D. (2001). *Online public relations*. London, UK: Kogan Page Limited.

Polyzois, C., & Garcia-Molina, H. (1994). Evaluation of Remote Backup Algorithms for Transaction-Processing Systems. *ACM TODS*, 19(3), 423–449. doi:10.1145/185827.185836

Poskitt (2002) recommended from Sarmad Alshawi, Ali Alahmary, Hamid Alalwany (2007) E-government Evaluation factors: Citizen's Perspective. *Proceedings of European and Mediterranean Conference on Information Systems* 2007.

Prates, C. A. (2001). *E-government – Realising the benefits of Information Technologies and improving public services delivering. A paper presented on the seminars preceding the III Global Forum – Fostering Democracy and Development through e-government*. Naples.

Pressman, R. S. (2004). *Software Engineering: A Practitioner's Approach* (6th ed.). New York: McGraw-Hill.

Quattrone, P., & Hopper, T. (2005). A time–space odyssey: management control systems in two multinational organisations. *Accounting, Organizations and Society*, 30, 735–764. doi:10.1016/j.aos.2003.10.006

Radha, R., & Murphy, C. (1992). Searching Versus Browsing in Hypertext. *Hypermedia*, 4(1), 1–31.

Rahman, H. (2007). Role of ICTs in socioeconomic development and poverty reduction. In Rahman, H. (Ed.), *Information and communication technologies for economic and regional developments* (pp. 188–219). Hershey, PA: Idea Group Inc.doi:10.4018/9781599041865.ch010

Rahman, H. (2008). An overview on strategic ICT implementations toward developing knowledge societies. In Rahman, H. (Ed.), *Developing successful ICT strategies: Competitive advantages in a global knowledge-driven society* (pp. 1–39). New York, NY: Information Science Reference.

Rahman, H. (2010). Local e-government management: A wider window of e-governance. In Rahman, H. (Ed.), *Handbook of research on e-government readiness for information and service exchange: Utilizing progressive information communication technologies* (pp. 295–323). Hershey, PA: IGI Global.

Rainey, H., & Steinbauer, P. (1999). Galloping elephants: Developing elements of a theory of effective government organizations. *Journal of Public Administration: Research and Theory*, 9(1), 1.

Rajagopal, P. (2002). An innovation—diffusion view of implementation of enterprise resource planning (ERP) systems and development of a research model. *Information & Management*, 40(2), 87–114. doi:10.1016/S0378-7206(01)00135-5

Rashmi, J., & Saini, A. K. (2009). How to Tap ERP's Hidden Potential in India? Proceedings of the 3rd National Conference; INDIACom- 2009, Computing For Nation Development.

Raymond, L., Uwizeyemungu, S., & Bergeron, F. (2006). Motivations to implement ERP in e-government: an analysis from success stories. *Electronic Government. International Journal (Toronto, Ont.)*, 3(3), 225–240.

Raymond, L., Uwizeyemungu, S., & Bergeron, F. (2005). ERP Adoption for E-Government: an Analysis of Motivations. Paper presented at the *Proceedings of the E-Government Workshop 2005*, West London, UK, Brunel University.

Raymond, L., Uwizeyemungu, S., & Bergeron F. (2006). ERP Adoption for E-Government: *Electronic Government, an International Journal, 3*(3).

Reddi, U. V., & Sinha, V. (2003). ICT use in education. In Farrell, G., & Wachholz, C. (Eds.), *Meta-survey on the use of technologies in education in Asia and the Pacific 2003-2004* (pp. 253–265). Maldives: UNESCO.

Reddick, C. G. (2009). The adoption of centralized customer service systems: A survey of local governments. *Government Information Quarterly*, 26(1), 219–226. doi:10.1016/j.giq.2008.03.005

Reddick, C. G. (2004). Empirical models of e-government growth in local governments. *e-Service Journal, 3*(2), 59-84

Reschenthaler, G. B., & Thompson, F. (1996). The information revolution and the New Public Management. *Journal of Public Administration: Research and Theory, 6*(1), 125–143.

Rikhardsson, P., & Kræmmergaard, P. (2006). Identifying the impacts of enterprise system implementation and use: Examples from Denmark. *International Journal of Accounting Information Systems, 7*, 36–49. doi:10.1016/j.accinf.2005.12.001

Robey, D., Ross, J. W., & Boudreau, M. C. (2002). Learning to Implement Enterprise Systems: An Exploratory Study of the Dialectics of Change. *Journal of Management Information Systems, 19*(1), 17–46.

Rodríguez, R. A., Welicki, L., Giulianelli, D. A., & Vera, P. M. (2008). Measurement framework for evaluating e-governance on municipalities websites. In *Proceedings of the 2nd International Conference on Theory and Practice of Electronic Governance* (pp. 381--387). Cairo, Egypt: ACM.

Rosacker, M., & Olson, L. (2008). Public sector information system critical success factors. *Transforming government: People, Process and Policy*, 60-70.

Sadagopan, S. (1999). *ERP: A Managerial Perspective*. New Delhi, India: Tata McGraw Hill.

Saleh, K., Abdulaziz, A., & Alkattan, I. (2006). A Services – Oriented Approach to Developing Security Policies for Trustworthy Systems. In *Emerging Trends and Challenges in IT Management*. Hershey, PA: IGI Global.

Sanchez, A., & Koh, C. (2003). The relationship between IT for communication & e-government barriers. Paper presented at Americas Conference on Information Systems, Tampa, FL.

Sandoval-Almazan, R., & Gil-Garcia, R. A. (2010). Assessing local e-government: an initial exploration of the case of Mexico. *In Proceedings of the 4th International Conference on Theory and Practice of Electronic Governance* (ICEGOV '10). ACM, New York, NY, USA, 61-65. DOI=10.1145/1930321.1930335

Sarker, S. (2005). ICT policy: Perspectives and challenges. *Information for Development, 3*(6), 6–7.

Saunders, M., Lewis, P., & Thornhill, A. (2007). *Research Methods for Business Students* (4th ed.). Upper Saddle River, NJ: Pearson.

Sayo, P., Chacko, J. G., & Pradhan, G. (Eds.). (2004). *ICT policies and e-strategies in the Asia-Pacific: A critical assessment of the way forward. United Nations Development Programme-Asia Pacific Development Information Programme (UNDP-APDIP) – 2004*. Reed Elsevier India Private Limited.

Scapens, R. W., & Jazayeri, M. (2003). ERP systems and management accounting change: Opportunities or impacts? *European Accounting Review, 12*, 201–233. doi:10.1080/0963818031000087907

Schellong, A. (2008). *Citizen Relationship Management: A Study of CRM in Government*. Frankfurt am Main: Peter Lang Publishing Group.

Scholl, H. (2005). E-government: A Special Case of ICT-enabled Business Process Change. *International Journal of E-Govemment Research, 1*(2), 27–49. doi:10.4018/jegr.2005040102

Scholl, H. (2005). "Organizational transformation through e-government: myth or reality?" *Electronic Government*: 1-11.

Schwester, R. W., Carrizales, T., & Holzer, M. (2009). An examination of municipal 311 system. *International Journal of Organization Theory and Behavior, 12*(2), 218–236.

Scott, J., & Vessey, I. (2002). Managing risks in enterprise implementations. *Communications of the ACM, 45*(4), 74–81. doi:10.1145/505248.505249

Scotti, E., & Sica, R. (2007). *Community management*. Milan, Italy: Apogeo.

Segars, A. H., & Grover, V. (1993). Re-examining perceived ease of use and usefulness: A confirmatory factor analysis. *Management Information Systems Quarterly, 17*, 517–525. doi:10.2307/249590

Selz, D., & Schubert, P. (1997). Web assessment: a model for the evaluation and the assessment of successful electronic commerce applications. *Electronic Markets, 7*(3), 46–48. doi:10.1080/10196789700000038

Serafeimidis, V., & Smithson, S. (2009). Information Systems Evaluation in Practice: a Case Study of Organizational Change. *Journal of Information Technology, 15*(2), 93–105. doi:10.1080/026839600344294

Sharma, S. (2006). Ecology of e-Governance. In Antorioko, A. V. (Ed.), *Encyclopaedia of digital government* (pp. 431–436). Hershey, PA: IGI Publications. doi:10.4018/978-1-59140-789-8.ch065

Sharma, S. (2010). Breaking mind inertia for humane business through ICT. In Chhabra, S. (Ed.), *Integrated e-models for government solutions: Citizen-centric service oriented methodologies and processes* (pp. 179–194). Pennsylvania: IGI Global Publications.

Shneiderman, B. (2000a). Universal usability. *Communications of the ACM, 43*(5), 85–91. doi:10.1145/332833.332843

Shneiderman, B. (2000b). Designing information-abundant Web sites: Issues and recommendations. *International Journal of Human-Computer Studies, 47*, 5–29. doi:10.1006/ijhc.1997.0127

Shubin, H., & Meehan, M. M. (1997). Navigation in Web application. *Interactions (New York, N.Y.), 4*(6), 13–17. doi:10.1145/267505.267508

Sia, S., & Neo, B. (2008). Business process reengineering, empowerment and work monitoring: An empirical analysis through the panopticon. *Business Process Management Journal, 14*(5), 609–628. doi:10.1108/14637150810903020

Siau, K. (2004). Enterprise Resource Planning (ERP) implementation methodologies. *Journal of Database Management, 15*(1), 1–6.

Siemens, G. (2003). *Learning ecology, communities and network extending the classroom.* Retrived on June 2, 2010 from http//: www.elearnspace.org/articles /learning communities.htm.

Signore O., Chesi, F. & Pallotti, M. (2005). E-governance: challenges & opportunities. CMG Italy - XIX annual conference.

Simeon, R. (1999). Evaluating domestic and international web site strategies. Internet Research. *Electronic Networking Applications and Policy, 9*(4), 297–308. doi:10.1108/10662249910286842

Singh, A. (2005). *Sidestepping Pitfalls. DataQuest*, May 21, 2005. Retrieved May 29, 2006 from http://www.dqindia.com /content/egovernance /2005/105052101.asp.

Siriginidi, S. R. (2000). Enterprise Resource Planning in re-engineering business. *Business Process Management Journal, 6*(5), 376–391. doi:10.1108/14637150010352390

Skietrys, E., Raipa, A., & Bartkus, E. V. (2008). Dimensions of the Efficiency of Public - Private Partnership. *Inzinerine Ekonomika-Engineering Economics, 3*, 45–50.

Smith, A. G. (2001). Applying evaluation criteria to New Zealand government web sites. *International Journal of Information Management, 21*(2), 137–149. doi:10.1016/S0268-4012(01)00006-8

Sprecher, M. H. (2000). Racing to E-governance: using the Internet for citizen service delivery. *Government Finance Review, 16*(5), 21–22.

Sri Sri Paramhansa Yogananda. (2002). *The bhagavad gita: The immortal dialogue between soul and spirit a new translation and commentary.* Kolkata: Publication of Yogoda Satsanga Society of India.

Sterne, J. (2002). *Web metrics: Proven methods for measuring Web site success.* New York, NY: John Wiley and Sons, Inc.

Stevens, T. (1997). Kodak focuses on ERP. *Industry Week, 246*(15), 130.

Stibbe, M. (2005). E-government security. *Infosecurity Today, 2*(3), 8–10. doi:10.1016/S1742-6847(05)70272-X

Subramanian, G. H. (1994). A replication of perceived usefulness and perceived ease of use measurement. *Decision Sciences, 25*(5/6), 863–873. doi:10.1111/j.1540-5915.1994.tb01873.x

Subramanian, G. H., & Hoffer, C. (2005). An Exploratory Case Study of Enterprise Resource Planning Implementation. *International Journal of Enterprise Information Systems, 1*(1), 23–38. doi:10.4018/jeis.2005010102

Symonds, M. (2000). Government and the Internet: The next revolution. *The Economist, August.*

Tansley, C., Newell, S., & Williams, H. (2001). Effecting HRM-stage practices through integrated human resource information in system. *Personnel Review*, *30*(3), 351–371. doi:10.1108/00483480110385870

Tarokh, M., Sharifi, E., & Nazemi, E. (2008). Survey of BPR experiences in Iran: reasons for success and failure. *Journal of Business and Industrial Marketing*, *23*(5), 350–362. doi:10.1108/08858620810881629

Thomas, J. C., & Streib, G. (2003). The new face of government: Citizen-Initiated contacts in the era of E-Government. *Journal of Public Administration: Research and Theory*, *13*(1), 83–102. doi:10.1093/jpart/mug010

Thong, J., Yap, C., & Seah, K. (2000). Business process reengineering in the public sector: The case of the housing development board in Singapore. *Journal of Management Information Systems*, *17*(1), 245–270.

Torres, L., Pina, V., & Royo, S. (2005). E-Government and the transformation of public administrations in EU countries: Beyond NPM or just a second wave of reforms? *Online Information Review*, *29*(5), 531–553. doi:10.1108/14684520510628918

Trenti, G. (2001). *Dalla formazione a distaza all'apprendimento in rete*. Milan, Italy: Franco Angelle.

Turban, A. (2008). *Information Technology for Management, Transforming Organizations in the Digital Economy*. New York: John Wiley & Sons.

Turban, E. (2002). *Electronic commerce- A managerial perspective* (2nd ed.). Prentice Hall.

Umble, E., & Umble, M. (2002). Avoiding ERP implementation failure. *Industrial Management (Des Plaines)*, *44*(1), 25–34.

Umble, E. J., & Umble, M. M. (2002). Avoiding ERP implementation failure. *Industrial Management (Des Plaines)*, *44*(1), 25–33.

UN. (2001). *Benchmarking e-government: A global perspective-Assessing the UN Member States*. New York, NY: United Nations.

UN. (2003). *Global e-government survey 2003: E-government at the crossroads*. New York, NY: United Nations.

UN. (2004). *Global e-government readiness report: Towards access for opportunity*. New York, NY: United Nations.

UN. (2005). *Global e-government readiness report: From e-government to e-inclusion*. New York, NY: United Nations.

UN. (2008). *United Nations e-government survey 2008: From e-government to connected governance*. New York, NY: United Nations.

UNDP. (2002). *Information and communications technology policy for Afghanistan*. Final Report, Asia-Pacific Development Information Programme, UN Development Programme, October 2002.

UNESCAP (Ed.). (1999). *Local government in Asia and the Pacific: A comparative study of fifteen countries*. Bangkok, Thailand: UN Economic and Social Commission for Asia and the Pacific (UNESCAP).

UNESCAP. (2003). *Country reports on local government systems*. Pakistan: United Nations Economic and Social Commission for Asia and Pacific.

Utting, K., & Yankelovich, N. (1989). Context and Orientation in Hypermedia Networks. *ACM Transactions on Information Systems*, *7*(1), 58–84. doi:10.1145/64789.64992

van den Bergh, J. C. J. M. (2007). *Abolishing GDP Tinbergen Institute discussion paper. TI 2007-019/3*. Vrije Universiteit Amsterdam, and Tinbergen Institute.

Van Den, B. L., Van Der, M. L., Van, W. W., & Woets, P. (2006). *E-governance in European and South African cities: The cases of Barcelona, Cape Town, Eindhoven, Johannesburg, Manchester, Tampere, The Hague, and Venice*. Ashgate Publishing, Ltd.

van der Merwe, R., & Bekker, J. (2003). A framework and methodology for evaluating e-commerce web sites'. *Internet Research: Electronic Networking Applications and Policy*, *13*(5), 330–341. doi:10.1108/10662240310501612

Velcu, O. (2007). Exploring the effects of ERP systems on organizational performance: Evidence from Finnish companies. *Emerald Group Publishing Limited*, *107*(9), 1316–1334.

Venkatesh, V., & Davis, F. D. (2000). A theoretical extension of the technology acceptance model: Four longitudinal field studies. *Management Science, 46*(2), 186–204. doi:10.1287/mnsc.46.2.186.11926

Victorian Auditor General. (2003). *Report of the Auditor General on RMIT's Finances*. Australia: June, State Government of Victoria.

von Dran, G. M., et al. (1999). Quality Websites: An application of the Kano Model to Website Design. *Proceedings of the 5th Americas Conference in Information Systems* (AMCIS'99).

Wagner, W., & Lederer, Y. (2004). An Analysis of the Imagine PA Public Sector ERP Project. *Paper presented at the Proceedings of the 37th Hawaii International Conference on System Sciences*, Big Island, Hawaii.

Wailgum, T. (2007). *ERP Definitions and Solutions*. CIO.

Wang, J. F., & Duo, H. (2009). Customer-centered e-government service quality evaluation: framework & case study.ISECS International Colloquium on Computing, Communication, *Control, &. Management, 8*(3), 198–202.

Wang, L., Bretschneider, S., & Gant, J. (2005). Evaluating web-based e-government services with a citizen-centric approach. Proceedings of the 38th Hawaii International Conference on System Sciences, 3-6 January 2005, Island of Hawaii (Big Island), 5, 1292.

Wang, X., & Feng, D. Lai, X., & Yu, H. (2004). Collisions for Hash Functions MD4, MD5, HAVAL-128 & RIPEMD. *Cryptology ePrint Archive*, Report 2004/199. Retrieved from http://eprint.iacr.org/2004/199.pdf.

Ward, C. J. (2006). ERP integrating and extending the enterprise. *Public Management, 35*(1), 30–33.

Wauters P., & Lörincz B. (2008). User satisfaction and administrative simplification within the perspective of eGovernment impact: Two faces of the same coin? *European Journal of ePractice, 4*, 1-10.

Webster, J., & Watson, R. (2002). Analysing the past to prepare for the future: Writing a literature review. *Management Information Systems Quarterly, 26*(2), 13–23.

Weikum, G., & Schek, H. (1992). Concepts and Applications of Multilevel Transactions and Open Nested Transactions, A. Elmagarmid (ed.), *Database Transaction Models for Advanced Applications*. San Francisco, CA: Morgan Kaufmann.

Weise, J. (2001). *Public Key Infrastructure Overview*. SunPSSM Global Security Practice, SunBluePrintsOn-Line.

Welch, E. W., Hinnant, C. C., & Moon, M. J. (2004). Linking government satisfaction with E-government and trust in government. *Journal of Public Administration: Research and Theory, 15*(3), 371–391. doi:10.1093/jopart/mui021

Welch, E. W., Hinnat, C. C., & Moon, M. J. (2005)...*Journal of Public Administration: Research and Theory, 15*(3).

Welch, E. W., & Pandey, S. (2007). Multiple measures of web site effectiveness and their association with service quality in health and human service agencies. In *Proceedings of the 40th Hawaii International Conference on System Science*, 3-6 January, 107.

Welling, R., & White, L. (2006). Web site performance measurement: promise and reality. *Managing Service Quality, 16*(6), 664–670. doi:10.1108/09604520610711954

Wentz, L., Kramer, F., & Starr, S. (2008). *Information and communication technologies for reconstruction and development: Afghanistan challenges and opportunities*. Washington, DC: Center for technology and National Security Policy, National Defense University.

West, D. M. (2004). E-Government and the transformation of service delivery and citizen attitudes. *Public Administration Review, 64*(1), 15–27. doi:10.1111/j.1540-6210.2004.00343.x

West, D. M. (2007). *Global E-government*, available at: http://www.insidepolitics.org /egovt07int.pdf.

Widdowson, H. G. (1979). *Explorations in applied linguistics*. Oxford, UK: Oxford University Press.

Williamson, O. E. (2002a). *The Lens of Contract: Private Ordering*. Berkeley: University of California.

Wilson, T. D., et al, (1999).Uncertainty in information seeking. Final report to the Birtish Library Research and Innovation Centre/Library and Information Commission on a research project carried out at the Department of Information Studies, University of Sheffield, December.

Wimmer, M., & Bredow, B. (2001). E-Government: Aspects of Security on Different Layers. In *Proceedings of the 12th International Workshop on Database & Expert Systems Applications* (DEXA'01. WorldBank (n.d.). *Definition of E-Government.* Retrieved from: http://go.worldbank.org

Windsor, D. (2006). Corporate social responsibility: Three key approaches. *Journal of Management Studies, 43*(1). Retrieved on May 23, 2010, from http://www.blackwell-synergy.com /doi/pdf.

Wittmann, C., & Cullen, M. (2000). *B2B Internet.* First Union Securities.

Wood, F.B. et al 2003. *A practical approach to E-government Web evaluation. IT Professional*, May|June 2003, 22-28.

World Bank. (n.d.). *World Bank* Retrieved Sept. 2009, from http://go.worldbank.org /M1JHE0Z280

Wrightsman, L. S. (1991). Interpersonal Trust and Attitudes Toward Human Nature. In Robinson, J. P. (Eds.), *Measures of Personality and Social Psychological Attitudes* (pp. 373–412). San Diego, CA: Academic Press.

Yamin, M., & Sinkovics, R. R. (2007). ICT and MNE reorganisation: the paradox of control. *International Business Review, 3*, 322–336.

Yang, C., Ting, P., & Wei, C. (2006). A Study of the Factors Impacting ERP System Performance from the Users' Perspectives. *Journal of American Academy of Business, 8*(2), 161–167.

Yazdifar, H., & Tsamenyi, M. (2005). Management accounting change and the changing roles of management accountants: A comparative analysis between dependent and independent organizations. *Journal of Accounting & Organizational Change, 1*, 180–198. doi:10.1108/18325910510635353

Young, D., & Benamati, J. (2000). Difference in public web sites: the current state of large US firms. *Journal of Electronic Commerce Research, 1*, 3.

Yücel, G., & Özok, A. F. (2008). A Methodology for Developing and Evaluating of Ergonomic Quality of Governmental Websites base on Fuzzy Approach. *Proceedings of the 2nd International Conference on Applied Human Factors and Ergonomics.*

Yusuf, Y., Gunasekaran, A., & Abthorpe, M. (2004, February). Enterprise Information Systems Project Implementation: A Case Study of ERP in Rolls-Royce. *International Journal of Production Economics, 87*(3). doi:10.1016/j.ijpe.2003.10.004

Zahedi, M. F., van Pelt, W. V., & Song, J. (2001). A conceptual framework for international Web design. *IEEE Transactions on Professional Communication, 44*(2), 83–103. doi:10.1109/47.925509

Zeithaml, V. A., Berry, L. L., & Parasuraman, A. (1996). The behavioral consequences of service quality. *Journal of Marketing, 60*(April), 31–46. doi:10.2307/1251929

Zhang, A., Nodine, M., Bhargava, B., & Bukhres, O. (1994). *Ensuring Relaxed Atomicity for Flexible Transactions in Multidatabase Systems*, Proc ACM SIGMOD Conf, pp 67-78.

Zhou, L. (2004). A dimension-specific analysis of performance-only measurement of service quality and satisfaction in China's retail banking. *Journal of Services Marketing, 18*(6/7), 534–546. doi:10.1108/08876040410561866

Zhu, K. (2002). *Information Transparency in electronic marketplaces: Why data transparency may hinder the adoption of B2B Exchanges.* Electronic Market.

Zwahr, T., Rossel, P., & Finger, M. (2005). Towards electronic governance – A case study of ICT in local government governance. *Proceedings of 2005 International Conference on Digital Government Research*, Atlanta, May 15-18, 2005.

About the Contributors

Susheel Chhabra is Associate Professor at Lal Bahadur Shastri Institute of Management (Delhi, India). His areas of research and consultancy include e-government, e-business, computer networks, and software engineering. He has published several research papers on international and national level journals. He has co-authored a textbook on human resource information systems, edited a special issue of International Journal of E-Government Research on strategic e-business model for government, and also co-authored the edited book Integrating E-Business Models for Government Solutions: Citizen-Centric Service Oriented Methodologies and Processes (IGI Global, USA). He is currently engaged in several consultancy and training assignments on social change for human development, e-governance, e-business, and ERP for ISID, NTPC, LBSRC, etc.

Muneesh Kumar is a Professor, at Department of Financial Studies, University of Delhi (India). His responsibilities include teaching banking and information systems related courses to students of Masters in Finance and Control (MFC) programme and supervising research. He has published several articles in international journals and presented papers in several international conferences. He has also authored three books and co-edited three books. He is associated with the several expert committees appointed by Government of India such as expert committee for IT projects of India Post and Market Participation Committee of Pension Fund Regulatory and Development Authority (PFRDA).

* * *

Catherine Equey is a Professor of Accounting and Finance at the Haute Ecole de Gestion of Geneva, Switzerland. After many years in Swiss audit firms as an accounting auditor, she took on a teaching role within a local management School. More recently, she has been CFO of a university for which she was equally in charge of the implementation of Oracle Financials. Professor Equey is specialized in ERP implementation, specifically the finance modules. Apart teaching, she devote a large part of her time at work coaching companies wishing to implement financial and management accounting systems. Her research areas are ERP and Accounting.

Emmanuel Fragnière, CIA (Certified Internal Auditor), is a Professor of service management at the Haute Ecole de Gestion of Geneva, Switzerland. He is also a lecturer at the Management School of the University of Bath, UK. Previously he was a commodity risk analyst at Cargill (Ocean Transportation) and a senior internal auditor at BanqueCantonaleVaudoise, the fourth largest bank in Switzerland. He Fragnière specializes in energy, environmental, and financial risk. He has published several papers in academic journals such as Annals of Operations Research, Environmental Modeling and Assessment,

Interfaces, and Management Science. His research is partly focused on the development of risk management models for decision-makers in the fields of energy and production. Mr Fragnière other research interests include modeling systems, for which he has also obtained considerable funding from the Swiss National Science Foundation.

Lars Frank has for 20 years been a database consultant for both private companies and organizations in the public sector. Since 1994 he has been Associate professor at the Department of Informatics in Copenhagen Business School. His research areas are System integration, Data warehousing, ERP architectures, Distributed health records, E-commerce, Distributed systems, Mobile databases, Transaction models, Work flow management, Multidatabases, and Data modeling. In 2008 he received Dr. Merc. Degree from Copenhagen Business School for a dissertation about integration of heterogeneous IT-systems.

Asmare Emerie Kassahun is currently a PhD student in the School of Business Information Technology & Logistics at RMIT University, Melbourne, Australia. His research title is "The effect of BPR on public sector organization performance in a developing economy". He obtained a Master degree in information science and a Bachelor degree in Accounting.

Sushila Madan is Associate Professor in Computer-Science department of Lady Shri Ram College, Delhi University. She is M.Sc. in Applied Maths from I.I.T. Delhi and M Tech from BITS Pilani. She has finished Research Project in "Security Risk Management in E-commerce funded by UGC. Dr. Sushila has taught in Indian and Foreign Universities. She has also authored SIX books in areas such as MIS, Information Technology, E-commerce, Multimedia and Web-Technology to name a few. She is also a corporate trainer and consultant to Industry for information security. She is Lead Auditor and Tutor for Information Security Management System standards in India and Abroad. She is member of several prestigious bodies such as the Computer Society of India, Faculty of Mathematical Sciences, University of Delhi, Gerson Lehrman Group CouncilsSM and Fellow member IETE.

Alemayehu Molla is an Associate Professor, School of Business IT, RMIT University. He holds a Bachelor degree in management, a Master degree in information science, and a PhD in information systems. He researches in the areas of Green IT, digital business, and development informatics with more than 80 publications including in the European Journal of Information Systems, International Journal of E-commerce, Journal of E-commerce Research, Information & Management, Internet Research, and The Information Society Journal.

D.N. Gupta joined Indian Administrative Service (IAS) in 1989. For the last one and a half decades he has been closely associated with development planning, and management of implementation of various social and rural development programmes. He has worked in various capacities in the state of Orissa and Govt. of India. He was Deputy Secretary, Ministry of Rural Development, Govt. of India, and before joining ISID, he was Special Secretary, Housing and Urban Development (H&UD), Government of Orissa. His specialization is in the field of development administration, e-governance and GIS. He has written several articles on development issues, and books on Rural Development System, Integrated Development Planning, and Decentralization.

Alan R. Peslak is an Associate Professor of Information Sciences and Technology at Penn State University Worthington Scranton campus. He joined the faculty in 2001 after 25 years of diverse manufacturing and service industry experience. He received his Ph.D. in Information Systems from Nova Southeastern University, Fort Lauderdale, Florida. His research areas include information technology social, ethical, and economic issues, enterprise resource planning, information privacy, and information technology pedagogy. Publications include the Communications of the ACM, Information Resources Management Journal, Journal of Business Ethics, Journal of Computer Information Systems, Journal of Information Systems Education, Team Performance Management, Industrial Management and Data Systems, Journal of Electronic Commerce in Organizations, Information Research, and First Monday. He is on the editorial boards of numerous journals. He currently serves as President-Elect for the Educational Special Interest Group of the Association for Information Technology Professionals.

Hakikur Rahman, PhD. is the Founder-Principal, Institute of Computer Management & Science (ICMS), and President of ICMS Foundation. He is currently serving as a Post-Doctoral researcher at the University of Minho, Portugal. He is the Chairman of SchoolNet Foundation Bangladesh, Adjunct Faculty of the Bangabandhu Sheikh Mujibur Rahman Agricultural University, former faculty of International University of Business Agriculture and Technology, Bangladesh, former Chair of ISOC Bangladesh Chapter (2000-2010) and former Secretary of the South Asia Foundation Bangladesh Chapter (2001-2008). He served Sustainable Development Networking Foundation (SDNF) as its Executive Director (CEO) from January 2007 to December 2007, the transformed entity of the Sustainable Development Networking Programme (SDNP) in Bangladesh where he worked as the National Project Coordinator since December 1999. Before joining SDNP he worked as the Director, Computer Division, Bangladesh Open University. Graduating from the Bangladesh University of Engineering and Technology in 1981, he has done his Master's of Engineering from the American University of Beirut in 1986 and completed his PhD in Computer Engineering from the Ansted University, UK in 2001.

Christopher G. Reddick is an Associate Professor and Chair of the Department of Public Administration at the University of Texas at San Antonio, USA. Dr. Reddick's research and teaching interests is in e-government. Some of his publications can be found in Government Information Quarterly, Electronic Government, and the International Journal of Electronic Government Research. Dr. Reddick recently edited the book entitled Handbook of Research on Strategies for Local E-Government Adoption and Implementation: Comparative Studies.

Geetanjali Sahi is an Assistant professor at Lal Bahadur Shastri Institute of Management, Delhi and a doctoral student of Banasthali Vidyapith, Rajasthan. She is an MCA and M Phil in Computer Science. She has over ten years of research and teaching experience and has published many articles in the areas such as data mining, E-governance, On-line shopping, cyber-crime and web usability. Her research interests are in the development and use of electronic commerce and E-governance applications. She is also a member of Computer Society of India.

Mamta Sareen is an Associate Professor in Department of Computer Science, Kirori Mal College, Delhi University. She teaches subjects like Management Information systems, E-commerce, IT for managers, Operating systems, computer architecture, DBMS, etc to both undergraduate and post graduate students in the field of management and computer science. Her main area of research relates to the role of technology played in e-commerce. She has a few international publications in the area of B2B e-commerce to her credit and also has presented paper in conferences. Presently, she is in the process of completing a book titled "Trust and Technology in B2B E-Commerce: Practices and Strategies for Assurance".

Pradip K. Sarkar is a lecturer at the School of Business Information Technology & Logistics, RMIT University, Melbourne, Australia. His research interests lie in the areas of Cloud Computing, Green ICT, Digital Supply Chains, and Enterprise Systems Implementation.

Sangeeta Sharma is Professor of Public Administration at the University of Rajasthan. India. Her works have appeared in various publications of National and International repute. Her research interests include E-governance, Ethics, and Socio-psychological experimentation. Her basic inclination is towards constructing the conceptual frameworks that are high in normative contents. She has authored book on Organization Change. The edited volume by her relates to the Transformative Pathways with collections from scholars around the globe on the prognosis of the future society. Her innovativeness to analyze various aspects of Governance from interdisciplinary perspective reflects scientific aptitude. Her conceptual frameworks have been well acknowledged and she has been invited to deliver keynote addresses on her conceptual constructs at various professional forums.

Girish H. Subramanian is Professor of information systems and Director of information technology programs at the School of Business, Penn State Harrisburg. His work has appeared in Communications of the ACM, Decision Sciences, Journal of Management Information Systems, Journal of Systems & Software, Journal of Computer Information Systems as well as several other journals. He serves on the editorial boards of International Journal of Business Information Systems and the Journal of Systems and Software.

Doug Thomson's research interests are multi-disciplined. As a Certified Practicing Engineer (Civil) he used computer aided design and PERT. After experience with the Australian and US Corps of Engineers, he managed and directed major infrastructure developments, benchmarked high tech major projects through business systems and processes including ERP, and developed new, innovative procurement and contracting methodologies. His applied global research included the examination of government/industry policies of Singapore, Israel, Holland, Sweden, Germany, UK, US and Japan. As Principal Consultant in e-business and corporate strategy, he researched e-business 'roadmaps' for MNCs and government. He has published four books, five book chapters, and 32 refereed conference/journal publications/papers.

Index